D0181875

THE OLYMPIC MYTH
OF
GREEK AMATEUR ATHLETICS

THE OLYMPIC MYTH
OF
GREEK AMATEUR ATHLETICS

BY

DAVID C. YOUNG

ARES PUBLISHERS, INC.
CHICAGO MCMLXXXIV

First Edition
© *Copyright 1984*

ARES PUBLISHERS, INC.
7020 NORTH WESTERN AVENUE
CHICAGO, ILLINOIS 60645

ISBN 0-89005-523-8

FOR JUDY
and
IN MEMORIAM JACOBI THORPE

"If the Thorpe case convinces the whole world of the need for a change, it will undeniably have rendered sports an invaluable service.... It is enough to remember the careful way antiquity allowed participation in the Olympics only to those athletes who were irreproachable. Ought it not to be the same in the modern world?"

Baron Pierre de Coubertin
Revue Olympique, April 1913, p. 59

PREFACE

This book began in 1971, when Bill Toomey stood his javelin outside my office and asked if I would collaborate with him on an 'Olympics, Ancient and Modern' project. I agreed to write a brief general account of the ancient Olympics (Toomey knew of my work on Pindar, author of the *Victory Odes*). I began the task rather lightly, with the usual preconceptions in mind and Gardiner's books in hand. But I soon found it a knotty assignment. After writing about thirty pages, I realized that the Greek texts did not support what I was writing, particularly on the subject of amateurism. I discarded the manuscript, and began a fresh study of the ancient evidence. By then both Mr. Toomey and I were so busy with other obligations that we mutually abandoned the general project.

In 1973 a teaching assignment again drew me to Greek athletics, and I resumed my study of Greek athletic profit. That study slowly grew into what is, in the main, Part Two of the present book. I summarized this work at the 1979 Meeting of the American Philological Association in Boston, suggesting that ancient Greece did not know amateur athletics. But my conclusions were so heterodox that they still left me ill at ease--and a few of my colleagues in open disbelief. Another kind of question seemed to need an answer. How could the popular belief be so far from the mark? How could the standard scholarship be so faulty? Is such a discrepancy even possible? Part One of the present book results from asking those questions.

Since both specialists and non-specialists have an interest in my topic I accommodate both kinds of readers. The text itself requires no knowledge of foreign languages or classical philology; yet there is more discussion and documentation than usual in a book for the general reader. A heterodox thesis such as mine could not stand without its concrete evidence. I could not make my notes brief references to the standard research. That research was often more than unusable; it was an added burden, compelling me to clear away nettlesome underbrush before continuing on my path. No scholarship is flawless, but that on ancient athletics contains an inordinate number of careless errors, impetuous assertions, and faulty readings of the sources. The distorting influence of the modern Olympics is not the only cause. Few classicists have taken up the subject of athletics. We tend to rely on just a few works from the hands of a few scholars.

Several technical works on special subjects are excellent (e.g., Ebert's *Epigramme auf Sieger* and Knab's *Periodoniken*). But most general works are badly out of date and weak in philology. Until more classicists accept athletics as an important feature of Greek society, progress in this field will continue to lag behind that in others. And we who do pursue it will experience especial frustrations.

When my experience with the evidence clashed directly with widely published reports--and with universal beliefs--there seemed no choice but to elaborate the discrepancy. Sometimes, however, the source of a universal belief was almost impossible to find, or so unsubstantial that I seemed to be shadow-boxing. I could only retrace circular arguments or catalogue a series of perpetuated misconceptions, misquotations, or misprints. Other difficulties were not related to athletic scholarship. I found no real precedents or simple formula for calculating the value of ancient athletic prizes, either in ancient drachmas, wages and buying power or in modern equivalents. It seemed necessary to present much of this material here (olive oil, sheep, and slaves). But again there was underbrush. The only recent attempt to correlate ancient athletic prizes with modern values founds its calculations on the odd notion that a skilled American worker nowadays makes only $8 a day ($2,080 annual). The burden fell on me--and on my notes--to record not only what a Platonic sheep cost but also what our own workmen actually earn (and what our government in fact enforces as a minimum wage). Finally, as is normal in any field, the evidence for some questions is indeed ambiguous, and thoughtful scholars have disagreed. A fresh investigation was then in order.

I am aware that this book will not be welcome in some classrooms--and locker rooms. Some may dismiss what I say without argument. It is not likely that they will dispute my evidence. They will not deny that the 1870 modern Greek Olympics took place and were successful; nor that Coubertin sought to cover them up. They will not deny that Caspar Whitney was President of the American Olympic Committee; nor that he called working class athletes "vermin" and urged their exclusion from amateur sports. They will not deny that the champion sprinter in Plato's Athens won a prize worth 1200 drachmas; nor that those 1200 drachmas would buy that sprinter six or seven people (or a luxurious house). Unless they find texts that I could not find, they will not claim there is any sound evidence that Astylos, Milo, and Theogenes were "noble aristocrats." Nor will they claim that the Greeks had, after all, the word and the concept "amateur." No one will deny that ancient texts call the early Olympic victor Polymnestor a "goatherd." And no one will deny that the San Francisco Olympic Club, before Coubertin's June 1894 Congress, received and published an eight-point version of Coubertin's 1894 circular--a version which explicitly denies the intention to inaugurate international legislation.

Rather they may dismiss what I have to say by stating (never so directly) that I am 'nasty' or that I 'oversimplify'; or that what I say is 'unimportant.' Or they may (quite wrongly) assert that I try to discredit the Olympic Movement. Parts of my *story* might be deemed nasty by some. But I sought to minimize my moral judgments (scholarly judgments are another matter) and to let my subjects speak for themselves. That is why I quote so extensively. On the issue of "evil," I think each reader should decide independently whether Gardiner's ubiquitous label is rightly or wrongly distributed. So also each reader must decide the question of importance. As for oversimplification: the matters which I investigate are indeed complex, and probably no one is fully qualified in the sundry fields where my study led--ancient Greece, Victorian England, poetry, athletics, epigraphy, modern Greece, America, the history of classical scholarship, several influential personalities, the Olympic Movement, and so on. I make no such claim. But much of this material does not need such subtle sociological interpretation--nor need we treat the bare facts so gingerly--as many suppose. When the facts are clearer, we may better perform the overall socio-economico-historical analysis. So long as what I say is true, it should not injure the cause of a more sophisticated treatment. As the Greek said, ἄγροικός εἰμι. τὴν σκάφην σκάφην λέγω. I leave the subtleties to others.

I happen personally to support the Modern Olympic Movement without a qualm. I view it as one of the world's greatest institutions--potentially, perhaps, its greatest hope. But my judgment (which scarcely bears on the contents of the book) is that the basic idea of the modern Olympics is so sound that they have often succeeded *despite* their historical origins and certain features of ideology, not *because* of them. I therefore think the Olympic Movement most likely to achieve its potential if we understand its history. I do not think it will help if we deceive ourselves and blindly idolize--or even protectively idealize--all the individuals and catch-phrases that have been associated with it.

I anticipate one potential misconception. My Part One should not be misconstrued as excoriating the Victorian English.

It tells an international story. Of the ten or so principals there, three are American, two are Greek, and the Irish and French score one each. That leaves only three for England, and only one of these (Percy Gardner, a pleasant enough man) was truly a Victorian Englishman. The greatest vehemence, the most obvious intolerance toward others appears not in Victorian aristocrats but in those who *wished* that they were Victorian aristocrats, such as Whitney and Mahaffy.

Similarly, my frequent disagreement with the work of H. W. Pleket must not be misconstrued as polemic. His work is almost the foundation of mine. Because Pleket investigates or broaches many of the same questions, his important studies provided a framework in which I could cast parts of my own. Furthermore, to identify the differences between his and my conclusions seemed a useful way to clarify the issues. Before Pleket's articles appeared, there was no forum for a serious discussion of this subject, and I acknowledge my genuine debt to him both on that account and in several important matters of detail.

My greatest debt, immense, is to Judy Turner, whose encouragement, criticism, and tolerance were nearly everything. Without her, there would be no book, no joy. οὐκ ἔστιν ἄλλη τῆσδε λωίων γυνή. For helpful criticism or valued encouragement I thank Hugh Lee, Frank Frost, Nicholas Richardson, Stephen Miller, Robert Renehan, Edward Tripp, Donald Kagan, Robert Potter, David Messick, and Ed Barton. And I thank those who typed and retyped various portions and many drafts of an ever changing manuscript: Randi Glick, Michiko Yusa, Judy Turner, Donna Althoff, Irene Cole, and Virginia Phillips. And I thank Joseph Maalouf, who set the final version from the scars and chaos that passed as a finished manuscript. Finally, I express my gratitude to Al. N. Oikonomides of Ares Publishers, who encouraged me to write the truth as best as I could determine it, whether or not it accorded with what he and others wanted to hear. His belief in the idea of scholarship and his integrity as a publisher are perhaps best indicated by the fact that he is also the current publisher of Gardiner's *Athletics of the Ancient World.*

Ann Arbor   David C. Young
December 24, 1983

CONTENTS

Chronological Foreward 1

PART ONE: *THE MYTH*

I. Introduction to Chronological Legerdemain 7

II. The Modern Origins of Amateurism 15

III. The Modern Greek Olympics and John Mahaffy ... 28

IV. The Ancient Greeks Turn Amateur 44

V. Coubertin and the Modern International
Olympics 57

VI. E. N. Gardiner, James Thorpe,
and Avery Brundage 76

VII. The Truth "almost" Told 89

PART TWO: *THE REALITY*

I. Introduction: Valid Questions about
Greek Athletics 107

II. Homer and Hesiod 111

III. Panathenaic Prizes in the Classical Period
(*IG* II² 2311) 115

IV. The Sixth Century and the Olympic Games 128

V. The Western Colonies and Croton's
Athletic Empire 134

VI. Modern Aristocratic Bias and the Question of
Ancient Athletes' Social Class 147

VII. Economic and Social Mobility within the
Greek Athletic System   158

VIII.   The Greek System Versus the Nineteenth-Century
         "Amateur Ideal" 163

  IX.   The Meaning of Greek Athletics 171

         Appendix 1 177

         Appendix 2 179

         Appendix 3 182

         Appendix 4 184

         Appendix 5 185

         Appendix 6 186

         Bibliography 189

INDICES

   I.   Modern 195

  II.   Ancient (General) 198

 III.   Ancient Athletes and Coaches 200

  IV.   Ancient Authors and Texts 201

Chronological Foreward

The Modern International Olympic Games are not yet a hundred years old (1896-1983). The ancient Greek Olympics lasted well over a thousand years, with a history thirteen times as long as our own (776 B.C.-ca. 400 A.D.). There were Olympic Games when Homer composed the *Iliad* and the *Odyssey*, the earliest works of literature known to Western man. The Olympics and many other large-scale athletic contests were an old but thriving institution when Greek tragedy was invented, and in the time of the Peloponnesian War. They continued through the time of Plato and Aristotle, the days of Alexander the Great, and of Julius Caesar in Rome. The Olympic Games were eight centuries old when Christianity was born. Indeed the Games enjoyed renewed vigor in the Roman Empire, at the very time Christianity struggled against many other religions, old and new, for its eventual place in the Roman Empire's sun. It took a special Imperial edict to stop the Olympics short of their twelve thousandth birthday near the end of the fourth century A.D., an edict which outlawed all pagan festivals, including the Olympic Games.

My study of the amateur-professional question focuses on just the first few centuries of that long span of time (776-ca. 350 B.C.). No classical scholar or modern Olympic official has ever denied the abundant evidence for what we call "professionalism" throughout most, the last two-thirds or so, of ancient Olympic history.[1] Rather,

---

1. For the large cash payments given to post-classical athletes see, e.g., Harris 1964, 42, Pleket 1974, 71, and 1976, *passim*. Harris reckons the prizes given at the games in Aphrodisias (Asia Minor) in the early Christian era as worth up to 3000 days' wages (i.e., ten years' work) for a working man. I shall argue that archaic and classical prizes were often comparable. For the later athletes' immense pensions see, e.g., Gardiner 1930, 113.

1

they have simply asserted that *for their last eight hundred years the ancient Olympic Games existed in a thoroughly corrupt and degenerate state.* The change from healthy sport to corruption (in their thesis, the change from amateurism to professionalism) is generally presented as abrupt, and chronologically well-defined. E. N. Gardiner, for example, our most prominent authority on the subject, says:

> Thus within a century [about 480-380 B.C.] the whole character of Greek athletics was completely changed. From this time there is little to record save that all the evils which we have described grew more and more pronounced.[2]

In contrast with that extended degeneration, Gardiner and his amateur partisans posit a shorter period of pure aristocratic "amateurism" preceding it--about three centuries (776-ca. 450 B.C.) when all Greek athletes came from families with hereditary noble blood and were born to such great wealth that they had no need of money prizes. Whether professionalism is or is not an evil is a moral question on which each reader must decide. But Gardiner's chronology and the rest of his thesis of aristocratic amateurism are scholarly positions, which I think the evidence denies. By the very thesis of degeneration Gardiner and his supporters have made chronology of the essence in the following pages. Their works teem with temporal words and phrases, such as "archaic," "late archaic," "Roman," "earlier," "later," "Hellenistic," "late fifth century," and "in

---

2. Gardiner 1930, 104. Both Gardiner (1930, 99) and Harris (1964, 37f) themselves observe that their chronological divisions and early period of pure aristocratic amateurism do not well accord with the evidence. But the inconsistency will not dissuade them from their chosen thesis. Even Pleket, who questions the thesis of the ancient amateur, still adopts Gardiner's precise chronology for the advent of full professionalism (i.e., the end of an aristocratic monopoly).

Pindar's time." These terms, then, do matter. In hopes of clarifying them for the reader unfamiliar with the customary divisions of ancient Greek historical time I provide a chart of these terms in Appendix One.

I also emphasize that my concern with modern athletics and with the modern International Olympic Games is limited to that chronological period when the amateur movement had its strongest formative influence on modern sport (1866-1913)--howsoever much that influence remains. I infrequently touch on more recent matters, but to assess the development of the modern Olympics after 1913 lies outside the scope of this book.

PART ONE: *THE MYTH*

"The ancient Olympic Games
were strictly amateur--and for many centuries,
as long as they continued amateur..."

Avery Brundage
Report of the United States Olympic Committee (1948), 23

"The winter of 1892-3 went by without the idea causing any stir among the general public.... I decided to keep the idea of a Congress, but to use a little deception.... Amateurism, an admirable mummy (*momie*) that could be presented ... as a specimen of the modern art of embalming. Half a century has gone by without it seeming to have suffered in any way from the unceasing manipulations to which it has been submitted. It seems intact. Not one of us expected it to last so long."

Pierre de Coubertin
Mémoires Olympiques (1931), 11f (= *Olympic Review,* 101-2, 159)

*   *   *   *   *

"Anyone who works in such a field as this must necessarily owe a great debt to his predecessors. In the study of Greek Athletics Dr. E. N. Gardiner towers high above all others," H. A. Harris, *Greek Athletes and Athletics, with an introduction by* The Marquess of Exeter, *Chairman of the British Olympic Association* (1964), "Preface," p. 20.

"It is a fitting circumstance that this book should have been produced under the auspices of Professor Percy Gardner, seeing that he was unconsciously the originator of it. My interest in the subject was first aroused by the chapter on Olympia in his *New Chapters from Greek History*," E. N. Gardiner, *Greek Athletic Sports and Festivals* (1910), xi.

"Mr. Mahaffy has more recently compared our English athletics with those of Olympia and the Isthmus," Percy Gardner, *New Chapters in Greek History* (1892), p. 272.

"[T]he contests were amateur performances, and...for centuries the glory and pride of Greece," John Mahaffy, "Old Greek Athletics," *Macmillan's Magazine* 36 [1879], 61.

*   *   *   *   *

"There were horse races (μονόζογοι καὶ δίζυγοι) also announced, but had to be postponed to another day," John Mahaffy, "The Olympic Games at Athens in 1875," *Macmillan's Magazine* 32 [1875], 326. (cf. p. 37, below).

I

Introduction to Chronological Legerdemain

Ancient amateurism is a myth. No victor in the Olympic Games of classical Greece would even be eligible for their modern counterpart.* Ancient athletes regularly competed for valuable prizes in other games before they reached the Olympics, and they openly profited from athletics whenever they could. Yet the public still imagines an idealistically motivated Greek athlete who never competed for more than an olive crown and some glory. And even classical specialists cannot say when professional athletes first appeared in Greece, nor precisely how they differed from the amateurs. The confusion is worse than we admit. I can find no mention of amateurism in Greek sources, no reference to amateur athletes--no evidence that the concept "amateurism" was even known in antiquity. The truth is that "amateur" is one thing for which the ancient Greeks never even had a word.[1]

N.B. For abbreviations and form of citation, see note at heading of the bibliography.
* The statement remains true, despite truly significant changes very recently made in the rules for Olympic eligibility.
1. The Greek word *athletes* ("athlete") literally meant, and always meant, "competitor for a prize" (*athlon* = "prize"). Gardiner (1910, 130; cf. Jüthner 1965, I.89ff) wrongly claims that *idiotes* was the Greek word for "amateur"; and others translate it as "amateur" (e.g., R. McKeon, *Basic Works of Aristotle,* New York, 1941, 978). But the two words are wholly unalike. "Amateur" always implies some involvement--some affection for, devotion to, or participation in an activity (no matter how slight). *Idiotes* (= essentially "layman") has, in the relevant contexts, the opposite meaning: a "non-participant," a person without involvement in an activity; "without any experience, wholly unskilled,"

Our conviction that there *were* amateur athletes of some kind at some time in antiquity does not come from ancient texts; it comes from works published in the past century, written by men who were promoting a modern cause and a modern idea. They wished to represent Greece as an ancient precedent for the athletic system which they themselves preferred. Among the first of these authors was a noted American classical scholar, Paul Shorey.[2] On the eve of what we call the "First Modern Olympic Games" held in Athens in 1896, Shorey lectured our first potential Olympic victors and the readers of *The Forum* (Philadelphia) on "the chief lesson" that modern man could learn from the ancient Greek Olympics.

1. **(continued)** even "raw hand, ignoramus" (LSJ s.v., III.3), whence English *idiot*. Even "rank amateur" would not help Gardiner's case. No rank amateur, no *idiotes* ever competed in the Greek Olympic games. (For Hdt. 8.26 see p. 173, below).

Unlike the common English compound "amateur athlete," the words *idiotes* and *athletes* never appear joined in Greek. For they are mutually exclusive terms, and the combination amounts to a contradiction. For the opposition see Xenophon *Hiero* 4.6: "An athlete (*athletes*) takes no joy in being better than a non-competitor (*idiotes*) but is pained if he loses to a fellow-contestant (*antagonistes*)." Even more telling is Dio Chrysostom 28.5-8, who says of the famous boxer Melancomas of Caria, "If he had remained an *idiotes*, and never taken up the activity [boxing] at all (μηδὲν ὅλως ἔπραξε)...." When the concept of amateurism finally reached Greece in the late nineteenth century, the modern Greeks were compelled to find a new word. They finally settled on ἐρασιτέχνης ("amateur" in Modern Greek), a translation from the French. There is no equivalent in ancient Greek.

2. Mandell 91f calls Shorey 'English," but wrongly. Born in Iowa, Shorey was educated at Harvard (Law) and in Germany (Classics). In 1895 he held the prestigious Chair of Greek at the University of Chicago (he had taught at Bryn Mawr before Chicago).

And here lies the chief, if somewhat obvious, lesson that our modern athletes have to learn from Olympia, if they would not remain barbarians in spirit.... They must *strive,* like the young heroes of Pindar, *only* for the complete development of their manhood, and their sole prizes must be the conscious delight in the exercise... and some simple symbol of honor. They must not prostitute the vigor of their youth for gold, directly or indirectly.... [T]he commercial spirit... is fatal, as the Greeks learned in their *degenerate* days.... Where money is the stake men will inevitably tend to rate the end above the means, or rather to misconceive the true end... the professional will *usurp the place of the amateur....*

Such was the experience of Greece after the brief bloom immortalized by Pindar had passed away. The noble scions of the victors, as Pindar says, "loved fair and honorable things, by the grace of God, and *strove only* for the attainable in the days of their youth".... But their place was gradually usurped by the professional "strong man,"... who won his victories by 1) breaking the fingers of his antagonist or 2) otherwise disabling him, and whose admirers eagerly recounted, 3) the number of pounds of raw flesh he could devour,4) the whipcords he could break by knotting the veins in his brow, 5) the oxen he could lift, 6) the chariots he could stay in full career-- the type of man, in short, whose repulsive, lethargic features are preserved for us in the late Roman statues of athletes. And so in place of Pindar's ideal strains... we hear from Plato to Galen an ever louder chorus of disparagement and contempt for the mere athlete. (321f; e[mphasis] a[dded], as are the item numbers)

By now this account may seem standard enough fare, even if a bit passionate. But it is all wrong. Shorey's version of "the experience of Greece" has no relation to the evidence. Shorey himself seems to have known very little about Greek athletics.[3] The comment which he attributes to Pindar is not in Pindar's text. It is, at best, a bad mistranslation of *Pythian* 11.50f, carefully

---

3. Shorey writes of such things as "the Greek record for the high jump" (314); there was no high jump. The article contains no indication that Shorey had studied athletics himself; it merely summarizes and paraphrases Gardner (see n. 47, below).

contrived to echo Shorey's own sermonizing ("strive only," "strove only")--and wrongfully to suggest that Pindar warned against money prizes. Pindar never did anything of that kind.[4]

Even worse are Shorey's violent misdatings, every one of them at least five hundred years--half a millennium--off the mark. Of Shorey's tales about "the professional 'strong man'" who "usurped" the place of the "amateur" not one concerns an athlete who dates from the "late Roman" period. Nor were the athletes at

---

4. Shorey cites no poem, but what Shorey's "Pindar" says seems closer to *Py.* 11.50f than to any other passage in Pindar. The subject at *Py.* 11.50f is not the enigmatic "noble scions of the victors" nor even athletics. The subject is the poet himself, and he speaks generally: θεόθεν ἐραίμαν καλῶν, δυνατὰ μαιόμενος ἐν ἁλικίᾳ. "May I pray for noble favors from the gods, seeking what is possible in my time" (translation of F. Nisetich, *Pindar's Victory Songs,* Baltimore, 1980, 223; cf. Theognis 461). Pindar's sentence has not the remotest connection to amateurism in athletics.

Long and loudly have the amateur partisans invoked Pindar as their ancient spokesman. Since his poems nowhere frown on athletic money and nowhere support the amateur creed, the amateur partisans simply put words in the poet's mouth. So the Pooles quote a "passage of Pindar that succinctly expresses the essence of Olympic victory" (107). But the words contained in the quotation are not in Pindar. The Pooles print, in fact, a garbled translation (credited to Edith Hamilton) of Hesiod's *Works and Days* 289-292. Hesiod's subject is not athletics, but farming.

So also Coubertin was wont to write, "'The gods are friends of the games,' said Pindar" (MacAloon 140). The sentence is not un-Pindaric, but I cannot find those words in Pindar. They must be traced back instead, through a complex chain of modern mis-quotation, to Plato's *Cratylus* (Mahaffy 1881, 24 with MacAloon 140: Mahaffy was a literary collaborator of V. Duruy, who was in turn Coubertin's source). Plato's *Cratylus* 406c reads φιλοπαίσμονες γὰρ καὶ οἱ θεοί. The topic at *Cratylus* 406c is not athletics but word-play, puns--and Plato's sentence means nothing like what Couber-tin says that "Pindar" says. Jowett's translation is, in fact, "For the gods too love a joke" (*Dialogues of Plato: Cratylus,* many editions).

issue even as late as Hellenistic. Items one, two, and six are stories told of various athletes from the archaic and classical period of Greece, not of those "with repulsive, lethargic features" from Greece's "late Roman" and "degenerate days."[5] And items three, four and five are not stories told about athletes who came "after the brief bloom" of the Pindaric "amateur" in the fifth century. Rather they are all feats attributed to Milo, the sixth century B.C. wrestler who won many Olympic crowns before Pindar was even born, decades before Pindar's "noble scions of the victors" (whatever that means) entered the Olympic lists.[6] Shorey's argument is quite

5. Item one (breaking fingers) is told of Leontiskos, who won his Olympic victories in the first half of the fifth century--in the midst of Pindar's career (M[oretti] Nos. 271, 285); it was told again of Sostratos, an athlete of Plato's time (M., No. 420). But the worst stories of "disabling" (Shorey's second item) come from the mid-sixth century, long before Pindar, when Arrichion, we are told, wrenched his opponent's ankle from its socket just as he himself succumbed to a fatal choke-hold (M., No. 102). I do not recall such stories about post-classical athletes. Shorey's item six, "staying chariots," concerns Poulydamos of the fifth century (M., No. 348), not a late athlete.

6. Milo (M., Nos. 115, 122, 126, 129, 133, 139), even more than our Babe Ruth, was a favorite subject for the story-teller (Part Two, VI, with n. 50). Harris himself collects (1964, 111) the very 'Milo-stories' to which Shorey refers. I repeat them in Harris' words: Milo's "daily diet, we hear, was twenty pounds of meat, the same weight of bread and eighteen pints of wine" (= Shorey item three); "He used to bind a ribbon round his forehead and break it by swelling his veins" (= Shorey item four); "He was reported to have carried a four-year-old bull round the stadium at Olympia and then eaten it in one day." Milo's final Olympic victory took place in 516 when Pindar was an infant. Shorey's descriptive phraseology for such late and "repulsive" types--as Milo--on "late Roman statues" comes directly from Gardner 280 ("repellent, if not absolutely repulsive"). But Gardner was not describing late Roman athletic statues; he was describing the fifth century classical Greek sculptures on the pediment of the temple of Zeus at Olympia.

preposterous. That is to say, his evidence for the degeneration that supposedly came "after the brief bloom immortalized by Pindar" actually dates from the period *before* that "bloom." In fact Shorey's evidence, if properly dated and taken seriously (which is another matter), proves the opposite of his case. Yet we shall find that our standard interpretation of Greek athletics in general is equally preposterous.

A general interpretation must rest on the interpretation of details. Matters have not improved since Shorey's day. Classical scholars still treat the evidence for Greek athletics in the same cavalier way. In his *Greek Athletes and Athletics* (London 1964), the British classicist H. Harris writes an account of Phayllos of Croton (an archaic Greek city located on the sole of the Italian boot). Phayllos won the pentathlon event (200 meters, long jump, javelin, discus, and wrestling) three times at the Pythian Games, and was famous for his extraordinary athletic ability. Harris tells us much more about Phayllos.

> With high hopes of an Olympic crown, he set out for Greece in the spring of 480, in order to put in the months of training at Elis demanded of competitors before the games in August. He must have been a man of considerable wealth, for he sailed in command of his own ship. But when he reached mainland Greece there were more important things than athletics to think of. The invading army and navy of Persia were approaching....Phayllus added his ship to the combined Greek navy....Phayllus stayed with the Greek fleet in the Aegean during the strategic moves of July and August, and in September fought in the crowning victory of Salamis....But by the time Salamis was fought the Olympic festival was over. Phayllus had seen where his duty lay and had done it. His Olympic hopes were still in the future. (Harris 1964, 114)

It is a fascinating story, well and vividly told. It is, unfortunately, also a sham. Harris' entire account, with its detailed itinerary and chronology, is outright historical fiction. And the athlete whom he represents is nothing but a creation of Harris' own imagination. Phayllos the Pythian victor did indeed command a ship at Salamis in 480. That is all we know.[7] There is no ancient source to suggest that Phayllos was still active in athletics in 480 or that he ever intended to enter the Olympic Games of that year. It is far more likely that he had already retired from athletic competition; his Olympic hopes, if any, lay behind him, not in the future.[8] In fact, our sources say nothing about Phayllos' "high hopes for an Olympic crown"; nor about his setting out "for Greece in the Spring of 480"; nor about his staying with the Greek fleet that summer or seeing "where his duty lay." All that is Harris.

Why would Harris invent such details? Why would he insert so elaborate a piece of historical fiction in the midst of a scholarly work? The answers are painfully simple. Harris' Phayllos is no ancient Greek athlete at all; he is a nineteenth century Englishman. And his imaginary career is not intended as classical history, but as a moral lesson to modern man. Harris' Phayllos is, in short, a fictitious archetype, an idealized character drawn to represent the values of Victorian gentleman amateur athletes. For they were the ones who embraced a code that placed country above personal glory; and they always knew that "there were more important things than athletics." Two thousand five hundred

---

7. Herodotus 8.47; Pausanias 10.9.2.

8. All evidence suggests an end to Croton's athletic activity before 480 (Part Two, V, below, with n. 33). Harris' confident conjecture that Phayllos was in 480 in the midst of his athletic career and "probably" won at the Pythian games in 482 and 478 is groundless or worse (unfortunately Miller 62 follows him). Herodotus' Greek clearly implies that all of Phayllos' known victories (three Pythians) antedated Salamis (Hdt. 8.47). He achieved his final Pythian victory, then, no later than 482.

years later Phayllos may now learn the same lesson, and sees "where his duty lay." All the little details of Harris' fiction aim at creating a context for those two highly emotional phrases. And to promote the values expressed by those phrases is the real goal of Harris' Phayllos-tale, not historical accuracy.

Harris' bogus Greek athlete and Shorey's false history of ancient athletics are not isolated cases nor mere instances of sloppy scholarship. They are representative examples of a far-flung and amazingly successful deception, a kind of historical hoax, in which scholar joined hands with sportsman and administrator so as to mislead the public and influence modern sport- ing life. We shall never know whether these men per- formed their deception consciously or unconsciously, nor does it much matter now. But the deception itself is still with us, and we need to inquire into its results and its causes. The introduction to Harris' *Greek Athletes and Athletics* is itself revelatory. It was not written by a classical scholar, but by someone eager to commend the book, anyway, someone "delighted" to

> commend it highly to those who are interested in sport and the Olympic Movement in particular .... May I in particular commend to readers the last chapter headed 'Conclusions.' The author's carefully argued and logical comments on the present day situation as regards *amateurism* admirably put in- to words what so many of us who are dedicated to this *move- ment* are trying hard to achieve. (e.a.)

It is not mere chance that this Introduction is signed by the Marquess of Exeter--a titled English nobleman and the Chairman of the British Olympic Association.

II

The Modern Origins of Amateurism

My main subject in the present study is ancient Greece. But we shall never look at Greek athletics with an unprejudiced eye, we shall never understand why amateurism is universally attributed to antiquity--nor why Shorey would so garble the facts--unless we first understand the modern amateur movement, both in its aims and in its history. For those aims and that history are by now almost inextricably wound into our view of ancient Greece. I hope the word "almost" is justified. For it is no easy task to untangle the current snarl of amateurism, ancient athletics, and our own Olympic Games. It will require that we look first of all at the history of modern athletics. There is more than one myth to be dispelled.

Amateurism is a strictly modern concept born in England not much more than a century ago. It began as the ideological means to justify an elitist athletic system that sought to bar the working class from competition. Most people nowadays think that amateurism was somehow the original state of our own organized sports, and that professional sports encroached on an earlier amateur system. The reverse is true. Because amateurism was the late-comer, it was forced to make inroads into an existing sporting system, or to invent alternatives. And amateurs regularly sought to displace existing professional athletes and professional institutions. The amateur generally usurped the place of the professional not, as Shorey has it, the other way around.

Athletics as we know them scarcely existed two centuries ago. But in the first half of the nineteenth century competitive sport suddenly grew in popularity, and various contests sprang up in England, Scotland, and

America.[9] "Professionalism"--that is, money prizes, cash payments, and wagers--was the standard practice in most early competitions of public interest. These contests included horse races, prize fights, rowing matches, and foot races. The purses even in rowing and running events were often large.[10] On the turf, an owner who rode his own horse was a "gentleman" and a professional rider a "jockey." Similarly, in cricket some members of a team were paid, others not, depending on their ability and need. The salaried members of a team were called "players," but no one thought to call the others "amateurs." For that term was not yet employed in sports.[11]

9. In a study of ninety-five modern sports, M. Egler found that the majority originated in the nineteenth century; about 65% began in England, France, or the U.S. (Lucas 1962, 60). If we considered only the twenty most popular sports, the percentages would be much higher. Scotland's importance has been neglected, but becomes apparent below.

10. Bailey, s.v., "pedestrianism." In America in the 1820's foot races for a prize, generally $100-$400, were especially popular. In a Long Island race in 1835 a farmer, Henry Stannard, won a $1,300 prize by beating a butcher, a carpenter, and a house painter (Holliman 152-154). These are not wealthy aristocrats. $1,300 in 1835 was far more than three years wages for any working man. In rowing contests of this period "purses ranged from twenty dollars to ten thousand .... Stakes sometimes reached the sum of ten thousand dollars and even fifty thousand" (Holliman 157; see also Menke 833).

11. Concise, accurate accounts of the pre-amateur state in modern sports appear in Menke 11-13 and esp. *Encyclopedia Americana*, 1952, s.v. "Amateur" (the excellent but unsigned historical study of the 1952 edition has by now been supplanted by an article [of no historical value] by Avery Brundage, who merely declares whom he will, and whom he will not give amateur standing). The word "amateur," first used (1803) in the arts (= dilettante), was first applied to athletics much later (*OED*, s.v.). Menke's conjecture (12) that the Latin word *amator* was first used in Roman times "to distinguish the Olympic champions who refused to capitalize on their fame" is badly anachronistic and wrong. The Latin word is never used of athletes, and athletes such as he describes never existed in antiquity.

The forerunners of modern track and field, the Highland Games of Scotland, always offered cash prizes to the victors in each event. About mid-century these traditional Scottish games spread to Scottish immigrant communities in America and Canada, forming a circuit of "Caledonian Games," as they were called here. Competitors traveled that circuit, the better ones collecting substantial amounts of money. There was then, on both sides of the Atlantic, a group of professional track and field athletes before anyone styled as an "amateur" ever practiced these events.[12]

By the 1860's, however, English university men began contests in track and field, the number of organized athletic contests burgeoned, and Englishmen of all stations increasingly sought to participate.[13] At first, men of the upper classes contended, as usual, side by side with the others. As Caspar Whitney (America's foremost apostle of amateurism) recounted it, "[F]or some time ... the amateur remained uncared for; he competed under his own name or a fictitious one for money

12. Redmond cogently argues the importance of these Scottish games to modern sport, and they are beginning to receive proper historical recognition (Lucas 1978, 107f). For their origin and spread to America see Redmond 15-41. The Braemar games of 1837 (Redmond 29) deserve especial note for their antiquity, program, and prizes.
13. The first track and field contest between two universities occurred in 1864 (Oxford vs. Cambridge; some intramural contests had preceded by a few years). The professional pedestrian contests and the Scottish-founded games (with cash prizes) were common on both sides of the Atlantic long before; "club" athletics did not yet exist. Whitney (225ff) traces the sketchy history of what he considers the antecedents to collegiate and amateur athletics in English schools, colleges, and military groups; the soundest claim to originality here seems to be hurdle races.

or trophies, and against whomsoever he pleased."[14]

Yet many of those who called themselves "gentlemen" (often, in fact, bourgeois parvenus[15]) found it distasteful to compete--and to dress[16] --with members of the working class. More importantly, they found it difficult to win.[17] They preferred to contend only

14. Whitney 229; the men whom Whitney here calls "amateurs" (i.e., men of good social standing) competed under fictitious names only because most of their peers still shared Mahaffy's view (below, IV), and regarded athletics as a rather "low thing." Cf. Anthony Trollope, British Sports and Pastimes (London 1868), 5, who notes that "Athletics" ("Racing, Jumping, Ball-throwing and Hammer-throwing, and the like") had by 1868 become so prominent as to merit "almost a claim to be reckoned among British Sports; but we have felt that they have fallen somewhat short of the necessary dignity, and have excluded them." The Greeks' modern Olympic series had already begun (and the successful 1870 Greek Olympics were but two years away: III, below) when Trollope refused to count track and field among British sports.

15. "It appears that those most recently qualified as gentlemen were the most assiduous in pulling up the ladder behind them; as one observer remarked, 'From enquiries I have made I find that nearly all the members of the athletic clubs calling themselves "Gentleman Amateurs", and who exclude tradesmen are, in reality tradesmen's sons'" (Bailey 136, emphasis in original). Bailey's observer was a correspondent in the Athletic Record and Monthly Journal, June 1876. The date reveals much.

16. "Some members of the new athletic clubs were anxious to keep out the lower orders to spare themselves the embarrassment of an unwonted physical intimacy in the dressing tent--'a matter of some importance to a sensitive person'" (Bailey 131; he quotes a contemporary press clipping). We may compare the American Whitney's 1895 reluctance "to dine or play football" with one of "the great unwashed" (below, II).

17. Every account of amateurism's origins underrates the amateurs' need to win. When an amateur lost a contest to a working man, he lost more than the race and the valuable cup. He lost his identity. His life's premise disappeared; namely, that he was innately superior to the working man in all ways, even without equivalent training. In this light we may understand the

against one another, as at college. They began to form limited membership athletic clubs in order to keep their competitions away from the working class. These exclusive clubs were the very origin of amateur athletics. "The amateur rule," as Allen Guttman aptly puts it, "was an instrument of class warfare."[18]

The first[19] amateur athletic organization in history, the Amateur Athletic Club (hereafter AAC) was formed by university men in London in 1866. Its expressed purpose was to enable "Gentleman Amateurs the means of practising and competing versus one another without being compelled to mix with professional runners." But "professional" did not mean to those men what it means to us. Those who coined the term "amateur athlete" did not define it, as we do now, strictly in terms of money or athletic profit. For them it was primarily a question of social class. Just as

17. **(continued)** vehemence of the amateurs' need (despite the stated code) to win at almost any cost or to abstain from the lists. See VI and Part Two, n. 69, below. Cf. the London *Times* comment on "the ridiculous nature of such a defeat" and its "social degradation" if a "base mechanic" should win an amateur athletic contest (26 April, 1880; quoted by Bailey 135). For the reaction of the British Football Association to a working class victory see n. 29, below.

18. Guttman 31; excellently documented by Steven Cohen in his (unfortunately unpublished) 1980 Brandeis University dissertation, "More than Fun and Games: A Comparative Study of the Role of Sport in English and American Society at the Turn of the Century," 34-98.

19. I leave aside a few problematic earlier rowing societies, for rowing requires a separate account that lies outside the scope of this study. See, e.g., "In the early days of English university boating, water-men--i.e., professional boatmen or employees of the various college boat clubs--frequently rowed under college colors" (Whitney 122; cf. 159). And I leave aside the Olympic Club of Sa Francisco, which was founded in 1860 along Germanic *Turne* lines, and did not affect Anglo-American style amateurism unt much later.

"Gentleman" and "Amateur" were synonyms, "professional" *meant* "working class." Besides nominally bar-
ring those who made money from athletics, the AAC--
by written rule--specifically excluded from amateur
eligibility any man who "is a mechanic, artisan, or
labourer."[20]

In the next decade many more class-exclusive
athletic clubs formed, adopted the membership restrictions of the AAC, and registered with it. Older, exclusive rowing clubs adopted the same wording or
something even more class-conscious:

> No person shall be considered an amateur ... who is *or has
> been* by trade or employment for wages a mechanic, artisan,
> or labourer, *or engaged in any menial duty.*[21]

In practice, restrictions against athletic profit were
not applied to men of the upper classes. They could win
as much money as they wished, and still preserve
"amateur" standing; for they were "gentlemen."[22] Con-

---

20. H. F. Wilkinson, ed., *The Athletic Almanack,* 1868 (quoted at
greater length by Bailey 131); cf. current editions of the *Encyclopedia Britannica,* s.v. "Amateur."
21. The rules for the famous Henley Regatta (e.a.), quoted with
high approval by Whitney 163. The Henley Regatta receives
especial attention because John Kelly, father of the late Princess
Grace of Monaco, was excluded for being of too low a social class
(Guttman 30f). See further Part Two, n. 69, below.
22. "Indeed, when an individual was recognized as an amateur,
he could then make money from sport and still be considered an
amateur. Dr. W. G. Grace ... was a doctor, a cricketer, and an
amateur. Since he was playing for the sake of sport and did not
need any income from the game in order to survive, Grace was
able to receive money openly and still retain his amateur status."
At two different public testimonials, Grace, a superb and adulated
cricketer, accepted checks for 1,500 and 9,000 pounds respectively
(a fortune in late nineteenth century England). "Yet, Grace was an
amateur; his background and his career made him so" (Cohen 91f;
cf. n. 26, below).

versely, working-class athletes, no matter how pure of athletic gain, could not enter amateur contests, for only "Gentleman Amateurs" were allowed. As one English sportsman wrote in 1872,

> [M]en of a class considerably lower must be given to understand that the facts of their being well conducted and civil and never having run for money are *not* sufficient to make a man a gentleman as well as an amateur.[23]

In 1880 *The Times* of London agreed with him that amateur sports should be wholly free of men from the lower social orders, who were regularly counted and should be

> counted as, in every case, professionals .... The outsiders, artisans, mechanics, and such like troublesome persons can have no place found for them. *To keep them out is a thing desirable on every account.*[24]

But in that same year English class-defined amateurism faltered, and the AAC faltered with it. Under pressure from northern clubs, which had dropped the "Mechanics Clause," the AAC was replaced by the Amateur Athletic Association (AAA). Amateurism itself was redefined. Under the new AAA rules all athletic profit was strictly forbidden to all amateurs, and social class was not specified.[25] But what working man could afford the time needed to train and to compete without

---

23. Bailey 136 (quoting from a letter in the July 1872 *Sporting Gazette*), q.v. for other revelatory comments of that time (emphasis in Bailey's quotation).
24. Quoted in Bailey 135 (e.a.). The *Times* even argues that the valuable prizes given at amateur contests must "fall into the right hands" (no "base mechanic arms") lest athletics become a means of redistributing the wealth of the upper classes to the working class.
25. Bailey 140.

any hope for remuneration? There was an obvious expectation that the new amateur rule would, in the main, achieve *de facto* what the old rule achieved by *fiat;* that is, the exclusion of the working class.

*   *   *   *   *   *   *

As the amateur movement was born in the late 1860's it spread quickly to this continent, where it met an immediate and ringing defeat in American League Baseball--which was unabashedly professional by 1869. Many in the more egalitarian America could not even grasp what "amateur" was intended to mean.[26] Our first amateur athletic organization, The New York Athletic Club (NYAC), was founded in 1868. Since no other amateur clubs were available, its members held their first contest against the professional New York Caledonian Club, a long-established Scottish-American

26. So when the Schuylkill Navy regatta (Philadelphia) officially turned amateur in 1872, many of the banned contestants claimed not to know what the word meant and the officials fared scarcely better (Menke 11). "The concept fitted easily into English society with its traditions of deference and its heritage of class rule. Englishmen knew who were amateurs. As a graduate of Oxford noted ... it was one's position in society which defined whether you were an amateur or a professional .... 'in his heart of hearts the Englishman who is born in the upper class still regards any one of his own sort as an amateur ... [*Outlook* 93 (1909)]'" (Cohen 64). "Such an argument was plausible in England. An amateur knew who his equals were, and--even more important--who his inferiors were.... In the United States such assertions were almost impossible to make. The line between gentleman and professional was always an object of intensive debate. The firm class basis and traditional bonds of society which enabled the English system to function were not present in the United States. The result was constant disagreement over what those terms meant....Americans had difficulty deciding who was amateur and who was professional" (Cohen 64, 92).

organization which had always offered cash prizes. But other amateur clubs soon formed, following the NYAC's lead. None yet contained the novel word "amateur" in its title.[27]

The first track contests among teams from American universities took place in the early 1870's. Ivy League students and others contended openly for large money prizes in meetings promoted along the traditional lines of American professional running ("pedestrianism"). As universities began track and field meets on campus, some at first offered valuable prizes or even cash. But some members of the press objected, and amateurism began to creep into academe. Many younger Caledonian college athletes were forced to abandon the professional games of their forebears in order to acquire amateur standing for university eligibility and for overseas contests in Britain. By 1879 the universities had turned amateur.[28]

This is not the place to detail all the class politics of sport in that tumultuous period from 1870 to 1888. I highlight just a few cases. In British Association Football (Soccer) a long and bitter class struggle ended in 1885, when professionalism won out and the partisans of amateurism suffered a stinging defeat equal to their earlier loss in American baseball. In America an

---

27. Redmond 50-53 (cf. 61, 66), 99f.
28. Redmond 81f, 84f, 90f; Whitney 231 ("$500 cup" prize). "When Yale U. announced its intention to award cash prizes at its Annual Games," proponents of the then novel notion of amateurism put up a howl (Redmond 61). "'Some of the younger members of the Caledonian Society of New York, realizing that the cash prizes that were awarded at the games would jeopardize their amateur standing, broke off from the parent club'" (R. Korsgaard apud Redmond 61). See also Redmond 93f, 102f. "At Cornell, cash prizes were offered, or a medal in lieu, 'if the contestant wished to retain amateur standing'" (Redmond 124).

"amateur" had proved to be impossible to describe, and there was no definition of the term that found general acceptance. Members of amateur clubs sometimes competed in professional meets, and they often made large side bets on amateur contests.[29] The amateur athletic clubs themselves bought and paid for professional athletes to compete under their banners.

> While some of the socially elite were top-flight performers, most were not....One method used by the socially elite club members was to sponsor outstanding athletes in amateur sports like track and field .... Athletic clubs began to hire the best athletes, including collegians, by offering them free room and board, and giving them valuable prizes including cash. (Lucas 1978, 156)

In 1888 the quarrels, power plays, and bidding wars among the various amateur clubs led to the downfall of the National Association of Amateur Athletes and to the creation of a new umbrella organization, the Amateur Athletic Union (AAU). The AAU formulated extremely strict rules, their core patterned after the 1880 revised "amateur" definition of the British AAA: no amateur could ever compete against a professional or make any money, however slight, from athletics.

But the AAU, it turned out, was not so interested in enforcing those rules as in controlling and dominating athletics in America.

---

29. In soccer the dates and events are typical: "In 1883, however, the working-class Blackburn Olympic team defeated the Old Etonians" (Walvin 88). "The football world was convulsed in ... 1884 when the governing body introduced a ruling effectively banning professionals .... The north formed its own British Association .... Faced with open secession ..., the Football Association executed a remarkable volte-face and gave official sanction to professionalism ... in 1885" (Bailey 141f). America: difficulty defining "amateur," n. 26, above; for club athletics see, e.g. (besides Lucas), Korsgaard *apud* Redmond 67, and n. 27, above.

The wealthy members of the AAU began to offer lucrative
prizes, as much as a quarter of an average laborer's yearly
salary for winners of track and field competitions. Athletic
clubs bid for recognized talent helping further to debase the
concept of amateurism with their hypocritical policies. (Lucas
1978, 157)

Such was the state of the amateur movement in
1895--embarrassing defeats in popular, major sports
such as baseball and British football, internal hypocrisy
and near chaos in its own strongholds, the universities
and track and field. Amateurism by 1895--then twenty-
nine years old--had scarcely ever had much actual existence in sporting life. Compared with professional
sports, especially, it had virtually no real history. It remained mostly a brief but fond dream dreamed by a
privileged few in the 1860's and 1870's, almost a
Platonic *idea* which they could glimpse now and then,
but seldom found in authentic form in this imperfect
world.

In 1895 Caspar Whitney, the most influential
American sportswriter of his time, wrote about his ex-
periences during a recent trip to England. Whitney was
an open elitist and zealously devoted to English class-
exclusive amateur sport. He repeatedly spit out his contempt for the "amachoors" of the working class, the
"great unwashed"--the "vermin" as he called athletes
from the "lower classes." It was "a class," he wrote,
"that, as a rule, is wanting in the true amateur instinct
of *sport for sport's sake.*" As Whitney put it, he was
"more than willing" to grant his "laboring brother of
lesser refinement" some of his own "advice, time, aid."
"But," he quickly adds, "I do not care to dine *or play
football* with him."[30]

30. Whitney's role in American sports has not passed wholly
unremarked: "the influential American sportsman," "Caspar
Whitney, the powerful, opinionated editor of *Outing*" (Lucas 1980,

Yet Whitney found the conditions of contemporary amateur sport in England no better than in America. The laboring class had infiltrated the ranks there, as well. In a fervent plea for a return to "the halcyon days" of the 1860's and an amateur rule that banned "mechanics, artisans, and laborers," Whitney in 1895 called for a separation of the classes in American sport for the twentieth century. Athletic participation might lead to a "purer heredity" (a high matter for Whitney[31]) in any of the social classes. But amateurism, he argued, should be restricted to "the better element," that is, the upper class. He founded it only evil

> to bring together in sport the two divergent elements of society that never by any chance meet elsewhere on even terms.... The laboring class are all right in their way; let them go their way in peace, and have their athletics in whatsoever manner suits their inclinations....Let us have our own sport among the more *refined* elements. (Whitney, 166f)

Whitney could hardly have known that he would soon find his dream-world of sport, a magnificent athletic festival intended for "the more *refined*

---

30. **(continued)** 50, 64); cf. Cohen 93. The words quoted above: *A Sporting Pilgrimage,* 287f, 280, 281, 285, 286, and 166, respectively (e.a.). Yet Whitney says (166) at the same time, "None is more democratic than I." Cf. "I hope no one will understand me as disparaging athleticism among the lower classes" (282f).

31. Whitney 285. Whitney placed great faith in heredity, and his racism was as open as his classism. We should not expect the lower class man to be able to abandon the "habits of a lifetime-- nay, of several generations of lifetimes." And it is "senseless" to expect "the negro, lifted suddenly out of generations of bondage, to fraternize and favorably compare with the race whose individuals have always been the refined and cultured members of the civilized world" (164).

elements." He would find it in the modern International Olympic movement of Baron Pierre de Coubertin. Whitney was to become, in fact, the second American appointed to the International Olympic Committee (1900-1905). He was President of the United States Olympic Committee from 1906-1910.[32]

32. An official IOC publication gives Whitney's term on the International Olympic Committee as 1900-1905 (IOC, *The International Olympic Committee and the Modern Olympic Games,* Aigle, Switz., 1950, p. 31). Some sources give 1906-1908 as the term of Whitney's presidency of the American Olympic Committee (later renamed United States Olympic Committee).

III

The Modern Greek Olympics and John Mahaffy

It might seem that we should now turn to the modern International Olympic Games and Baron de Coubertin, whom we regularly credit with the idea of reviving the ancient Greek Olympics in 1896. But that credit is all by Coubertin's own careful design. We must turn next to Greece--not ancient Greece, as one might expect, but to modern Greece, a neophyte nation which our study has already left unfairly behind. There were many Olympic revivals that antedate Coubertin's and our own Olympic Games. But I focus on the pre-Coubertinian modern Olympic games which have had the most historical impact on our own world--the modern Greeks' Olympic Games of the nineteenth century. They are now virtually forgotten, even in Greece. That too is by Coubertin's careful design.

What Coubertin wrapped in darkness was a series of modern Olympic Games which began in Athens in 1859, several years before either Coubertin or the concept of amateurism had been born. In order to press his own claim to priority the Baron himself feigned amnesia about these Greek games (MacAloon 150f). He liked to give his articles titles such as "Why I revived the Olympic Games." His supporters, eager to preserve his claim, wholly ignore the pre-Coubertinian modern Greek Olympics. Or else they systematically seek to discredit them.

Thus Georges Bourdon, Coubertin's associate from the start (Mandell 80), once wrote an account of the subject. In summary he claims that the modern Greeks' Olympic Games amounted to "nothing." They were "more country-fair amusements [*amusements forains*] than serious sporting competitions" (which is surely untrue). Bourdon scarcely conceals his motive for denigrating the Greek Olympic revival: "It is to a French initiative that the lofty credit for re-establishing the Games would redound" (Bourdon 21). But Bourdon's damning account is uninformed, incomplete, openly biased, and full of errors. In journalism it would be called a 'hatchet job.'

Yet for half a century historians of the modern Olympics have relied on nothing but Bourdon's brief article (supplemented only by Mahaffy's own 'hatchet-job' on the 1875 Greek Olympics studied below). Embellishing it with further errors they conclude that the modern Greek games were "completely unsuccessful," "good examples of what not to do." But their judgments are founded on almost total misinformation. Coubertin's reputation has indeed prospered, but history has been dealt a nearly fatal blow.[33]

As the nineteenth century began, Greece was still under full Turkish rule. But the Greek War of Independence put much of southern Greece in Greek hands by 1829. The Greeks' allies, France and Germany, installed a teenager from Bavaria as Otto the First, King of the Hellenes. In 1858, E. Zappas, a wealthy Greek then living in Rumania, gave King Otto a large sum of money for the "restoration of the Olympic Games, to be celebrated every four years, following the precepts of our ancestors." A veteran of the War, Zappas believed that a return to the glorious days of ancient Greece would help to restore national pride. Most of Otto's Greek advisors, however, argued that nineteenth-century Olympics should focus on nineteenth-century concerns; specifically they should be limited to competition in such categories as industrial and agricultural progress. Athletic contests, they informed him, were

33. *See Excursus I, pages 39-40 below.*

bygone affairs of the primitive past. From that time on the Olympics funded by Zappas contended with an anti-athletic faction that sought to divert the Games and the Zappas fund away from competitive athletics.

Yet when Olympic Games were held in Athens in 1859, athletic contests, as Zappas had specified, were included in the program. They took place in a flat city square not far from Omonoia. Most people, including the reporters, complained that they could not even see the athletes. Police roughly removed them from the central scene, and the games were marred by disorder. But the athletic events occurred (running events at three distances, jumps, discus and javelin throws, and a pole climb); and the winners were rewarded with substantial cash prizes, as Zappas had specified. An Olympic revival had indisputably happened.[34]

Zappas soon died, leaving his immense estate for the continuation of the Olympic Games. The Greeks

34. The Plateia Loudovikou (Grombach's "Louis Square") lies between Aiolos and Athina Streets (bounded by Efpolis and Kratinos Streets) a few blocks south of Omonoia. (Renamed Plateia Kotzia some time ago, it has recently been renamed again). Its old-time habitues know nothing of the origin of the Olympic Games in their square, and will assure the inquiring visitor that Baron Coubertin first restored the Olympic Games, with Greek help, in the Panathenaic stadium in 1896. It is still a flat, open square (dotted with flower shops, fountains, and *kapheneia*); if a crowd stood round it, only those in the front rank could see events within it. Because the reporters could not see well in 1859, even contemporary accounts of the 1859 athletic events are sketchy. One highly critical newspaper indeed states that a distance runner died ('Αθηνᾶ, November 18, 1859); but the others are remarkably silent on the matter. No blind beggar won an event (as Santas 94 claims); nor can I discover why Grombach (and thus Mandell, MacAloon, and others; above, n. 33) says that the blind beggar sang a song to the multitude (or to the king and queen), "for which he was not (un)recompensed (unrewarded)." It seems that he merely ran.

soon ran Otto off the throne and out of Greece; their allies rewarded them with another teenage prince for a king, this time a Dane. Olympics at four-year intervals proved impossible. But in 1870 the Greeks held another edition of the restored Olympic Games. This time the site was, as many wanted in 1859, the ancient Panathenaic stadium in Athens. It was still damaged and not fully excavated. But at least the spectators--and reporters--could see from their seats on its long, steep sides.

To judge by today's standards the athletic program of the 1870 Athens Olympics was the most modern and sophisticated that the world had seen at that time. It included ancient Greek Olympic events (such as the discus and javelin throws--unknown in England, America, and France--foot races, long jumps, and wrestling) and modern gymnastic events (such as a rope climb and a pole climb). Athletes from all around the Greek world, as in antiquity, assembled in the stadium and contended, in orderly fashion and as best they could, for Olympic victory. The winners were rewarded with their olive crowns and cash prizes, generally a hundred drachmas for each victor and fifty for second place. A large crowd of about 30,000 spectators looked on with great appreciation and perfect order. The Games ended with dignity and virtually everyone, even the reporters, joined in praise of the restored Olympics (Chrysafis 51f, 77-83). These 1870 Games mark a high point in Olympic revivals prior to 1896, in most ways perhaps superior to several IOC editions after that date. A historian might seriously consider whether they should be reckoned as a legitimate descendant of the ancient Olympics and an ancestor of the successful 1896 Games held in that same stadium, the Games which we count as the beginning of our own.

Yet not quite all joined in their praise. The 1870 Olympics were an athletic and public success without doubt. But the 400 meter race was won by a butcher; an ordinary laborer won the wrestling; and victory fell to a stone-cutter in a gymnastic event, the pole climb. Even in Greece a few men rose to complain. A university professor, Philippos Ioannou, belonged to the anti-athletic faction, but still served as a judge at the games. After the games he and two fellow judges filed a complaint with the Olympic Committee, and expressed strong dissent from the general satisfaction with the Games. "Some laboring men," they noted with contempt, had competed.[35]

It is well to mark the date, 1870. The idea of amateurism had scarcely left its cradle, but it had traveled far and fast. Already it had reached America, and now it made its first step ever onto Greek soil: "[S]ome laboring men scarcely pried away from their

---

35. Ioannou's and the judges' Report is paraphrased (and partly quoted) in Chrysafis 84f. Ioannou's attachment to the anti-athletic faction (for which see further Μέγα ... Λεξικόν I, 396-416 [from οὐχί ... ἀθλητῶν, ἀλλὰ ... βιομηχανίαν ... καλλιτεχνίαν; "not athletes ... but industry ... fine arts," 396]) was already clear from an "Olympic Speech" which he made before the Games. There he argued that the "useful arts should be valued ahead of a demonstration of strength and physical dexterity." In this world of scientific, mechanized warfare, Ioannou claimed, "physical strength and the athletic development of physical powers have lost a large part of their former worth [ἀξία]" (apud Chrysafis 76). Apparently both Chrysafis and Bourdon believed that working class men should indeed be excluded from Olympic competition. For they both subscribe fully to the spirit and recommendation of the Judges' Report, and editorialize accordingly (ὀρθότατα, "quite correctly," Chrysafis 84; "Cet intelligent et substantiel rapport," Bourdon 21). Chrysafis was Phokianos' pupil (below) and repeatedly defends his master's principles.

The working men, whose presence at the Games offended Ioannou and the judges, were Evangelis Skordaras, Theophanis Trounkas, and K. Kardamylakis, the 1870 Olympic champions in the 400 meters, pole climb, and wrestling, respectively (Chrysafis 78f).

wage-earning jobs" had entered "impromptu and for the most part for the money prize." Even worse, apparently, they had won. These men from the working class, Ioannou's group decided, had turned the Games into a "pointless parody of the ancient games."[36] They proposed that any future Olympic Games should ban entries from the public at large, restricting eligibility to the "educated youth" (εὐπαίδευτος νεολαία) of Greece. These men had no intention of excluding money prizes. They merely wanted to exclude working men and to encourage physical education among the students at the university and schools, who tended to come from the upper social orders. To that end they recommended the funding of gymnasiums, staffed with coaches, for the young men of academe.

Ioannou's party carried the day. A corps of gymnastic instructors was appointed, Ioannis Phokianos at its head. His goal was to attract to the gymnasium the youth "from the cultured class (ἐκ τῆς μορφωμένης τάξεως) ... instead of the working men (ἀντὶ τῶν ἐργατικῶν) who had competed in the two previous Olympiads" (Chrysafis 89). Olympic Games were announced for 1875, still offering money prizes (150 drachmas for first, fifty for second place). And the program was much as before, yet with fewer track and field events and more Germanic gymnastic events (Phokianos later deemed the Olympic events of his ancient ancestors of little use

36. This remark that the Games were "a parody of the ancient games" is often quoted (e.g., Bourdon 21, Santas 94) as a means summarily to dismiss the entire Greek Olympic series and to imply that it was the general judgment even of the Greeks themselves. It is well to remember that it refers specifically to the participation of the working class, not the athletic or public success of the Games; and that it was the opinion filed by three men against the prevailing judgment. It should not be taken from context and generalized.

and undignified). But the 1875 Olympic Games were for educated youths only. Prospective competitors, "students at the University and upper schools," were to enroll in preparatory training at their academic institution.

A crowd of ten to fifteen thousand assembled in the stadium for the Olympic Games. But the track and the seating arrangements were ill prepared. And very few young men actually competed for the prizes. They were of a much "higher social class" than their 1870 Olympic predecessors. But neither they nor the officials seemed to take the Olympic Games very seriously. There was disorder on the field, disorder in the stands. The athletes did not come quickly when their events were called. Miscues on the field drew laughter. The music which punctuated the events was not Greek, but polkas and other "frivolous" tunes from the North. Worst of all, the interval between events was stretched out by long, boring speeches of the judges. The patient crowd grew impatient, and the Games ended.

In sharp contrast to the successful Games of 1870--to which the newspapers insistently compared them--the 1875 games were universally judged as a failure. Of this, too, there can be no doubt. Phokianos was blamed for the disorder, felt disgraced, resigned, and left town (he returned to preside over one last Olympic debacle [1889], again for an elite--this time a small, elite audience sitting comfortably away from the large, empty, unused Panathenaic stadium where the 1870, 1875, and 1896 Olympic Games took place). In short, the modern Greek Olympic games had turned amateur and run aground.[37]

Yet the Olympic Games of 1875 were fated for worse than failure. In the stands sat a fateful spectator, John Mahaffy--a classical scholar and prolific author of

37. *See Excursus II, pages 40-43 below.*

books on Greece. He was freshly arrived in Greece. He knew nothing of the successful 1870 Games, nor of Ioannou's and Phokianos' efforts to turn the Olympics into an enclave for the "cultured class." In Mahaffy's eyes a Greek was a Greek. In so democratic a society, he wrote sarcastically, even the "richer classes" could not be called "upper."[38]

Though his family was Irish and he lived in Ireland, Mahaffy professed to be English. And Mahaffy adulated everything that was associated with the English royalty, nobility, and upper class--which to his mind represented all proper values. He was proud to be an English chauvinist. And even his defenders agree that he was a pretentious social "snob."[39] He belittled the ancient Greeks whom he studied and contemned the modern Greeks whose hospitality he accepted. And, he tells us, he strongly disliked track and field athletics.

---

38. Mahaffy 1875, 324. His ignorance about the details of the previous Greek Olympics shows in his phrase "the first contests (eight years ago)" (326). It had actually been fifteen years since the 1859 Games, to which Mahaffy's quotation, "almost ridiculous," explicitly refers (unattributed, but taken from the Ἐφημερίς, May 20, 1875). Mahaffy makes no note of the "second, somewhat better Games" of 1870, which his same source mentions in the same sentence. Mahaffy did not know who Zappas was, nor could he even spell or inflect his name ("[A]n old gentleman called Zapa," 324).

39. "'The Anglo-Irish are a curiously snobbish people, and Mahaffy was a prime specimen of his kind. He was an out-and-out social snob: that is he would rather have sat down to a bad meal with a stupid aristocrat than to a good meal with an intelligent tradesman....He loved a lord, adored a duke, and would have worshipped a prince...[Hesketh Pearson, Life of Oscar Wilde, 1960 edn., 30].'

...'Castle-lackey', 'tuft-hunter', they called him....[E]ven some of his friends conceded that he was something of a snob, but a dazzlingly successful snob," W.B. Stanford and R.B. McDowell, Mahaffy: A Biography of an Anglo-Irishman (London, 1971) 89.

They were not aristocratic enough. They smacked of "the city." The track, like the gym, was no place for an aristocratic "country gentleman." "Running races round a short course," Mahaffy declared, "is no proper out-of-door game." The only "proper" sports, he maintained, were cricket and fox hunting to hounds.[40]

It is no wonder that Mahaffy saw nothing to praise in the Olympic Games at the Panathenaic stadium that day in 1875. His account of his observations appeared in *Macmillan's Magazine* the same year. It is a brutally satirical, derisive attack on the Greeks and on their restored Olympics.

It bristles with patent exaggerations and quarter-truths. But even worse, it is full of mistakes and arrogant ignorance. The 1875 games themselves were bad enough. But the very idea of reviving the Olympic Games--an idea we now would not question--seemed absurd to Mahaffy:

> The burden of great names and of a noble past seems to sit lightly on the modern Greeks. Were we to propose the resuscitation of the Olympic Games in the Panathenaic stadium at Athens, we should be in anxious dread of comparisons with the victors of Pindar's day .... Nay, we should fear an accusation of absurdity in transferring Olympia to Athens..... But the modern Greeks seem in no ways daunted by these sentimental difficulties.

Mahaffy described the stadium as being like "a huge, oblong stewpot" (he apparently had not seen a stadium before). He observed quarrels in the stands, but decided that they were "inevitable, when ten or eleven thousand people of all classes are gathered together" (they had not, however, happened when

---

40. Mahaffy 1881, 23: cf. 1879, 63; Stanford (above, n. 39) notes Mahaffy's excellence in "cricket and field sports" (i.e., hunting and fishing, not track and field, which he regularly disdained).

nearly 30,000 attended the 1870 Games). Mahaffy ridicules the Greeks for reviving the discus throw. The event, he thought, should be buried in history never to be re-enacted. The Greeks should emulate English models. "[W]e never throw the discus," he remarks with smug pride. He has little to say about the contests themselves, and almost nothing good to say about the competitors (he did not know they were the cream of the cultured class). He found the dogs that entered the field more interesting, and gave them equal space.

A man of Mahaffy's aristocratic preferences would surely have applauded the ban on working men and Phokianos' singular efforts to attract the social elite. But, alas, Mahaffy did not even know who Phokianos was. He faults "some single master," who had trained the athletes: "[W]e could not help wishing that some slight flavour of English system and form had been known to him."

He was naturally quick to censure the national authorities and organizers of the games. But he chides them for the wrong reasons. "There were horse races (μονόζογοι, καὶ δίζυγοι) [sic] also announced, but had to be postponed to another day." But Mahaffy should never have expected to see horse races in the stadium that day. For μονόζυγον and δίζυγον are the modern Greek words for "horizontal bar" and "parallel bars," respectively.[41] Mahaffy ridiculed the Greeks in 1875 for their lack of athletic sophistication. But he himself was so ignorant of modern athletics (and of Greek) that he did not even *recognize* modern gymnastic events on the

41. Gymnastics were Germanic, and generally unknown in Britain. Mahaffy's *δίζυγοι and *μονόζυγοι are not even words, neither ancient nor modern Greek (the words for 'parallel bars' and 'horizontal bar' are neuter gender, but Mahaffy unwittingly inflected them as masculines, adding a further misspelling in the latter).

program. He expected "horse races." The error is typical of Mahaffy's work.

Such then is the nature and reliability of the Western World's only eye-witness account of the modern Greek Olympics. It is the account on which recent Olympic historians, such as Mandell and MacAloon, have necessarily depended for their evaluation of these pre-Coubertinian modern Games. Had they not been so full of mischief, Mahaffy's mistakes would be ludicrous. But his errors have caused worse mischief than our faulty vision of early Olympic history. To James Thorpe, Paavo Nurmi, Karl Schranz, Brian Oldfield, Bill Toomey, and countless others, "amateurism" has been no laughing matter. And they owed their difficulties in some part to John Mahaffy and his errors. For Mahaffy founded the academic myth of ancient Greek amateurism, on which other amateur partisans relied.

EXCURSUS I: *Bourdon and the falsified history*
of the "Zappas" Olympics (= note 33)

Perhaps most revelatory of Bourdon's aims is this sentence:
"C'était plus qu'il n'en fallait pour discréditer les jeux olympiques
[grecques]" 20. The words "completely unsuccessful" and "good
examples of what not to do" come from Lucas 1962, 18f and
Grombach 13 (each author knows of only two of the four Greek
Olympiads). So Mezö 19 writes that the Greeks' Olympics "had
no sport-value." Mezö belonged to the IOC, Grombach is tied to
the USOC; Bourdon is their source.

It is no surprise that sports historians cannot obtain other,
more accurate information on these games (so MacAloon 151, can
only quote Grombach, and openly despairs [319, n.135] of
discovering Grombach's own source). The only reliable source,
apart from old Athenian newspapers, is Chrysafis' book. But it is
written in an exceptionally difficult style of modern Greek, and is
unavailable outside of Greece. None of the accounts readily
available (such as Grombach 13f, Bianculesco, Mandell 34ff, and
MacAloon 150ff) is trustworthy. They are fourth and fifth hand
versions so garbled by errors (a tradition of mistranslation, confusion of Olympiads, lost contexts, embellishment, omission,
moralizing, and editorializing) that they bear little relation to the
games which actually took place. Mandell, for example, indeed
paints a picture of *amusements forains,* the rude affairs which
Bourdon described. In the 1859 Games, he tells us, "The winner
in wrestling took home a milk cow" (34). But there was no wrestling
event in the 1859 games, and certainly no milk cow for a prize.
(The error comes from a misreading of Bourdon 19f.) The pole for
the 1875 pole-climb event, Mandell writes, was "a tall greased
pole at the top of which honked a fat goose. It was the prize for the
athlete who was the first of the many who simultaneously tried to
seize it" (35). Fortunately, we need not try to visualize this impossible action. For there was no goose at the 1875 Olympics nor
at any other. Mandell has confused the 1875 pole climb with the
1859 pole climb, where the prizes did rest at the top of the pole for
the victor's taking. But Mandell's fat, honking "goose" was in
reality a valuable watch, a silk belt and silk handkerchiefs, two
wine goblets, and a pair of silver candlestick holders (so the contemporary Athenian newspaper, Αἰών, November 16, 1859). The
Greek Games begin to appear not so rude, after all (goose-pulls
were still held in the American South at this time). These errors
are not exceptional; rather they are typical of the rest of Mandell's
account, and of all the versions of the others. The historically accurate sentence is the exception rather than the rule. This is not

Excursus I: (**continued**) the place for a full analysis of these errors nor a full, documented account of the Greek Games. I intend to offer a separate article on the question elsewhere. My own source here is, in the main, Chrysafis (despite his prejudice for the amateurs' and Coubertin's case), supplemented by contemporary Greek newspaper items, the Μέγα...Λεξιχόν, Mahaffy's article, and some items preserved (but displayed untranslated) in the IOC's Museum of the Modern Olympics in Olympia, Greece.

EXCURSUS II: *The 1875 and 1889 "Zappas" Olympics* (= note 37)

1875 Games: Chrysafis 89-111. "Higher social class": Οἱ ἀγῶνες οὗτοι ἐφέτος ἀνυφοῦνται πολὺ διότι ἡ κατερχομένη εἰς αὐτοὺς τάξις τῶν νέων εἶναι πολυτιμοτέρα βεβαίως, the newspaper 'Εφημερίς, May 15, 1875; μορφωμένης νεολαίας, *ibid.*, May 20 (Chrysafis 99, 103). There were noticeably fewer contestants than before. The Αἰών says there were only "about fifteen"; but the 'Εφημερίς says, "very few, twenty-four in all," and Mahaffy says "not above twenty-five." "There was no order, no reverence" shown in any respect, "but everything assumed the color of comedy .... The crowd seized every chance for merriment .... Neither the judges nor the contestants themselves had any interest in the form (ἰδέα) of the proceedings," Αἰών, May 19, 1875. The parallel bars and horizontal bar events were cancelled: "the hour was late, and the crowd had had enough of the sight ('Εφημερίς, May 20; Phokianos disliked the events, as well--Chrysafis 118, n. 1, etc.). For the explicit, highly unfavorable comparison with the successful 1870 Games: Chrysafis 100 (and quoted newspapers). The newspaper accounts devastated the 1875 Games. "They were viewed in general and by everyone as a failure" (Chrysafis 109).

Quoting Mahaffy's (erroneous) perceptions (including his "all Athens was perfectly satisfied" and his misspellings of Greek), MacAloon writes, "The papers ... were for the most part 'in high delight and admiration'" of the 1875 Games. "Unfortunately," MacAloon continues, "I have failed to turn up eyewitness accounts of the 1889 (?) festival, but improvements were likely made and the outpouring of civic joyfulness unabated" (152). But MacAloon's guess is far from the mark. The opposite was true.

There is an eye-witness report of the 1889 Olympic Games by Chrysafis, who includes two more (118-127). Chrysafis not only attended but also participated. Although he was devoted to Phokianos and to the amateur movement in Greece and has nothing but praise for them, he makes no attempt to cover up their failure in this case (nor his own contribution to it).

Excursus II: (continued) Olympic Games were announced for Autumn 1888 (the cause of all the confusion over the date: see MacAloon 319, n. 136: Mezö 19 wrongly says there were games in both 1888 and 1889). They were to be directed by the Swiss gymnast Borel--Panhellenic Olympics, "public games, ... in the Panathenaic stadium." Borel died. Phokianos was recalled, and once again drew the "youth of the cultured social class" to his gym. The Olympic Committee dropped their former plans, turning the matter over to Phokianos. Phokianos produced the whole affair on his own. For he wanted "to encourage the young *amateurs* of his gym" (Chrysafis 117, e.a.). There were no games in 1888. But in May 1889 "instead of Panhellenic Games in the stadium" Phokianos held "a simple contest among his gymnasium trainees" in his gymnasium. "[O]nly the students and pupils and some other habitues of [Phokianos'] gymnasium" participated (Chrysafis 117). They were dressed in white shirts with tie, dark blue belts, and long white trousers.

The spectators were greeted by Phokianos' pupils demonstrating precision group drills with Indian clubs and barbells (which Phokianos preferred to competitive athletics and gymnastics, which he associated with danger, vulgar acrobatics, and the abhorred "professional" [Chrysafis 118, n. 1, and *passim*]). But the spectators were too many for the small place; idle participants blocked their views. Phokianos' pupils crowded round the arena and "shoving and being shoved, we too indisputably contributed to the failure" of the 1889 Olympics (Chrysafis 119). Athletes apparently began to do impromptu, unofficial demonstrations of their ability in the events. "The crowd was large, the seats few." It seems that panic (or a melee) began. There was "a flood of humanity, jostling one another helter-skelter ... ladies and young women were made uneasy ... contestants mixed with the crowd, and no one knew what was happening" ('Ακρόπολις *apud* Chrysafis 121). The disorder could not be stopped, the Government Ministers left, and the games were stopped, "postponed until Tuesday." On Tuesday, a "small, select audience" was allowed to observe the restaging of the Games. "[Perfect] European order! You would have thought you were in a gymnasium in Germany," the 'Ακρόπολις now wrote in high approval. The small, select crowd applauded especially a fifteen-year old winner in a weight-lifting event (A. Philadelpheus-- "from," Chrysafis notes in praise, "an old and prominent family"). It applauded Phokianos, and two newspapers

Excursus II: **(continued)** applauded the second try as a success. But it is clear that the Olympics had, in violation of Zappas' intention and will, been removed from the Greek public. First, ordinary citizens were excluded from competition; now they were not even allowed to watch.

Grombach (not knowing that Zappas died before amateurism was invented) claims that the Greek Olympic Games failed because Zappas "was naive and inexperienced in both promotion and amateur athletics. Unlike Baron de Coubertin, he did not first seek out the leaders of school, college and amateur athletic organizations throughout the world and solicit their help." In view of the sequence of events, a historian might argue the reverse: that precisely when the leaders of school, college, and amateur organizations took over the direction of these (once successful) Games, they faltered. Mandell, too, misses the mark badly when he caps off his dismal account of the Greek games thus: "The modern Greeks ... lacked an established festive or ceremonial sporting tradition of their own" (36). Again the details suggest exactly the opposite. The Greeks, if any one, had an established festive and athletic tradition in this period that was all their own; Western Europe was only beginning to pick it up. But when the Greeks abandoned their own authentic tradition in favor of Northern European models, they produced games that indisputably failed. MacAloon says that the Greek "'Olympics'" (n.b. the safe quotation marks) were "apparently" discontinued "for want of money and organization" (152). His version is less inaccurate, but confessedly uninformed and obviously simplistic.

A more likely version appears between the lines in Chrysafis' book. Chrysafis confesses that the 1875 and 1889 Olympics were disastrous affairs, but seeks to salvage something from them. On the positive side, he relates: "In a word, there arose a small but not wholly inconsiderable gymnastic and agonistic movement, sufficient to provide the requisite elements for a very dignified (εὐπρόσωπος), for that time, competitive athletic festival--far more perfected (τελειοτέρα) and diversified than any of the preceding ones; because, as it turned out, all the amateur gymnasts and *amateur athletes* [φίλαθλοι--the translation of "amateur" in vogue then, now abandoned] of the period occupied, *without exception, the very highest social positions* (ἀρίστας κοινωνικὰς θέσεις)." "Yet the Olympic Committee," Chrysafis continues in apparently genuine wonder, "for reasons that I have never been able to discover, left this opportunity entirely unexploited" (130, e.a.). It did not occur

Excursus II: (continued) to Chrysafis (excellent at documentation but perhaps slow at perception) to inquire whether the very class-exclusiveness of the Ioannou-Phokianos movement (his object of praise)--along with its twice-demonstrated failure--might have contributed to the public disaffection with the games, and to their end.

IV

The Ancient Greeks Turn Amateur

Mahaffy was not content to stand the modern Greeks in head-hanging shame beside the modern Englishman. A year later, in 1876, the ancient Greeks felt precisely the same sting. In *Old Greek Life* Mahaffy wrote, "I believe that the Greeks did not understand athletics at all so well as the English do" (77). And in 1879, apparently as a sequel to his piece on the 1875 modern Greek Olympics, Mahaffy wrote a second article for *Macmillan's,* this time on "Old Greek Athletics." The old Greeks, too, were the Englishman's inferior. Mahaffy expresses his

> suspicion that ... Greek athletic performances were not greater, if even equal to our own....(64) [T]hat the Greeks did not box on sound principles, and that any prominent member of the P. R. would with his naked fists have easily settled any armed* champion of Olympia. (67)

But the ever inventive Mahaffy found a silver lining in the cloud which he saw hanging over ancient Greek sport. The more intelligent Greeks, he asserts, despised athletics as much as he did; and what is more they even had--clear back in ancient Greece--something of that grace that saves any sporting contest from evil: the *"amateur".* Mahaffy's paragraph here deserves a close look. For it is, so far as I can discover, the *first assertion ever that ancient Greeks were "amateur"* in their sports. And the entire Myth of Ancient Greek Amateur Athletics seems to descend from Mahaffy's very words:

---

* Mahaffy wrongly thought archaic Greeks used a caestus.

> [T]he term *athletic* was used by the Greeks for that **profes-sional** development which they reprehended as the exaggera-tion of the older *gymnastic,* with its accompaniment of public games (*agonistic*) at which the contests were **amateur** perfor-mances, and which were for centuries the glory and the pride of Greece. Thus *athletics* was rather a low thing among the Greeks, who looked upon "running for the pot" with a highbred contempt. (61; Mahaffy's italics, my emphases)

This is utter nonsense. Despite Mahaffy's authoritative tone, his argument is as preposterous as Shorey's, with which we began. A glance at the stan-dard Greek dictionary (LSJ) will reveal that the words ἀθλεύω, *'contend for a prize'* and ἀθλητής, *'athlete'* (whence ἀθλητικός *'athletic'*) antedate γυμνάζω, *'exercise the body'* and γυμναστής, *'trainer '* (whence γυμναστικός *'gymnastic'*). The ἀθλεύω / *athletic* group antedates the γυμνάζω / *gymnastic* group by centuries. So also do the concepts and the practice of the former antedate the latter. Mahaffy has the chronology of his evidence backwards. So far as we can separate the two items *athletic* and *gymnastic,* the evidence clearly suggests that *athletic* came first.

And *athletic* was "a low thing among the Greeks," who looked on running for the pot with "highbred contempt"? These are Mahaffy's *own* responses; they are certainly not those of an archaic Greek such as Pin-dar or Simonides. To prove that athletics were a low thing among the Greeks, Mahaffy rejects Pindar, turn-ing to later authors. Although Pindar indeed sang the glories of the victors, "even then":

> [E]ven then men began to think of *more serious* rivalries, and more exciting spectacles, than the festive meetings at Olym-pia. In the very next generation the poets had drifted away from them, and Euripides despises rather than admires them. The historians take little notice of them. (62; e.a.)

Mahaffy's text of the historians seems to differ greatly from our own.* As for Euripides, Mahaffy seems to know frag. 282 Nauck well enough. But he is patently guilty of the most fallacious step known to literary criticism. He takes the remark of one character in one of Euripides' plays--wholly out of context--and makes of it the author's own considered and unswerving personal philosophical belief. There is plenty in Euripides to confound Mahaffy at that low level of scholarship. In Euripides *Hippolytus* 1016f, e.g., we read "I would like to be first in winning the athletic games of the Greeks, but have a secondary place in the city." But to quote *Hippolytus* 1016f against him is to proceed as pointlessly and fallaciously as Mahaffy. More to the point, and apparently quite unknown to Mahaffy, is Euripides frag. 755 Page (*PMG*). There Euripides himself writes a poem to praise a victor in those "festive meetings at Olympia" which Mahaffy tells us Euripides "despises."[42]

---

* And from that used by T. S. Brown, "Herodotus' Views on Athletics," *Ancient World* 7 (1983), 17-29, who has just now taken up the subject of Herodotus' "many references to sports" (18), concluding, "This examination of Herodotus' references to individual athletes and to the great athletic festivals leaves no doubt that ... he had a soft spot in his heart for the games" (29).

42. For translation of Euripides frag. 282 Nauck see Miller 95f; its much milder antecedent is Xenophanes 2 (Miller 95; see also Part Two, IV, below [end]) and its humorous descendant is Plato *Apology* 36d (Part Two, n. 26, below). We do not know the speaker's identity in Euripides' fragment. Euripides *Hipp.* 1016f (ἐγὼ δ᾽ ἀγῶνας μὲν κρατεῖν Ἑλληνικοὺς/πρῶτος θέλοιμ᾽ ἄν, ἐν πόλει δὲ δεύτερος) not only contradicts Mahaffy's point but it also runs directly counter to the amateur creed; see D. C. Young, *Three Odes of Pindar* (Leiden 1968), 18. Euripides frag. 755 Page *PMG* (his poem in honor of Alcibiades' Olympic victory) is not translated in the sourcebooks and is generally ignored in the textbooks (but cf. Yalouris 144).

Yet by far the most pernicious of all Mahaffy's misrepresentations was his discovery of the "amateur" element in the early days of ancient Greece:

> [I]t is to the honour of the Greeks, who were otherwise fond enough of lucre, that the distinction of a parsley, fir, or bay crown should have (in theory at least) been the only reward for long and arduous labour....There seems to have been no second prize in any of the historical games, a natural consequence of the abolition of material rewards. (61, 65)

Mahaffy either did not consider the Panathenaic Games at Athens as "historical," or he was simply ignorant of *IG* II^2 2311. That inscription shows that even second prize at Athens paid, in fact, a material reward equivalent in value to thousands of our dollars (Part Two, III, below).[43]

But by his own admission such things as ancient inscriptions and scholarly accuracy were never of much importance to Mahaffy. He found it more important to promote his own aristocratic values--and to impose a kind of imaginary history of Victorian English sport over a kind of imaginary history of ancient Greece.[44] In early Greece, "among the aristocrats of epical days" and among the Spartans, hunting and fishing were, Mahaffy claims,

---

43. This inscription was in print in Mahaffy's day; the relevant portion was published by Sauppe in 1858 (*IG* testimonia). But Mahaffy ignores the classical inscription, and cites (irrelevantly) a passage in St. Paul instead. A case for second and third place at the Olympics is made by Buhmann 13ff.

44. Mahaffy was repeatedly judged a poor scholar by his peers. "He was accused of superficiality, irrelevancy, rash judgement, and inaccuracy. For example, Basil Gildersleeve...declared: '...the book is not to be taken in dead earnest .... Mr. Mahaffy's *Greek Life and Thought* is hardly intended to be anything else than a running commentary on the latter half of the nineteenth century ....' Monro ... remarked: 'Mr. Mahaffy has ... at least the Greek freedom from the domination of hard fact.' Both of these critics

quite the leading amusement, nor ought competitions in a
gymnasium to be compared for a moment to this far higher
and more varied recreation. The contrast still subsists among
us, and our fox-hunting, salmon-fishing, grouse-shooting
country gentleman has the inestimable advantage over the city
athlete ... whose special training for a particular event has a
necessary tendency to *lower* him into a professional. There is
even a danger of some fine exercises ... being vulgarised by
the invasion of this professional spirit, which implies such attention to the body as to exclude higher pursuits, and reward
by special victories (*sic*) and by public applause, rather than
by the intrinsic pleasure of sport for its own sake. (63f, e.a.).

Many of these remarks become catch-phrases of later
scholars and of the amateur movement: namely, the objection to "special training" for an event (later called
"over-specialization"); the phrase "to lower" someone
"into a professional" (which judges the professional to
be, *ipso facto,* debased); and the notion that such "attention to the body" somehow "excludes higher pursuits."
Then there is that bittersweet phrase, the "pleasure of

44. (**continued**) struck at one of Mahaffy's greatest failings--
inaccuracy. It was a surprising, indeed a humiliating, weakness in
a classical scholar .... Productivity, not perfectionism was his ideal
.... When a reviewer in an English classical journal charged him
with serious inaccuracies, he defended himself on the grounds
that in works of genius errors in matters of detail were not only
forgivable but inevitable, ... Inaccuracy was not the only fault
alleged. He was also charged with superficiality and exaggeration,
with indulging in reckless generalizations, and with sprinkling his
works with prejudiced and irrelevant allusions to current personalities and events. ... There was one other foible .... He con-
stantly used ancient history as a vehicle for moralizing and
preaching .... A scholar of less self-confidence and resilience
might well have been daunted by the running fire of rebuke and
censure that almost all his major works provoked from 'pure'
scholars. In fact Mahaffy seems to have enjoyed the ... conflict,"
Stanford 145-148. I seek not to denigrate Mahaffy but to show the
scholarly atmosphere whence the myth of Greek amateurism
emanates. I also emphasize that Stanford (Mahaffy's biographer)
is one of his friendliest judges.

sport for its own sake." The last, in fact, has remained a catch-phrase from Mahaffy's day onward, throughout the modern International Olympic Movement--even after Avery Brundage retired from its presidency a few years ago.[45]

Indeed our brief trip to Greece and our meeting with Mahaffy could direct us straight back again to the 1890's in America, when Whitney urged us to limit our amateur sports to men from "the better element," since they alone possessed "the true amateur spirit of sport for sport's sake"; and where Shorey, our Professor of Greek, lectured our own first potential Olympic victors on the "lesson" they should learn from the ancient Greek "amateur" at Olympia. But Mahaffy could not leave the Greeks alone, and we have not yet fully plotted his influence on classical athletic scholarship--nor indeed his possible impact on *fin-de siècle* sport. He wrote again on our subject. One classical scholar found a challenge in Mahaffy's comparisons of the Greeks and the English. And it is possible that Pierre de Coubertin found in them a clarion call.

Mahaffy now saw ancient Greece as the ground on which to attack the French and, most of all, the Germans. So Mahaffy writes in his *Old Greek Education* (New York and London, 1881):

---

45. For training as a negative quality, see below, VI (Gardiner). For a perceptive analysis why his contemporaries viewed "attention to the body" as negative, opposed to "higher pursuits," see Coubertin's observations (below, VI, "Préface"); cf. Harris' statement that Phayllos knew "there were more important things than athletics" (above, I). For the catch-phrase "sport for its own sake" cf. Whitney (above, II, end); it was used by Whitney, Shorey, Coubertin, Gardiner, Brundage, Harris, and countless others. It is still promulgated throughout the literature which has emanated from the IOC even in the 1980's.

> [T]he English schoolboy is physically so superior to the
> schoolboys of other European nations that we may count
> him, with the Greek boy, as almost a distinct animal. (30)

But the Greek, too, must predictably drop out of this
uneven contest. England wins in the finals:

> [T]he [English] public-school boy...enjoys a physical training
> which no classical days ever equalled.... that kind of exercise
> which vastly exceeds in value any training in gymnasia. The
> Eton and Harrow match at Lord's is a far more beautiful sight
> ... than [was] the boys' wrestling or running at Olympia. (21ff)

Even the "ideal types," the highly-developed
bodies of adult Olympic victors represented in ancient
statues, left Mahaffy unimpressed (29) and afforded
him another chance to rail against athletic training in
general--ancient Greeks and modern continentals,
French and German, in particular.

> [T]he finest English schoolboy is not inferior to the best Greek
> types in real life....The Greeks were like the French and the
> Germans, who always imagine that the games and sports will
> not prosper or be properly conducted without the supervision
> of a *Turnlehrer*, or overseer....If the zealous and learned
> reformers who write books on the subject in modern Europe
> would take the trouble to come [to England] and see this for
> themselves, it might modify both their encomia on Greek
> training and their suggestions for their own countries. (29-32)

Mahaffy did not know that an earnest French
reformer would actually answer his call almost im-
mediately, and come to see English sports in person
with all the awed approval that Mahaffy thought they
deserved. That Frenchman, of course, was the young
Coubertin, making his first visit to England in 1883.[46]

46. I do not claim that Coubertin came in a direct response to
Mahaffy's printed, rather rhetorical invitation. The situation and
the sequence was as described above. It does not make much difference whether the youthful Baron actually read Mahaffy (there is

Four years later Coubertin's Anglophilia had become as devoted as Mahaffy's and he was making, at the age of twenty-five, many suggestions for his own country. But the scene is still not fully set for the dramatic entry of Baron Pierre de Coubertin, "Reviver of the ancient Olympic Games."

As Coubertin was visiting England, to see English sport for himself, a real Englishman named Percy Gardner read Mahaffy's account of "Old Greek Athletics" with keen interest. Gardner too was a classical scholar, an Oxford don. He shared Mahaffy's aristocratic preferences. But he did not wholly share his contempt for track and field athletics. And he shared none of Mahaffy's contempt for the ancient Greeks. And he said so.

Although Mahaffy founded the myth of ancient amateurism, he never idealized the Greeks. It was Gardner who created Greek athletics in the image of his own Victorian ideal. It was Gardner who gave us our fully idealized picture of the ancient Greek amateur athlete, whose noble world of amateur sport crumbled and collapsed at the advent of a creeping and sordid professionalism. It was Percy Gardner whom Shorey paraphrased in the item which begins the present book. And it was Percy Gardner who inspired E. N. Gardiner, the source of all our own gross misconceptions about

46. **(continued)** no explicit evidence either way); but it is not at all unlikely. Coubertin read anything dealing with education, Greece, and England--precisely Mahaffy's topics. Mahaffy's works were translated and used widely in French schools. His literary collaborator, Duruy (above, n. 4), was (only a few years later, at least) associated with Coubertin (MacAloon 103). And Coubertin picked up Mahaffyisms almost certainly through Duruy (MacAloon 140-144 with n. 4, above). A twenty-year old was as likely to read Mahaffy's simple little pamphlet, *Old Greek Education,* as he was to read Taine.

our subject.[47]

Gardner was quick to defend the ancient Greeks against their detractor. "Mr. Mahaffy has more recently compared our English athletics with those of Olympia and the Isthmus, and decided far more favourably for the moderns....In some matters he is distinctly unjust" (272). After centuries of athletic tradition, Gardner concludes, "the skill of the Greeks" was probably equal to that of the neophyte breed, the English amateur. But Gardner adds an odd and historically crucial twist. The ancient Greek athlete could be the equal of the Victorian English amateur for only one reason: namely, because the ancient Greek athlete *was a Victorian English Amateur.* Sixth and fifth century B.C. bruisers such as Milo and Theogenes were now to walk the High Street at Oxford. All the ancient Greeks were now English amateurs, the athletes as well as Sophocles and Thucydides (who would have felt at home at Oxbridge).[48]

47. "Paraphrased" is a bit generous. With Shorey's "the hammer of the Christian monk, the lime-kilns of the Turk" (318) cf. Gardner's "ravages of the Christians, who used the materials of the buildings ...; and then Turkish times, when lime-kilns ..." (288f), etc. For Shorey's "The height from which the thronging spectators looked down upon" (319) cf. Gardner 291; and so on, *passim.* For P. Gardner's influence on E. N. Gardiner, see Gardiner 1910, xi: "It is a fitting circumstance that this book should have been produced under the auspices of Professor Percy Gardner, seeing that (sic) he was unconsciously the originator of it. My interest in the subject was first aroused by the chapter on Olympia in his *New Chapters from Greek History.*" For Gardiner, see below, VI.
48. In defense of the Greeks Gardner (272) notes that Mahaffy's judgment of Greek boxing ignores the abundant evidence from Greek art and literature, while it founds itself on one mythical passage in Latin poetry (Vergil *Aeneid* 5.425ff--which actually depicts not Greek boxing but the Roman caestus bout: see Gardiner 1910, 431).

On ancient Greeks as Victorian Englishmen cf. Jenkyns or F. Turner, *Greek Heritage in Victorian Britain* (New Haven, 1981).

On two points Gardner and Mahaffy fully agreed: first, that their own Victorian aristocratic values were superior to any others the world had known; .second, that they as Hellenic scholars should promote those Victorian aristocratic values through a re-interpretation of Greek history. Thus Gardner found much to borrow and to elaborate in Mahaffy's talk of early Greek "amateur performances" and in his topsy-turvy chronology. And he was eager to second Mahaffy's attacks on the "professional spirit," as Victorian gentlemen called it when their brief attempt at exclusivist sport seemed near collapse after a decade or two. Ancient Greek history must necessarily follow its English prototype.

Thus Gardner paints a vivid picture of what he calls

> the rise and fall of Greek athletic sports. The chapter is a short one. The bloom of all the promising institutions of Greece was short. Abuse soon succeeded use; excess supervened on moderation; and the same causes which had made the greatness of the people, in matters athletic as in other matters, also caused its decline and eclipse. (266f)

"When the Olympic festival was at its best," Gardner writes, further on, the aristocratic victor returned to his home city through a breach in the city walls....

48. (continued)In the age of muscular Christianity the Greeks became muscular pagans .... Now the Athenians of the fifth century were essentially amateurs .... Socrates was an amateur philosopher, Sophocles an amateur playwright, Thucydides an amateur historian .... Richard Livingstone was confident that an ancient Athenian ... would appreciate the 'athletic grace' and 'easy condescension' of the upper-class [Oxford and Cambridge] undergraduates. (Jenkyns 217, 221)

> [A]ccording to ancient usage, a part of the city wall was thrown down in order that the hero might pass by a way not made vulgar by other footsteps. And so he entered to the notes of a triumphal song, written by a Pindar or Simonides and sung by the *noblest-born* of the city .... The proudest and *wealthiest* houses sought an alliance with him in marriage. (299, e.a.)

It boggles the mind to imagine the city walls coming down for each Aeginetan celebrated in Pindar's *Victory Odes,* or for every Crotoniate victor of the sixth century. There is no evidence whatsoever for this so-called "ancient usage" in Pindar's time--nor, indeed, for anywhere in the Greek world at any time.[49] The first 'ancient Greek athlete' to enter the city in this manner, according to our sources, was the Roman singer, charioteer, and Emperor, Nero. After his tour of the Greek games, Nero wished to have his return to Rome celebrated as if a great military triumph of a Roman general. And (at least so we read in some later sources)

---

49. Even E. N. Gardiner would not be taken in with this error. In his *Olympia* (1925), 67 he writes "As for the purple robe and the breach in the city wall, the first mention of them occurs in the account of the triumphal entry of Nero into Rome after his notorious tour in Greece, and even if some precedent could be found for them in Hellenistic times these excesses cannot be urged as evidence of early Olympic custom." The sources, all post-Neronian, are: Suetonius *Nero* 25, Dio Cassius 63.20, and Plutarch *Symp.* 2.5.2. Gardner's sentence at first appears to be a paraphrase of Plutarch, but where Gardner sees avoidance of the "vulgar" Plutarch gives a wholly different motive, "on the grounds that a city with men so able to fight and win had no great need of walls." Despite Plutarch, it is not likely that any Greek athlete ever entered his city through a hole made in the city wall. There is a confusion here of a Roman triumph with classical Greece. Even the term *iselastic* (common in the Roman Empire as a metaphorical and technical classification of the major games) does not imply the breaking down of walls but simply "solemn entry" (Pleket 1976, 62; Pleket states that the designation began in Hellenistic times, but the matter seems in some doubt).

the city wall came down. But it is absurd to extend a tale about the Roman Nero--infamous for his ludicrous idiosyncrasies--into a regular custom of Greek athletics five hundred years before Nero's time. But Gardner's absurdities are now our own history of the ancient Greek Olympic Games (the breach in wall error is in Kieran 13, and countless others). His historical account gets only worse.

Having illustrated the "Olympian festival at its best" in Pindar's time (ca. 470 B.C.) with a story about Nero (ca. 67 A.D.), Gardner sadly informs us that

> It was not long before *evil* days came. The *degradation* of Greek athletic sports may be traced to several causes .... The pancratium must always have been a sport unfitted for gentlemen.... It was only by degrees that the *professional* element among the competitors came in and the *gentlemanly* spirit went out ....[I]t was Herodicus of Selymbria, a contemporary of Socrates, who ruined athletics .... In fact, he first made training into a system. (300; e.a.)

Mahaffy has prepared us for the notion that systematic training is bad. But it is odd to see Herodicus blamed for the ruin of Greek athletics; for the same Herodicus may be the academic father of Hippocrates, our own 'Father of Medicine.' But Gardner has no time to examine such interesting questions--or to notice any of the abundant evidence for the systematic training of athletes before Herodicus.[50] He must hurry on to his real aim, to project the class war in contemporary British athletics onto Socrates' Greece.

> After his [Herodicus'] time, victory at Olympia became a thing which had to be worked for by special methods .... The competitors ceased to be drawn *from the better classes* ....

50. For Herodicus see Part Two, n. 42, below (end). For the strict diets and training programs of Greek athletes--long before Herodicus--see Part Two, V, below (end, with n.41).

> [T]he Olympian victory went more and more to the *profes-
> sional* .... At the same time a complete change comes over ...
> the leaders of Greek thought in relation to the games. Among
> *ourselves* there has been a great revival of athletic sports ....
> Surely we need not apply the *lesson* to English sports, or point
> out to our own youth the danger and discredit which threaten
> their favourite pursuits, unless they take to heart the *teaching
> of history.* Socrates' disciple, Euripides, makes one of his
> characters declare athletes to be one of the greatest pests of
> Greece....Alexander the Great cared not for athletics...
> (301-304; e.a.).

Words such as "degradation" and the empty appeal
to Euripides come directly from Mahaffy. Greek
"history" as a "lesson" for our sport reminds us of
Shorey (it should: Shorey copied from Gardner). But
such phrases as "the better classes" may remind us
even more of Caspar Whitney's monotonous concern
for protecting the "better element" from the lower-class
"vermin" who had, he thought, taken over athletics in
both England and America. Indeed one cannot find in
the annals of ancient Greece the "history" from which
Gardner draws his "lesson" for English sport. But it is
all there in Whitney's *Sporting Pilgrimage.* Gardner's
history of Greece is really nothing other than the history
of Anglo-American sports from the 1860's to the 1890's,
seen through the gentleman amateur's eye.

Despite their common cause and vocabulary,
Whitney and Gardner were in most ways worlds apart,
the one an American sportswriter, the other an Oxford
don. It is not likely that their ideas would have ever
united effectively had there not been a catalyst. That
third element was that idealistic Frenchman who had
the money, the ability, and the obsession to achieve his
own aims as he satisfied the aims of others. He would
soon be called *"renovateur."* Gardner would soon see
the Olympian victory *never* going to the professional;
and Whitney would find those games he wanted--and
himself--"among the more *refined* elements."
Amateurism had not, after all, shouted its last
"hurrah."

V

Coubertin and the Modern International Olympics

Games for the *elite:* an *elite* of contestants, few in number, but comprising the champion athletes of the world; an *elite* of spectators, *sophisticated* people, diplomats, professors, generals, members of the institute. For these people what could be more *refined (délicat),* more ravishing than a garden party at Dampierre .... (Coubertin, *Mémoires Olympiques* 50; e.a.)

Such is the view of the development which ought to take place in the institution of the modern Olympic Games....to exercise over the sports of the future that necessary and beneficent influence which shall make them the means of bringing to perfection the strong and hopeful youth of our white race,[51] thus again helping towards the perfection of all human society. (Coubertin, "Why I revived the Olympic Games," *Fortnightly Review* 90 [1908], 115)

51. With some misgiving, I have reprinted this unfortunate remark of Coubertin's; for it reveals that, howsoever fair Coubertin tried to be, neither James Thorpe nor Jesse Owens was the athlete whom he had in mind. Such men were not supposed to happen. But I hasten to add that Coubertin himself was far less racist and elitist than many who surrounded him in the amateur and Olympic movements, such as Whitney (Mandell 32f, 178, n. 20; MacAloon 168; Lucas 1980, 21-24, 31). In his youth Coubertin actively opposed anti-Semitism (no matter how he ended: Mandell 173 and Lucas 1980, 133). Perhaps he thought a racial remark might attract the Anglo-American sporting world just when he needed its support most, 1908. I assume that the French original (which I have not seen) for "white race" was "race blanche" (Coubertin's translator here was Helen Chisholm). For racist reaction, especially in England, to Thorpe and his red and black 1912 teammates, see Lucas 1980, 93; "'red Indians' and Negroes that violated the spirit, if not the letter of the Olympic ideal" (the sentiment is not Lucas').

Those are surely games of the kind that Caspar Whitney had in mind.

*   *   *   *   *   *   *

Baron Pierre de Coubertin was a French aristocrat, born to great wealth and a family titled since 1477. He did not start out to revive the Olympic games. He hit upon that idea as an afterthought, a brilliant substitute for his original aim of reforming French education. He wished to build physical fitness in his country's youth (France had just lost a war with Germany). But the young French patriot became an undisguised Anglophile, who saw the remedy for France's weakness in the educational system of the English privileged class. The social customs of the English upper class, its "muscular Christianity," and especially its amateur athletics all appealed to the idealistic French Baron. Unlike the rest of Mahaffy's "zealous and earnest reformers" on the Continent, Coubertin did "take the trouble" to go to England in 1883 and "see for [him]self" English amateur sports. When he returned, he began a vigorous campaign to introduce British-style athletics in French schools and to form French amateur athletic clubs after English models.[52] He was following

52. Mandell 49-73, MacAloon *passim,* and Lucas 1980, 13-27 rather elaborately and consistently recount Coubertin's background; his mission ("[T]he weight of a distinguished ancestry fell heavily" on him, Mandell 51); his education and intellectual formation (a rather uncritical devotion to what he saw as the educational principles of Thomas Arnold of Rugby coupled to an extreme Anglophilia and affection for titled nobility); and his early efforts to form a movement (athletic organizations that existed mostly on paper, a voluminous amount of writings, most published at his own expense). There is no need, then, to document these details here, nor would it be relevant to our purpose. Almost all the material contained in the next few pages here will be found in more detail and documentation in those three books. I give my own sources for the few exceptions.

Mahaffy's prescription to the letter.

But French educators generally turned him a deaf ear, and his success in forming athletic clubs was no better than mediocre. Most Frenchmen thought British-style athletics ill-suited to Gallic refinement. And Coubertin's frequent praise of "the Anglo-Saxon race" scarcely helped his cause in a country of Anglophobes. He began to direct his efforts more toward competitive athletics and a vision of international sports. He still had no notion of Olympic games.

He traveled to America in 1889 and visited England again in 1890. There he attended his first Olympics, the annual "Olympic Games" sponsored by Dr. W. Brookes in Shropshire. Brookes' "Olympics" were traditional English village games, hardly anything like their ancient namesake or even like contemporary British amateur athletics. But Coubertin loved their trappings of pomp and ceremony, and was entranced. Thus it seems that even the name of his "Olympic Games," like their philosophy, came more from England than from Greece.[53]

In 1892 Coubertin staged a "Jubilee" for his umbrella organization for French athletic clubs, the Union

53. For Brookes' Olympics see MacAloon 147-151 (cf. Mandell 32, 77). Such events as "tilting at a ring from horseback," "cricket," and "tentpegging" hardly suggest the ancient Olympics. At Shropshire Coubertin saw compete, according to his own account, "plucky young farmers"--not the Gentlemen Amateurs of Oxford and London. But in this same account, according to his later English version (a portion published by Mandell 32), Coubertin seems (first?) to have associated Victorian England with ancient Greece: "since ancient Greece has passed away, the Anglo-Saxon race is the only one that ...." Coubertin never set foot in Greece until he went to Athens to negotiate arrangements for the Greeks' 1896 Olympics; his knowledge of ancient Greek history, culture, and literature was superficial, at best (cf. n. 4, above; etc.).

des sociétés françaises des sports athlètique (USFSA). It was not even five years old at its "Jubilee." His movement was not progressing well. But the Baron now had a surprise up his sleeve. After a woman sang some Sophocles and his friend Bourdon read some translations of Pindar, Coubertin solemnly proposed that "we re-establish...the Olympic Games." What we call "The Modern Olympic Movement" had suddenly been born-- but no one seemed to care. Coubertin expected either cheers or catcalls. He reaped nothing but quizzical apathy.[54] We might recall that (perhaps unknown to the Baron) Mahaffy had already predicted the scenario:

> Were we to propose the resuscitation of the Olympic games ..., we should fear an accusation of absurdity.... (Mahaffy, "The Olympic Games at Athens in 1875," 324)[55]

Yet Coubertin was a dauntless man, and by now he had his mind set on starting an international athletic festival. When the august name "Olympics" failed to excite support, he turned to the fetish of the aristocrats whom he regularly courted, the concept of amateurism. Early in 1894 amateur athletic organizations in Europe and America received from Coubertin an invitation to attend an "International Congress of Amateurs" (sic) in Paris that June "for the consideration and extension of

54. "They thought I was merely speaking in symbols" (Coubertin, Une campagne de 21 ans (Paris 1908); "[H]is auditors failed to grasp the significance of the idea thus first put into words" (Henry 21f); "The young French baron was crushed" (Lucas 31). But cf. MacAloon 162-164.

55. Mahaffy, however, completes his clause thus: "accusation of absurdity in transferring Olympia to Athens." He thought that it was geographically and chronologically absurd to revive "Olympics" in 1875 Athens. He would have gasped at the thought of St. Louis in 1904 or Seoul in 1988.

the principles which underlie the idea of amateur sports." Other Olympic historians say that the invitation listed ten agenda items for the Congress; that the last three items "boldly stated the Olympic project" (MacAloon)--even mentioning "conditions to be imposed on the competitors," the nomination of an "International Committee" to administer the Olympic "revival," and so on. But those historians seem to be wrong. A text of the invitation appears in *The Olympic* magazine (San Francisco) volume 1, No. 6 (May 17, 1894), published before the Congress met in June 1894 in Paris. It is not the same document as that which appears in MacAloon's history, in the IOC annals, and in Coubertin's later publications. The discrepancies are major. I follow the contemporary document before my eyes, the pre-Congress 1894 *Olympic* version. (Coubertin himself spoke of two versions: see Appendix 2.)[56]

56. *The Olympic* was the magazine of the Olympic Club of San Francisco, an athletic organization founded before Coubertin was born and bearing no relation to his own Olympic movement (although the Baron visited the club in 1893). The May 1894 *Olympic* issue which printed Coubertin's circular printed along with it a covering letter written by Princeton professor William Sloane. Sloane was Coubertin's man in charge of American operations (in America, Coubertin said, Sloane "alone was my counsel and confidant in all this business," employing his "ingenious activity" in Coubertin's cause: MacAloon 166). I reproduce *in toto* the exact text of the circular along with Sloane's letter, just as the *Olympic* prints them, in Appendix 2; for they seem to have historical value (the last part [re]published here for the first time).

   Sloane's letter was written April 20, 1894 (a typographical error in the *Olympic* makes it "April 20, 1893," an impossible date; for the USFSA did not even decide on the eight-point program until August 1893 [MacAloon 166], and Sloane's "this late date" ill suits 1893). In his letter Sloane complains that "It is, I think, about three months since I addressed *this circular* to the Secretary of the Olympic Club .... I never received a reply" (e.a.). This sentence proves two things. First, the text of the circular is presumably the same as that of another previously sent. Second, that previous circular--with the eight-point text--was sent in mid-

The advertised name of the Congress was, as printed under the letterhead of Coubertin's own USFSA, "International Congress of *Amateurs*" (e.a.), not "International Athletic Congress." The invitation contained not ten articles for the agenda, but only eight. The first seven items concerned controversies that hovered around amateurism, such as, *"1. Definition of an amateur," "3. Can a professional in one sport be an amateur in another?," "4. The value of the medals or other prizes. Must it be limited?,"* and *"7. Does betting on himself disqualify an amateur?"* Each of these items was elaborated with some particulars. An eighth, brief, and final item (*"8. The possibility of re-establishing the Olympic games. Under what conditions would it be feasible"*) seemed so awkwardly appended that it hardly belonged in the

---

56. (**continued**) January, "about three months" before April 20, 1894. MacAloon's date, January 15, coincides perfectly with Sloane's (even if the documents do not). Finally, it is clear that on April 20, less than two months before the Congress was scheduled to convene (when prospective delegates would need to make final plans for the long voyage), Sloane was *still* sending out the innocuous, *eight-point* version.

Both MacAloon 166f and Mandell 84f omit the word "Amateurs" from the title of the Congress; and both scholars expressly state that the January 1894 document contained "ten articles" for discussion at the Congress, the last three concerning the re-establishment of the Olympic Games. MacAloon even reprints items eight through ten "from the official program sent out in January 1894." Something has gone awry with the evidence here. For the document which was sent to at least one club, namely, the Olympic Club of San Francisco, does not merely differ from that printed in MacAloon--it also contradicts it in important matters of the Congress' *stated intent.* For these crucial differences in the closing statements of the two documents see note 58, below. Here I merely observe that both MacAloon and Mandell cite and quote from later reprintings of what purports to be the January 1894 text, not from an original exemplar of the text itself. (They cite Coubertin's *Mémoires Olympiques* [1931] and especially the Carl-Diem-Institut's collection, *The Olympic Idea* [1967]).

same list as the others. But item number eight was obviously, as we say, "last on the agenda," and must have seemed so unrealistic as to be innocuous and negligible (Coubertin, we shall see, wanted it that way).

Yet when the delegates arrived that summer for the "International Congress of Amateurs" they found that their tickets read instead "Congress for the Reestablishment of the Olympic Games." The minor item, number eight, had become major item, number one. The delegates quickly resolved the questions of amateurism just as Coubertin wished: a "strict" but contemporary definition should prevail, *absolutely no money of any kind.* But the British delegates failed in their attempt to have "amateur" formally limited by social class. Obviously if the "no-money" rule was strictly applied, the expense of international competition would discourage the working class, anyway.[57]

But amateurism seems never to have been Coubertin's main motive in calling this 1894 Congress in the Sorbonne. He indeed parroted the usual catch-phrases, noting that amateurs need "to defend themselves against the spirit of lucre and professionalism" (*apud* MacAloon 166). But "amateurism," he later confessed, was his "camouflage" (1931, 11f).

> The programme for the Congress was drawn up in such a way as to disguise its main object: "the revival of the Olympic Games"; it merely put forward questions on sport in general. I carefully refrained from mentioning such an ambitious project, afraid it might raise such a storm of contempt and scorn

57. For the change in the title of the Congress see Coubertin, 1931, 18. For the British delegates' unsuccessful attempt to have "amateur" defined by social class see Mandell 88f, MacAloon 321, n. 43. Yet an odd and unforeseen circumstance allowed this very question (class defined amateurism) to raise the nastiest controversy of the first International Olympic Games at Athens in 1896; see n. 62, below.

as to discourage beforehand those favourably disposed towards it. For whenever I had alluded to my plan at meetings in Oxford and New York etc. I had always been sadly conscious that my audience considered it utopian and impracticable. (Coubertin, *Olympic Games of 1896,* 6f).

MacAloon chooses not to believe Coubertin here, and claims that the Baron's Olympic intentions were "quite clear" from the start in January. But MacAloon also believes in a January ten-point agenda. The above paragraph does not sound like the deceptive Coubertin; rather it sounds like authentic, candid Coubertin--the man who so exulted in his "little deceit[s]" that he eventually confided them to the world (MacAloon 162). But "little deceit" is MacAloon's term; Coubertin called it "switching babies." In the above paragraph the Baron can hardly refer to the ten-point program which MacAloon thinks he has in mind; for that version indeed "boldly stated the Olympic project." Rather, I suspect, Coubertin refers to the eight-point version of the agenda which the San Francisco Olympic Club received early in 1894; and that he here exults in no "little deceit," but in a Great Deceit, successfully executed through the ploy of *"amateurism."* (As for the date of the ten-point version--perhaps we have another case of "switched babies" or "amended birth certificates").[58]

58. MacAloon 167 somehow writes off Coubertin's confession printed above as a kind of glory-grabbing, and then comments:

"While true enough for the preliminary program approved by the union [USFSA] in 1893, only one of whose eight articles mentioned the Olympic Games, the official program sent out in January 1894 made Coubertin's intentions quite clear. After seven topics dealing with amateurism, articles VIII, IX, and X boldly stated the Olympic project."

I make short a long story, which others have now told more fully. Delegates at the Congress were wined, dined, and entertained lavishly--with refinement. Almost without noticing it they found that they had voted to re-establish the Olympics, games open only to amateurs. Coubertin had already formed a committee to administer the "Revival," namely, The International Olympic Committee (IOC)--with the Greek delegate Vikelas[59] as its head. Coubertin was its Secretary. The

58. (continued) MacAloon then prints Articles VIII, IX, and X, as if from the January 1894 invitation (citing Coubertin 1931) as follows:

> "VIII. Possibility of restoring the Olympic Games-- Advantages from the athletic, moral and international standpoints--Under what conditions may they be restored?
> IX. Conditions to be imposed on the competitors-- Sports represented--Material organization, periodicity, etc.
> X. Nomination of an International Committee entrusted with preparing the restoration."

The 1894 version in *The Olympic* --immediately after Article VIII (which itself differs significantly from its equivalent in MacAloon's text)-- actually closes with an explicit disclaimer of any such intentions:

> "Associations which participate in the Congress do not bind themselves to observe the regulations adopted. Its object is to express opinions on the different questions submitted to it, to consider measures for international legislation, *but not inaugurate it"* (e.a.).

That the two documents seek to give two very different impressions is obvious. For possible explanations see Appendix Two and n. 56, above.
59. For Demetrios Vikelas ("Bikelas" in most Olympic histories), a Greek then living in Paris, see MacAloon 172f, 153, and Mandell 88. Vikelas was an historian and scholar, an influential poet and prose writer, who translated such modern authors as Shakespeare and Racine into Modern Greek; C. Dimaras, *A History of Modern*

other delegates had come to haggle over fine distinctions[60] of "amateurism," over "Suspension, disqualification, and rehabilitation" of amateur athletes
(advertised agenda item no. 2). Coubertin and Vikelas
had come to deal in Olympic Games. The Baron had used
amateurism as an instrument to his ends. Yet the
amateur movement would emerge as the biggest winner of all; the Sorbonne conference was, perhaps, even
its very salvation.

At the closing session Coubertin stunned everyone
except Vikelas by announcing that the first of his revived
Olympic Games need not, after all, wait until Paris in
1900, the date and venue he had already announced in
print the week before. No. The Olympics could be
revived even sooner, and sprout up once more from
their own native soil. *Athens in 1896!* The motion passed
like a flash. The earnest Baron, "transported into a
euphoric state by the atmosphere he created,"
delivered his closing speech, coining a new word
"Olympism" as he began to define its novel concepts.[61]

59. (**continued**) *Greek Literature,* Mary Gianos, transl. (Albany,
N.Y., 1972), s.v. Vikelas. Vikelas was probably the only delegate
to whom Olympic Games were no novel idea (MacAloon 153,
citing Grombach, says that he "had been associated with the Zappas Olympic Games"). See also n. 61, below.
60. "Can a professional in one sport be an amateur in another?"
(Coubertin's agenda Article Three) was linguistic nonsense when
amateurism was a mere matter of social class: obviously, "no" (cf.
notes 26 and 22, above). The more confused phenomena of
French and American amateurism, along with the 1880 ruling,
made the question possible. Coubertin's Congress still answered,
"no." The same question became James Thorpe's nemesis; the
answer was still "no." Now, as I write, it is once more before the
IOC in the case of professional football player and amateur
hurdler (a situation the founders of amateurism could never have
grasped), R. Nehemiah.
61. Olympic histories are confused and vague about the change
from Paris in 1900 to Athens in 1896, and about whether it was
made at Coubertin's or Vikelas' initiative. Most (MacAloon 173)
make it Coubertin's suggestion, and indeed in 1908 Coubertin

> [W]e voted unanimously for the restoration of an idea that is
> two thousand years old .... the Olympism of ancient Hellas
> has reemerged in the world after an eclipse of many cen-
> turies. I raise my glass to the Olympic idea which, like a ray
> of the all-powerful sun, has pierced the mists of the ages....

The course was clear. As Coubertin had used amateurism as a devious means to achieve his own ends, so now he would use the myth of amateur Greece in the same way. Greece had an appealing aura.

*   *   *   *   *   *   *

"The mists of the ages!" Suddenly amateurism had come of age, aged beyond its fondest hopes. The legitimacy, the history, the *priority* which amateurism so sorely lacked lay in ancient Greece and in arcane, archaic texts that few could or cared to read. It was there for the taking. The classical scholars were already allies.

61. (**continued**) published a (1894) "note from Bikelas, in which Bikelas wrote, 'I ... was touched by your suggestion to begin with Athens'" (Mandell 183, n. 27). But Mandell notes that "[S]ome versions ... have Bikelas as the initiator." Indeed they do. In 1896 Coubertin himself wrote, "We proposed to fix the year 1900 for their first celebration, but *it was thought* advisable to advance that date to 1896 and *at the proposition of M. Vikelas*, Athens was chosen as the place for their inauguration" (Coubertin, *Olympic Games of 1896*, 8 [e.a.]). The words quoted above in my text ("transported," etc.) come from Mandell 90. For a brief account of Coubertin's original ˙ concept "Olympism" (there was no equivalent word in antiquity) see Lucas 1980, 78ff. The concept became for Coubertin an actual "religion" ("The author of the Olympic code flaunted heresy in pronouncing Olympism to be his religion, 'a religion with church, dogma, and cult,'" Lucas 1962, 141); it is now spread throughout the IOC movement and literature. In the United States Olympic Academy VI conference (Malibu, June 1982), the term "Olympism" was ubiquitous, and the topic occurred in virtually every session. Coubertin's closing speech is available in *The Olympic Idea*, 5-7.

The hybrid seed which Mahaffy planted and Gardner nurtured was now to bloom as a lovely flower before the eyes of the world. It was no longer the private conceit of a few reckless academics.

Coubertin was a master of the press. *Myth was now reality.* In less than two years the ancient Greek Victorian amateurs would again perform in the flesh and in their spiritual homeland. But only a handful knew who they were. It was time for all amateur partisans to come to the aid of their cause.

There was no time--it was no time--for scholarship. Shorey seems to have digested Gardner's chapter just in time to regurgitate it. But there was now a difference. In 1895 when Shorey lectured the ancient Greek Victorians of Chicago, Boston, and Philadelphia on the chief "lesson" which they needed "to learn from Olympia," he did not merely look back at the "brief bloom" of ancient amateurism, which Gardner saw with nostalgia. Shorey looked forward to a lofty modern aristocratic institution, one which Coubertin claimed could--in reality--provide international "games for an elite." His motivation was even more patently topical than Mahaffy's or Gardner's. For Shorey, a specialist in Plato's philosophy, is not likely to have broached the topic of Greek athletics had he not been inspired by the Frenchman's "Conference of Amateurs" at the Sorbonne. But Shorey was pessimistic about the Games' potential for success. As he himself observed, "The only classes in the modern world whose interest in athletics is wholly genuine and unfeigned are professionals, *idle amateurs of wealth,* a few educators, and the least studious among our college youths" (323; e.a.).

The first International Olympic Games were held in Athens in 1896 as Coubertin planned, or nearly as

Coubertin planned.[62] There was no actual team from France or England, the two countries which he cherished most.[63] America provided a team composed mainly of Shorey's "wealthy amateurs."[64] Although these men were not our best athletes--far from it--they captured a majority of first places and the hearts of a generous Greek nation. They contributed much to make the games a success.

Yet these 1896 games were not wholly different from the 1870 Olympics. They were international, and that difference is crucial. But the stadium was the same-- *so were many spectators.* Most of the athletes were Greeks, 230 of 311 (Yalouris 299). To his frustration, the Greeks left Coubertin almost wholly out of their

62. No Association Football or equestrian contests took place. Furthermore, a nasty incident occurred because many upper class Englishmen had never accepted the liberalized "amateur" definition of 1880. Some English athletes at Athens asked the officials to bar two of their own fellow-citizens from the bicycle race. The would-be cyclists, they argued, were not "amateurs" but professionals: for they worked for a living--namely as salaried employees in the offices of the British Embassy at Athens. The officials rejected the argument and allowed the men to compete, but only after the hubbub "had made all Englishmen in Athens look ridiculous" (Mandell 113f).

63. Of the six members of the British "team" which competed in Athens three were present for other reasons (a tourist and the two embassy employees mentioned above, n. 62); another was really Australian (Mandell 113f). For the French "team" see Mandell 110.

64. Mandell 115-119. All, even Connolly, had attended either Harvard or Princeton. "As was expected of young men with their positions in society, they all travelled first class on the *Fulda.* At their disposal they had dozens of waiters, pages, and other minions....Amateur sportsmen in the 1890's were drawn from a tiny, pampered minority....Few of the foreign athletes in Athens were of championship caliber even by the American, English, or German standards of the time" (Mandell 117, 157f, excepting four of the Americans, who were "tops or nearly so").

preparations. The Greeks provided the organization, the site, almost all the officials--and *all the money*.[65] Since they already had an established recent tradition of modern Olympic Games in Athens, it is no wonder that most Greeks saw these 1896 games in some ways as another edition in their continuing series of revived

65. Coubertin (who in advising the Greeks about the cost had underestimated it something like tenfold, a harbinger of Montreal) could get no money from France. Many Greek citizens contributed substantially from their own pockets. A crucial gift of nearly a million drachmas came from an Alexandrian Greek philanthropist, George Averoff. But a neglected element of the financing bears strongly on the question of these 1896 Olympics' continuity with the previous Modern Greek Olympic games (see above, Sec. III). Coubertin induced a young, wealthy, titled Greek, Count Mercati (boyhood friend of the [Danish] Greek Crown Prince) to cause the Crown Prince to appropriate the Zappas fund--legally bequeathed to finance the series of Greek National Olympics begun in 1859--to finance what Coubertin claimed as his own Olympic Games ("my claim to be sole author of the whole project," *Olympic Games of 1896*, 8). This information on the use of the Zappas fund is disclosed by Coubertin's own lieutenant, Professor Sloane (in: *Report of the American Olympic Committee: Seventh Olympic Games, Antwerp, Belgium, 1920*, Greenwich, Conn., n.d. [but 1920 or 1921], p. 79).

I have seen no general accounting of the expenditures of the Zappas fund. Some was spent on the Olympic Games of 1870, but obviously more was spent on the funding of Phokianos' gymnastic training for the "cultured class" and students. Little was spent on the Olympic Games of 1875 and 1889 (for the former the stadium was not even well prepared; the latter were little more than a gym-class exhibition, perhaps staged without any Zappas monies). A large amount was spent on the opulent Zappeion building. Some was spent on industrial and agricultural exhibitions (in the name of Olympic Games), and their promotion. Then too we are told that there were no Zappas' funds in 1896, for the Rumanian government "froze" them (MacAloon 183); Ketseas says that they had been reduced to "nothing" because of Rumanian laws and confiscations upon the death of Zappas' brother (in 1892; further elaborated in the Μέγα....Λεξικόν 417). This account does not fully accord with Sloane's version.

Sloane is in serious error, however, when he states that the Zappas fund was merely "designated for the furtherance of

Olympic Games, now expanded into an international athletic festival. Nor is it surprising that, when Coubertin sought all the credit for the 1896 games and for the entire idea of a modern Olympic revival, the Greek press called him "a thief."[66]

The Greeks tried vigorously, before, during, and after 1896 to keep the Olympic Games in Greece. The American Olympic athletes and others supported their case for the permanent site, but in vain. The Greeks actually won more medals than any other nation in these First International Olympic Games (and the first unofficial point count). But they were by far the biggest losers. As the 'no money of any kind' style amateurism touched their hallowed soil for the very first time--1896-- they lost the Olympic games themselves. Coubertin spirited the "Official" Olympics away to Paris for 1900,

65. (continued) physical culture" and only later (1896), through Mercati, "appropriated for Olympic purposes." Zappas specifically bequeathed his estate for the purpose of Greek National Olympic Games (athletics, and the government had, in fact, used them for that purpose before Coubertin ever came to Greece). Sloane's phraseology--and his error--may relate to Coubertin's attempt to consign the Greek National Olympics to oblivion (above, Sec. III), lest knowledge about them taint his claim to be sole author of the modern Olympic revival. A more important consideration in Sloane's disclosure and the use of the Zappas funds is this: If the 1896 Games were a continuation of the earlier Greek national series (with an international feature and Committee added), the Zappas money was perhaps properly used. But if Coubertin was "the sole author of the whole project" (Zappas himself, e.g., no author of it at all) and the 1896 games were to no degree a continuation of the existing Greek Olympic series, the use of the money might well be questioned, perhaps even in its legality. Whatever the case, the next year Count Mercati was appointed to the IOC. "The enterprise," as Sloane concludes, "was therefore brilliantly launched."

66. Lucas 1980, 42; see also n. 65, above.

never to return home again.[67]

Despite mediocre marks, the Athens games of 1896 were judged to be a success. The attendance had generally been excellent (a crucial factor), as was the hospitality. The Greeks had admired the talented, enthusiastic American college boys, who, in turn, admired the Olympic enthusiasm of the Greeks (and their marathon victor, Loues). The happy combination was reported in the press, and international Olympic games had indeed been born. But Coubertin turned away from Greece ("So much for Greece"[68]), and began to plan for his Parisian Olympics in 1900. Vikelas' term on the IOC ended in 1897 during the struggle for control of the games.

67. For a tally of 1896 Olympic medals awarded to the competing nations, see Santas 101. There is no adequate account of the Greeks' struggle with Coubertin for control of the Olympics, but cf. Mandell 112, 152-6, 167 (for the 1906 Greek "rump" Olympics, see below); MacAloon 150f. See also n. 66, above, and n. 68, below. The official publication of the 1896 Olympics, *The Olympic Games: B.C. 776.--A.D. 1896*, S. P. Lambros and N. G. Polites, edd. (Athens: First Section, 1896; Second Section 1897) captures the rift in still motion. Coubertin ends his article announcing, "Their next celebration is to be in Paris in 1900, and then they are to be held ... in every large capital of the world in turn" (2.8). Philemon ends his adjacent article, "We look forward with confidence to the next festival, to be held in our dear capital" (2.29); and Anninos closes his with a quotation from the King's speech, "May Greece be destined to become the peaceful meeting ground of all nationalities, and may Athens become the permanent seat of the Olympic Games" (2.116).
68. Lucas 1980, 48f; a real war with Turkey distracted the Greeks from their battle with Coubertin, and "[t]he Baron admitted that he felt more comfortable in an Anglo-Saxon environment." He held the 1897 meeting of the IOC in Normandy, "turning his back on the Greek-Turkish War,...dismissing any possibility of Athens as the next Olympic site." Cf. Lucas 1980, 55f. Coubertin's familiarity with Greece was always superficial, and his devotion to Greece perhaps more theatrical than profound (his heart is entombed at Olympia).

Coubertin wanted new committee members. It was time for Caspar Whitney to find his place among the more "refined elements." Whitney, the American who wanted to segregate athletes by social class and called working class athletes "vermin," was appointed to the IOC for 1900. Sitting beside him there he would find no "mechanics, artisans, or laborers." Of Coubertin's dozen most recent appointees before Whitney, eight were titled nobility or better: five Counts, two Barons, a Duke, and the Prince of Romania.[69] Here, if anywhere, was an athletic institution that ought to instill qualities which, as Whitney put it, "bespeak a better heredity."

Coubertin himself had begun to promulgate his own nonsense about the ancient Greek "amateurs": athletes participating in an aristocratic monopoly founded on heredity and dedicated to "sport for sport's sake":

> How little athletics and paganism have in common! The young Greek spent the eve of the contest in the solitude of the marble porticos of the gymnasium, far from the noise. He also had to be irreproachable personally *and by heredity*, with no blemish either in his own life or *that of his ancestors*. He associated his act with the national religion, consecrating himself before an altar and receiving as token of victory a simple wreath, the symbol of *genuine disinterestedness*. (*Souvenirs d'Amérique et de Grèce* [1897] 111f; e.a.)

There is no history here, just pure fancy. Every sentence, without exception, is in serious error.[70]

---

69. IOC 1950, 31; Vikelas, the same publication notes, left the IOC in 1897.
70. There was no gymnasium at Olympia in the period to which Coubertin refers. There was absolutely nothing in the Olympic regulations about "irreproachable personally and by heredity" (competitors needed to be Greek citizens, that is all). Nor is there any ancient source for the notion that Olympic athletes were required to be "without a criminal record" (Finley and Pleket 61) or

Coubertin's athlete is no ancient Greek. But he is a model Victorian amateur, and these are the words that Whitney and Shorey wished to hear.

Yet the 1900 Olympics in Paris were an embarrassing fiasco, and the 1904 Olympics in St. Louis failed badly, as well. Coubertin did not even bother to attend. In Athens in 1906 the Greeks held the best modern Olympics to that date, calling them "The Second International Olympic Games"; Coubertin managed to write them off as "unofficial." Yet some Olympic historians believe that the success of these 1906 Greek Olympics may have been the salvation of Coubertin's own Olym-

---

70. (**continued**) "[a]ll contestants had to swear...that neither they nor their immediate relatives had been guilty of any outlawry or sacrilegious act" (Henry 15). "Those who had committed murder or stolen from a temple" (Drees 41) were no doubt banned, since they were banned from all social intercourse in Greece. But that is far from Coubertin's false claim about impeccable heredity. The erroneous statements quoted above are founded, if not on pure fancy, on a truncated and quite erroneous mistranslation of Krause's German translation (Krause 133) of Pausanias 5.24.9 (not 5.24.2, as printed in Krause)--which simply says that all swear they *will not cheat in the games.*

Modern literature (especially from the earlier USOC) teems with similar errors: "From the earliest days, alcoholic beverages...were taboo" in ancient Greece (Grombach 11). "In the use of wine, all athletes were more than temperate and many were total abstainers" (Sloane in: *Report of the American Committee, 1920,* 68). "--and nothing else except water! And all this was 2,500 years ago" (Kieran 15). On the contrary, the one ancient source touching on the question of Olympic athletes and alcohol explicitly states that the Olympic officials are most careful that no competitor in the *boys'* events be over age: "But whether he possesses self-control or not, whether he is a *drunkard* or a glutton, whether he is brave or a coward, the regulations say nothing about any of those things" (Philostratus *Gym.* 152; e.a.). Milo's reported daily ration of two and a half gallons of wine (Harris 1964, 111) proves that ancient authors, too, often exaggerate (but Grombach, Sloane, and Kieran are quite serious).

pic movement. The 1908 London Olympics were scarred by loud and bitter charges of cheating and professionalism hurled back and forth between the British and the Americans. These London games reminded observers more of the American Revolutionary War than of Coubertin's idealized young Greeks who preferred to be "far from the noise" in their pursuit of "genuine disinterestedness."[71]

71. "[T]he Olympic Games of 1900 and 1904 were polyglot circuses, and the London Games of 1908 were more a contribution to international acrimony than to harmony" (Mandell 168). Even Coubertin's sympathetic biographer "called these crippled Olympic Games of 1900 'the country fair,'" and the St. Louis Olympics were embarrassing (Lucas 1980, 49, 55). Both Olympiads were "failures" (Lucas 1980, 70). For the 1908 London games see Lucas 1980, 62, 72 ("near disastrous"), and especially 57f. For the independently held Greek Olympics of 1906 as by far the best modern Olympics before 1912--perhaps the salvation of Coubertin's movement--see Mandell 167 ("the breadth of international participation and the performance levels were, as a whole, superior to the Olympic Games of 1896, 1900, 1904, and 1908"); Lucas 1978, 403 ("the concept of sport internationalism was saved"). The Greeks called the 1906 Games the Second International Olympic Games, for they did not recognize the Paris or St. Louis fiascos.

VI

E. N. Gardiner, James Thorpe, and Avery Brundage

Into this milieu stepped a gigantic figure in the history of Greek athletic studies, the Englishman E. N. Gardiner, another classical scholar of the second rank. Seldom has the work of one man so dominated all later interpretations of his subject. Since 1910 all modern accounts of Greek athletics, popular or scholarly, have descended--with *very* few exceptions--from this man and his writings. His philological abilities were limited, but his dedication to the contemporary cause of amateurism was absolute.

Gardiner made no pretense of disinterested scholarship. He opens his first book, in 1910, stating that his aim is to mold public opinion on the modern athletic controversy (vii). He speaks openly of "the evils of professionalism" in modern football (soccer) and of the "striking resemblances between the history of modern athletics and Greek" (5f). And his first chapter is laced from start to finish with tendentious sentences about Coubertin's modern Olympics, attacks on professional athletes, and encomiums of Victorian amateur ideology. His historical analogies can be falser than Mahaffy's. And, like others before and after him, he views ancient Greece mainly as a "lesson" (6) for modern man.[72] "History repeats itself strangely," he says (5). Strangely indeed, as we have seen, and shall now see again.

---

72. Apparently first among the "striking resemblances" between ancient Greek and nineteenth century English athletics is their common origin "in the public schools and universities" (5); a more false or anachronistic claim is hard to imagine (there were

The Greek archaic period, Gardiner argues, saw "genuine amateurs" (Whitney's "*bona fide* amateurs") competing, "men of position" drawn from the aristocracy.[73] All athletes were of noble birth and

72. (**continued**) no public schools and universities in Greece in the time in question). Gardiner never feigned scholarly detachment, even in his later work; and he never mitigated his Mahaffy-like use of cavalier historical analogies, such as, "Here again the history of modern sport tells the same tale" (1930, 105). Perhaps most revelatory of all of Gardiner's analogies is his comment on athletes of the later period: "They had no more claim to represent any Hellenic state than hired football *professionals from Scotland* have to represent an English town" (1930, 50; e.a.). For my placement of Gardiner's scholarship in the second rank, cf. also n. 80, below. For Greek history's use as a modern "lesson": "[T]he history of the decline of Greek athletics is an object-lesson full of instruction" (Gardiner 1910, 6); "The lesson of Greek athletics" (*ibid.*); "instruction for the present day" (1930, 107, and *passim*).

73. Despite "decline" Gardiner writes, "At all periods we find *men of position* competing as *genuine amateurs* in a manner worthy of the old tradition" (1930, 104; e.a.). He cites the cases of Aratus of Sicyon and Gorgus of Messene but no source. There is nothing in the reports of either man to suggest that they were amateur athletes of any kind. Aratus is rather irrelevant, for his known Olympic victory (Moretti No. 574) occurred in an equestrian contest, which he perhaps did not even attend (below, VII, end). The vague "won crowns" (στεφάνων τυχεῖν) in Plutarch *Aratus* 3 is almost certain proof that Aratus never won a non-equestrian Olympic victory (which Plutarch would surely specify). Gorgus won an Olympic pentathlon victory (Moretti No. 573) and later entered politics, but that is no proof whatsoever that he was an "amateur" (see below, Part Two, VII).

Gardiner's misleading statement here is apparently the sole source of the Pooles' remarkable claim that, during the "decline," a "few amateurs clung to the glory of the past, reflecting the shining example; *according to Pausanias, amateurs* 'kept alive the old traditions...'. Records ... are highlighted with exciting contests between the amateurs and the professionals" (Pooles 111; e.a.). I know of no record of an Olympic contest between an amateur and a professional in any Greek source, nor any mention of an amateur in Pausanias. The quoted words which the Pooles falsely place in Pausanias' mouth are apparently their own, prompted by Gardiner's page (which faces a page which cites Pausanias on another matter).

amateur. But then Greek athletics suffered a "decline," a "degeneration." Lower class athletes were permitted to compete, and the aristocracy began to withdraw from athletics.

> [T]he well-born youths and princes for whom Pindar sang were actuated by no mercenary motives, but by that pure love of physical effort and of competition which is natural to all healthy youth. (1910, 110)
> Before the end of the fifth century the excessive prominence given to bodily excellence and athletic success had produced specialization and professionalism. From this time sport, over-developed and over-specialized, became more and more the monopoly of a class, and consequently ceased to invigorate the national life. (1910, 4)

There lurks behind these words an attitude fundamental to amateur ideology, but unnoticed by everyone except the astute Coubertin. *The amateur philosophy is essentially anti-athletic.* "Bodily excellence" and "athletic success" might easily become *negative* characteristics. The reason is this: in the amateur partisan's view, athletics were still (as Mahaffy put it) "rather a low thing." To be good in athletics is good. To be *very* good in athletics is bad. So also Gardiner continues:

> Sport has too often become an end in itself. The hero-worship of the athlete tempts men to devote to selfish amusement the best years of their lives, and to neglect *the true interests* of themselves and of their *country.* The *evil* is worse with *us,* because our games have not the practical value as a military training....Still more grievous than this *waste of time and energy* is the absorbing interest taken by the general public in the athletic performances of others. (1910, 6; e.a.)

All this harks straight back to Mahaffy, who warned us that there were "more serious rivalries" than athletics, "higher pursuits," namely, war and the service of one's country. Harris' fictitious Phayllos knew all that.

Athletics, in amateur ideology, is something that exuberant young boys get out of their systems before taking over the family's affairs, or entering government service or military careers. Athletics should never absorb the interest of grown men, and athletic excellence should never be prized on a par with excellence in other fields. This anti-athletic attitude of his amateur associates always nettled the Baron, whose Gallic idealism told him that if a man participated in athletics he should hope to be the best. With penetrating insight, Coubertin identified the mediaeval origins of amateurism's anti-athleticism as it survived from Mahaffy to Brundage:

> The pedagogues are always moved to teach *measure;* it is their instinct; it is somewhat their *raison d'être* ....a systematic opposition resulting from the contempt which physical exercise attracts. It is the reaction of the early days of Christianity that always remains; it is the unconscious hatred of the flesh. (Coubertin, *Préface*, 1896, 150, 154)[74]

That, at least, attributes the amateurs' suspicion of training and success to a better motive than mere jealousy of those who trained harder and won.

74. Coubertin, "La préface des jeux Olympiques," *Cosmopolis* 2 (1896), 145-159 (emphasis Coubertin's): "Les pédagogues sont toujours portés à enseigner la *mesure:* c'est leur instinct; c'est un peu aussi leur raison d'être" (150). "...une opposition raisonnée issue du mépris qu'inspire l'exercice physique. C'est la réaction des premiers temps du christianisme qui dure toujours; c'est la haine inconsciente de la chair" (154). Cf. "rival claims," Gardiner 1910, vii.

Coubertin's insights and visionary powers on many larger questions should never be judged by his scholarly inaccuracy and his pettiness in prosecuting his critics and athletes suspected of professionalism (Mandell 171). There is much on those pages of "La préface" (153ff) that now appears downright prophetic, e.g.: "La 'renaissance athlètique' sera considérée, plus tard, comme l'une des caractéristiques du XIXe siècle. Aujourd'hui le mot fait sourire."

Sometimes, in fact, Gardiner seems to identify the "professional" as the man who practices, and the "amateur" as one who refuses to train. But in general, even in his 1930 book, he wavered indecisively between the two more official meanings which we have already seen.

For Gardiner the word "amateur" referred primarily to social class and only secondarily to money; that is, he generally followed the original 1866 definition that excluded mechanics and others of the working class. Thus his "genuine amateurs" are "the wealthy" of ancient Greece, the "sons of noble families," and "men of position." But he is not thoroughly consistent, and sometimes uses the 1880 modification which turned on the acceptance of money. Sometimes he uses the two differing definitions simultaneously, producing seemingly contradictory terms. So Gardiner writes of "the professional amateur" (by which he means an upper class athlete who trains and makes money from sport); and of the "true professional" (a lower class athlete who trains and makes money from sport).[75]

But Gardiner vehemently set his face against all athletic money, ancient or modern, whether coming into the hands of the rich or the poor. When the subject of money enters the ancient Greek evidence, Gardiner formally drops his historian's role and becomes merely a spokesman for the contemporary amateur cause. He lectures his audience directly, like the chorus in an Aristophanic parabasis:[76]

75. For "genuine amateurs" as "men of position" see n. 73, above. For "the wealthy" and the "sons of noble families" and for the distinction between the "professional amateur" and the "true professional" see Gardiner 1910, 81 (and Appendix 3, below).
76. For Gardiner's Aristophanic *parabaseis* cf.: "Indeed the Olympic crown is a lesson in sportsmanship for all time, reminding us that the true sportsman contends not for the value of the prize but for the honour of victory and not for his own honour only but for that of his country, his state, his school, his side" (1930, 36).

> [T]he Nemesis of excess in athletics is professionalism, which
> is the death of all true sport (1930, 99; cf. 1910, 134). The
> worst *evil* of professionalism is corruption.... When money
> enters into sport, corruption is sure to follow. (1910, 134;
> repeated 1930, 103; e.a.)

Gardiner could draw no clear distinction between prize-
money honestly won and bribes taken to 'throw' a contest. All athletic money was "evil" and corrupt, the
"death" of all sport. He was as quick to censure the
"evils" of ancient Greece as to curse the "evils" of
British Association football (1910, 6). "Evil," it seems,
was almost everywhere.

Yet Gardiner's entire case for a period of pristine
aristocratic amateurism later corrupted by the "evils"
of money and professionalism rests on something by
now familiar, a Shoreyesque kind of chronological
sleight of hand. When recounting the sins of ancient
Greek professionalism, the period of decline, Gardiner
cites the stories told of Croton and Sybaris. These two
ancient Greek cities of Magna Graecia, Gardiner sadly
reports, offered large cash prizes to athletes.

> [T]he increase of rich prizes was soon to put *the poor man on a
> level with the rich*....For this result states like Sybaris and
> Croton were largely responsible. They thought to encourage
> athletics by offering large money prizes; in reality they killed
> the spirit of the sport....These *evils*, however, did not yet exist
> in the sixth century. (1910, 81f; e.a.)

My omissions here make Gardiner's social argument more patent, but they do not misrepresent it:
Social equality in athletics is evil. But Gardiner's
historical argument here is manifestly false. For the
very stories which he employs to illustrate the evils of
later professionalism (which "did not yet exist in the
sixth century") indisputably refer to *sixth century* Croton
and Sybaris. That is, Gardiner cites the very period
which he praises in order to get the evidence for the

period which he condemns.[77] The methodology is as preposterous as Shorey's. It recurs repeatedly and consistently, misleading readers far worse than ordinary sloppy scholarship. The modern interpretation of Greek athletics depends on the same misleading methodology, indeed on the same book.

In 1912, two years after Gardiner's definitive work on Greek "amateur" athletics (533 pages), Coubertin held his first truly successful International Olympic Games in Stockholm, now known as the Fifth Modern Olympiad or the "James Thorpe Olympics." Thorpe's exceptional ability and his stirring achievements lent a new prestige to Coubertin's amateur Olympics; for they had not previously been known as an arena for the highest athletic quality. Thorpe was the toast of the world, and the International Olympic Games finally basked in the global limelight which they have enjoyed ever since. What is more, the IOC's successful prosecution of Thorpe's delinquent amateurism at the same time served to reaffirm the amateur restrictions and to answer once and for all the amateur *versus* professional controversy. Olympic Games were for amateurs.[78] No

---

77. Athenaeus tells the story of Sybaris at 522a and of Croton at 522c, citing fourth century B.C. historians (Part Two, n. 28, below). Sybaris was destroyed by Croton around 510 B.C., and any story referring to athletics at Sybaris must of necessity refer to the sixth century. The height of Croton's interest in athletics was the sixth century, and all association of Croton with athletics ends early in the fifth century (484 B.C.; see Part Two, V, below). It surprises that Gardiner could be ignorant of all these details.

78. Mandell 168, Lucas 1980, 91. Thorpe's role in this success is told in many histories of the Modern Olympics, e.g., Dick Schaape, *Illustrated History of the Olympics* (New York, 1967), 125-135 ("The World's Greatest Athlete"). Others--like the IOC official records and publications--expunge his name entirely from the lists. Jack Newcombe, *The Best of the Athletic Boys; The White Man's Impact on Jim Thorpe* (Garden City, NY, 1975) is a sympathetic biography of Thorpe, who was voted by sportswriters

one could doubt it now. Thus the IOC capitalized on Thorpe as it rejected him. An impecunious American Indian was, after all, not the kind of athlete that Coubertin, Whitney, and Gardiner had in mind. Avery Brundage was far closer.

With Thorpe disqualified, his teammate and 1912 opponent, Brundage--who had finished sixth in the 1912 pentathlon behind Thorpe--climbed up to fifth. That place he proudly claimed and zealously guarded till the day he died. He moved from sixteenth to fifteenth in the decathlon. And he soon began to climb the Olympic administrative ladder, as well. He quickly became a millionaire in business. Having acquired the Presidency of the AAU early in the 1920's, he was on the American Olympic Committee by 1924. He moved to its Presidency (later renamed United States Olympic Committee) in 1929.[79]

78. (**continued**) and broadcasters the outstanding American athlete of the first half of this century. Menke (1975[2], 766) briefly, accurately, and dispassionately gives the details of Thorpe's Olympic achievements (including all his Stockholm marks) and the aftermath. He notes that efforts by many to effect restoration of Thorpe's medals have failed. But with Brundage gone but a decade, the new IOC executed a full turnabout, voting in October 1982 to restore Thorpe's name to the Olympic record book.

Addendum: On January 18, 1983 (after I had completed this note) the IOC gave (replicas of) Thorpe's medals back to his survivors. It had been, after all, more than 62 years since his notorious misdeed (which consisted of accepting a few dollars a week for playing baseball).

79. In his panegyric of Brundage, Schoebel notes Brundage's "fifth place in the pentathlon" and speculates that there was a possibility that Brundage "would have won" in 1916 had those Olympics not been cancelled by the war (p. 12). Sources differ as to Brundage's precise placement in the decathlon (only three places were awarded). Most sources give 16th or 15th, but Brundage's obituary in the city where he lived (*Santa Barbara News Press,* May 9, 1975, page 1) claims that he finished "14th in the

The following year Gardiner published his "short
and simple account of the history and practice of
athletics in the ancient world" (Gardiner 1930), a con-
densation of his 1910 book aimed at the general public.
This is the book from which popular histories of the
Modern Olympics crib their brief, confused notes--often
their outrageous errors[80] --on the ancient games. In 1932

79. (continued) decathlon." I do not know how large the field of
decathlon competitors was. Brundage, of course, became the principal obstacle in the movement to have Thorpe's medals restored
to him. Thorpe's and Brundage's relative rank in the original 1912
decathlon results, juxtaposed to the courses of their later parallel
lives, provides an interesting study in contrasts (both within the
Olympic movement and in general).

There is a more comprehensive and less sugared account of
Brundage and his strictly amateur principles in Lucas 1980,
161-172 (where Professor Lucas notes that "Brundage has been
called a scurrilous capitalist, a fascist, a communist [for the cause
see Schoebel 16], a Nazi-lover, a bigot, a racist, an unfeeling
millionaire and a thoroughly unlikeable old curmudgeon"). Brundage is usually represented as a "self-made man," largely by his
own representation (cf. Schoebel, 11); and Lucas writes, "Plung-
ing into the business world, Brundage, a poor boy, made a million
dollars by the time he was thirty." Yet the photograph printed in
Schoebel (photograph 2) of Avery Brundage "At the Age of Five"
scarcely looks like the picture of "a poor boy"; and it is hard to
imagine how a "poor boy" could belong to a social fraternity in
college (Schoebel 7), visit Russia without subsidy, and begin to
collect expensive artworks at the age of 25 (Schoebel 15, 24)--and
own his own major construction company by the age of 28
(Schoebel 8). I cannot resolve the incongruity. Equally in-
congruous, to one who has read Lucas' version, is Schoebel's an-
nouncement that "narrow mindedness, jealousy and everything
that might injure the cause of sport is foreign to him" (14). Reports
of Brundage are mixed.
80. For example, the Pooles place an incredible caption (p. 12)
under a reproduction of a sixth century Greek painting of an
athletic scene (Attic red-figure kylix, British Museum E. 6): "pot-
bellied, obese boy ridiculed and taunted by athletes in gymnasium." It becomes credible when one sees that the outrageous

the 1936 Olympics were awarded to Berlin. There lies another story, and I defer to Richard Mandell's exemplary account of those games and of Brundage's role in them. By the end of the Berlin Olympiad Brundage's rigor in enforcing "strict" amateur principles was well known. He had joined the IOC earlier that year.[81]

When the games resumed after World War II, Brundage had become Vice-President of the parent IOC, as well as President of the USOC. There was a movement to restore Thorpe's Olympic medals and achievements to him. But Brundage, first from his post in the USOC, then in the IOC, held firm against Thorpe's case. In 1948 he defended his strict construction of the amateur eligibility rules by appealing to the amateurism of ancient Greeks. Obviously, his argument runs, we moderns could not break so hallowed a tradition, even if we wished it. Liberalism of the rules spells ruin. Look at the Greeks:

80. **(continued)** mistake comes from Gardiner 1930, 58f: "On the left two ill-developed youths, one lean and skinny, the other pot-bellied, are wrangling." Gardiner's caption under the painting reads "To 1. altercation between a fat and a lean youth." But the unpleasantness is all in Gardiner's own mind. The "lean youth" on the far left is not, in fact, ridiculing, taunting, wrangling, or altercating at all; he is a runner standing in the normal starting position, which position Gardiner did not recognize. Nor is the figure next to him ("fat youth") "wrangling" in any way; he is merely watching the runner at the start. Virtually all scholars in the field rate Gardiner's ability to interpret the monuments most highly. I cannot.

81. R. Mandell, *The Nazi Olympics* (New York, 1971). Brundage found nothing to censure in Hitler's government (Mandell [above], 71-74, 81f. [cf. 164f], and see esp. Lucas 1980, 164ff [on Brundage's "darker side"]); but he found much fault with the amateur principles of some of his American athletes (see Mandell [above], 243-247, the Eleanor Holm Jarrett case; n.b.: "He had tried two years earlier to have her amateur status taken away and had just prevented her from securing first class passage on her own").

The ancient Olympic Games...were strictly amateur...and for
many centuries, as long as they continued amateur, they
grew in importance and significance.... Gradually, however,
abuses and excesses developed....Cities tried to demonstrate
their superiority...by establishing special training camps...,
by recruiting athletes from other communities, and by sub-
sidizing competitors. Special prizes and awards and all sorts
of inducements were offered and winners were even given
pensions for life. What was originally fun, recreation, a diversion, and a pastime became a business....The Games
degenerated, lost their purity and high idealism, and were
finally abolished....sport must be for sport's sake.[82]

Brundage obviously availed himself well of am-
munition provided by the classical scholars. I do not
bother to cite chapter and verse, for the phrases will by
now ring in the reader's mind. Finally, Brundage even
attributes "the decline and fall of the Greek Empire" to
professionalism in athletics. "When they lost their
idealism, became materialistic, and could not even play
for fun, the Greek hegemony vanished." They took
athletics seriously, and the nation crumbled.[83]

As it was to Gardiner, athletic money was to Brundage the root of all evil. Brundage's liberality never
passed beyond the 1880 modification of the 1866
amateur rule. But the date of his remarks quoted above

82. "Why the Olympic Games," by Avery Brundage, Vice-
President, IOC, President, USOC, in: USOC, *Report of the United
States Olympic Committee: Games of the XIVth Olympiad, London,
England* (New York, 1948), 23ff.
83. Brundage (above, n. 82), apparently implying that vast em-
pires rise and fall dependent upon whether or not the athletes are
paid or not. The same argument is found in the Pooles' book
(whose material comes from Brundage when not from Gardiner
[above, n. 80]): "The increase in gold-rich awards to athletes coin-
cided with the decline of Greek culture and democracy, with the
decay of the very nation. Greece ... became lax in character and
morals. The way was open to foreign invasion, occupation, and
rule .... Slowly Greeks became members of a socialized state,"
Pooles 109 (the chapter titled "Creeping Professionalism").

was 1948. He continued to spread these notions on the world, to enforce them on the Olympic Games--and to lay the responsibility for his own acts at the feet of the ancient Greeks--until he retired from the Presidency of the IOC in 1972. *Any* profit of *any* kind made an athlete a professional.[84]

84. Brundage's "strictly amateur" stance became stricter and stricter, often embarrassing and discomfiting even his sympathetic colleagues on the IOC. Just before the 1956 Games in Melbourne, "a controversy almost split the IOC. Avery Brundage had tried to change the Olympic Amateur Oath by adding a controversial clause involving a commitment by every Olympic athlete to swear that he or she *would never become* a professional, as well as swearing that he or she *had never been* a professional" (Grombach 25; e.a.). Olympic champion hurdler Lee Calhoun lost his amateur status because he was married on the television program "Bride and Groom" (he received wedding gifts). Full details are impossible here. I refer to other books, such as Geoffrey Miller, *Behind the Olympic Rings* (Lynn, Mass., 1979): "This American multi-millionaire....expressed himself in forthright language; but towards the end ... it became a little monotonous....He was near to being a dictator .... When he passed into his eighties ... his obstinacy led more and more often into trouble and he developed prejudices that seemed almost pathological. He conceived a bitter dislike, for example, of the Winter Games." He so disliked the Winter Games--because he could not stop the athletes in an "equipment" sport from getting something worth money--that he "made a scapegoat" of the Austrian skier Schranz and banned him. "The skiing world...saw Brundage as an iron-fisted executioner....The bitterness felt against Brundage in Austria ... is difficult to describe" (Miller 17ff). At the IOC meeting at the 1972 Sapporo Winter Olympics, Brundage "delivered an uncompromising tirade against the Winter Games in general and wished them a speedy 'decent burial' in 1976. We all listened to this speech with some embarrassment, and by the time it was completed many in the audience felt that the old man had stayed in office long enough" (Miller 19). The full vehemence of Brundage's attacks on athletes whom he suspected of somehow making some small amount of money--and the infighting of the IOC when he prosecuted such an athlete--will probably never be known. I include these details here, for Brundage always, figuratively at least, shrugged his own shoulders and

And to this day Gardiner is still the principal source, both in the generality and in the detail, for Greek athletics. His 1930 book has scarcely ever gone out of print, and as I write, it is used as the fundamental text-book in college classrooms across this country. A new generation born during the Viet Nam War is receiving at this very moment a calculated indoctrination into nineteenth century amateur ideals under the guise of ancient history.[85]

84. (**continued**) pointed to the "strictly amateur" Greeks. People who could not read Greek believed him. People who could read Greek remained silent. Most were so uninterested in athletics that they did not even hear.

85. Most instructors in Ancient Athletics (or Sport) courses in major universities and colleges on both coasts tell me that they use Gardiner as the basic textbook (there is, as they explain, little alternative). My information is current (1983). And comments such as the following still abound in classical scholarship: "Even as professionalism more and more dominated the Greek athletic scene, there still remained, at least in principle, opportunity for a skilled *amateur* to make his mark" (H. Benario, "Sport in Rome," *Ancient World* 7 [1983], 39; e.a.). This sentence clearly (but perhaps unwittingly) descends from Gardiner 1930, 104 (see n. 73 above, where also cf. the Pooles' version of Gardiner's same sentence). Gardiner's sentences are by now so incorporated into traditional Greek athletic criticism (Benario lists Gardiner first in his bibliographical note) that later authors rephrase them unconsciously, without attribution (cf. Sec. VII, para. two, below [Harris], etc.).

VII

The Truth "almost" Told

The notion of a "degeneration" was always the cornerstone of the Greek amateur thesis. But always, too, there was an ironic contradiction. The supposedly "strictly" amateur period of archaic Greece lacked evidence for amateurism. But, even worse, the most palpable evidence for Gardner's "degradation of Greek athletic sports," Shorey's "degenerate days," and Gardiner's "decline" actually dated from the archaic period itself. These scholars eliminated the contradiction, as we saw, by violently misdating the early evidence, transposing pre-Pindaric materials to the post-Pindaric period--even into the Roman Empire. They then used the same early materials, misdated by five hundred years, to illustrate the very downfall which they deplored in later times. Their method was so simple and heavy-handed as to be obvious. It left their position wholly vulnerable to objections from any classical scholar who cared to object.

Yet the objections did not come. No classicist cared.[86] A mere decade ago the myth of Greek

---

86. The acquiescent tone of disinterested classical scholarship was set in C. Manning, "Professionalism in Greek Athletics," *Classical World* 11 (1917), 74-78. Manning begins with an astute comment: "[O]fficially the Greeks never made any distinction between amateur and professional athletics." Yet on the same page he incongruously imposes that very distinction on the Greeks and divides Greek athletics into two periods according to those very terms: "from the institution of the games to the Peloponnesian War, *the age of the amateur;* and from the Peloponnesian War to the suppression of the festivals, about 400 A.D., *the age of the professional"* (e.a.). And Manning's final paragraph reads as if a summary of Gardiner's 1910 book: "perhaps nowhere else

amateurism still passed without challenge or examination. It was even fortified in 1972, when Harris reiterated his views in a second book, *Sport in Greece and Rome*--replete with subconscious echoes of Gardiner's canonized 1910 phraseology: "When money comes in the door, sport flies out the window" (Harris 1972, 40; cf. Gardiner, above). But in 1974 the Dutch classical scholar H. W. Pleket published the first of two scholarly papers on related subjects, the prizes and the "sociology" of ancient Greek athletics.[87] Taking Harris' new book as representative, Pleket first remarks on "the inevitable classicist 'bias'" of a man such as Harris, who styled himself as "an old-fashioned don." Harris,

---

86. (**continued**) is the decay of Greek civilization so clearly seen. The competitors, originally members of the foremost families of Greece...became finally men with undeveloped brains and unnaturally developed bodies." More than half a century later, W. Rudolph took up the same subject in his "Zu den Formen des Berufssports zur Zeit der Poliskrise" (E. C. Welskopf, ed., *Hellenische Poleis* [1974], III, 1472-1483). He too begins by noting that, by ordinary definitions, all Greek athletes were professionals. Yet he then proceeds to talk about a hypothetical ancient Greek "Amateur." Rudolph's article contains much excellent and useful scholarship, but in the end, on the amateur-professional question, it differs little from Manning's. Jüthner (1965, I, 89-93), despite his detailed knowledge of Greek athletics, also talks about Greek "Amateurs" and seems to have taken Gardiner's nonsense seriously. I note finally that the selections under the heading "Amateurism and Professionalism" in Miller's 1979 sourcebook contain not a phrase about amateurism (*Arete*, pp. 83-95). The heading comes from the assumption that, if there is professionalism, there must be a complementary amateurism; it does not come from any word in any of the Greek texts which Miller prints.

87. Pleket 1974 ("Zur Soziologie des antiken Sports") and Pleket 1976 ("Games, Prizes, Athletes and Ideology"). I note also Pleket's contribution in Finley and Pleket, *The Olympic Games* (1976; a popular book which touches on the amateur question only in passing, but presents the most accurate view available in English).

Pleket says, "liked his college boys, i.e. amateurs and disliked professionals--which was his good right--but he retrojected his own views and sympathies into the ancient world" (1976, 51). For the first time Pleket exposes the myth's link to the Modern Olympic Movement: Harris' conception of "the noble Greek amateur closely resembled the views cherished by Pierre Baron de Coubertin and his followers." But, Pleket continues, "[i]t is hard to find a phrase that would have shocked *the* ancient Greeks more than the modern Olympic credo 'to participate is more important than to win'" (Pleket's emphasis).

> [A]rchaic nobles are not known to have rejected remuneration for athletic successes either in theory or in practice....[P]articipation at Olympia did not prevent them from participation in games with 'value prizes'...and from ca 600 B.C. onwards cities are known to have awarded money or bullion to their victorious athletes. (Pleket 1976, 59)

That effortlessly Pleket explodes much of the amateur myth. Following I. Weiler, Pleket observes that all Greek athletes, from the start, placed a very high value on winning and accepted whatever prizes they could earn.[88] The amateur and Olympic policy forbidding all athletic profit was as foreign to archaic Greek athletes--to "Pindar's nobles"--as it was to the "professionals" of later days.

And Pleket explodes one more part of the myth, the monotonous "degeneration"-theory of later Greek sports. Following a suggestion of Louis Robert, he removes the stigma of moral "corruption" (the

---

88. Ingomar Weiler, *Der Agon im Mythos* (Darmstadt 1974); Weiler has very recently come the closest to saying what I say here in his *Der Sport bei den Völkern der alten Welt* (Darmstadt 1981), esp. 96-99.

"depraved condition," Pooles 111) from the later professional athletes, who unquestionably dominated
Greek games for most of antiquity. Pleket argues that
later "professional" athletes accepted the athletic ideals
of their "aristocratic" precursors, whom they sought to
emulate in a kind of *"imitatio domini"* ("emulation of
one's master"). The "old values," Pleket adds, "the
value systems of Pindaric *kaloikagathoi*" were always
the values of Greek athletes, even those of lower class
origin in Hellenistic and Roman times.[89]

It might appear that Pleket has set the record
straight merely by bringing the touch of a realistic
historian to a field long ruled by prejudice and sen-
timental fancy. If all athletes accepted prizes of value,
even in archaic times, and all shared the same value
systems, even in Roman times, then the amateur thesis
would appear to evaporate. What could be left?

To our surprise, Pleket refuses to question the
amateur myth as a whole. On the contrary, he em-
braces it in its very essence. What he left intact lies at its
very heart. That heart is social elitism. Harris' bias was
not a "classicist" bias but a class bias. As Pleket rejects
Harris' case for Brundage-style 'no-money' amateurism,
he accepts the principal premise; namely, that all archaic athletes came from the noble class. Even as he
defends the integrity of "lower class" athletes of later
times (1976, 87) he quietly purchases the unproved
assertion that all archaic athletes belonged to "the upper class" (1976, 72f). What was for Gardiner a mere
conceit is for Pleket a *datum,* embedded in our scholarly
apparatus.[90] So tenaciously does he argue for archaic

89. Louis Robert in *Entretiens Fondation Hardt* 14 (1968):
L'épigramme grecque, 181-295 (288); see also Pleket 1976, 76f, 87.
90. Pleket does not normally cite ancient sources when categoriz-
ing such athletes as Theogenes, Pantakles, Milo, and Astylos as
"nobles" or "aristocrats." Rather he cites twentieth-century

"exclusivist sport" (1974, 79 and *passim*) that it passes beyond a belief and becomes Pleket's procedure of research. Each case must fall into line.[91] And, what is more--in spite of all else--Pleket somehow manages to deny that accursed thing "professionalism" to the athletes of archaic Greece.

*   *   *   *   *

When confronting the question of "amateurism" and "professionalism" in ancient sport, Pleket himself first warns, "These are modern, almost anachronistic concepts" (1976, 80). But behind the word "almost" there lies a fatal error and a program. Even Pleket could not free himself from the nineteenth-century elitists' lingering grasp. He *almost* freed himself. But the ghosts of the Gard(i)ners march across many a page.

Pleket does not heed his own warning and proceeds to apply those "almost" anachronistic concepts to the Greeks anyway.[92] He states first the modern definition

90. (**continued**) scholars, who are influenced by the amateur myth (such as Pouilloux, Moretti, Jüthner, Bilinski, and Hönle, whose proclivity for the aristocratic case even Pleket finds remarkable, 1974, n. 60). I have found no ancient author who mentions the class or social origins of these men. For Pantakles and Astylos there seems nothing that could even be twisted into evidence for a noble birth. For Milo and Theogenes modern scholars indeed invoke ancient texts, but what they offer is truly ridiculous (Part Two, VI, below, with notes 49-50).
91. This research procedure is not unusual or culpable in itself. It is what Thomas Kuhn (*Structure of Scientific Revolutions*[2] [Chicago 1970]) calls "normal research"; that is, a serious attempt to make the available data conform to a theory whose validity is no longer in question.
92. "...'professionalism' versus 'amateurism'. These are modern, almost anachronistic concepts, but this does not imply that they cannot be useful heuristic tools in the hands of the historian..." (Pleket 1976, 80). To employ invalid concepts as "heuristic tools"

of "professional": "Nowadays by professionals we
mean sportsmen who make money from their sport."
That definition was enough for Avery Brundage, the
AAA, AAU, and IOC for many decades. But in the next
sentence, Pleket abandons that modern definition, to
which he never returns. As he writes of other matters
instead, his argument becomes more and more difficult
to follow. His definition of "professional" changes so
often and so quickly that, like Proteus, it is almost impossible to grasp.[93] But this much is clear: the definition

92. **(continued)** too often becomes a means of having things both
ways. As a non-technical term "professional" need not be
anachronistic, and Pleket's eventual definition "to make a living"
could normally be accepted. But "professional athlete" has
always been a technical term, raising issues and controversy
beyond normal usage (witness Pleket's own work).
93. From the modern definition "make money" Pleket im-
mediately jumps to a very different definition, "make a living,"
"daily bread" (80). The difference is crucial; for Pleket here an-
ticipates his final definition, not to *make* money but to *need* money
(81). He then jumps back (80) to the subject of *making* money,
noting with examples that ancient Greeks never disapproved
when athletes made money from sport. It is hard to see how their
approval or disapproval relates to the question of "professionalism." Apparently Pleket offers their failure to disapprove as
his grounds for quitting the modern definition, "make money" (I
discern no other relevance nor any other grounds).
"Professional," it seems, can only be a term of disapprobation (if
that is indeed Pleket's logic, Mahaffy's ghost hovers overhead--"to
lower him into a professional"). But at this point (80) Pleket denies
that all ancient athletes were basically professionals on the
grounds that, "firstly, it would be unwarranted to assume that all
recorded athletes devoted all their time and their entire youth to
training and games" (yet another definition of "professional"). He
then cites the case of a Greek youth (from the first century, not the
archaic period) who quit athletics to study rhetoric and philosophy.
Again the case bears little relevance to the main question. A formal
"secondly" never appears in Pleket's discussion, but it is apparently
the case of Theogenes, to which Pleket here turns.

which we use "nowadays" has no bearing on Pleket's argument. To make athletic money, even large amounts, will not make an ancient athlete basically professional. "By no means" (Pleket 1976, 80).

Having found no earlier athlete (such as Milo) to fit the "professional" label in any sense, Pleket eventually identifies the early fifth-century athlete Theogenes as a candidate:[94]

> It is undoubtedly among late archaic aristocrats like Theogenes of Thasos that the first professionals are to be found. They would have accepted the title of professional if one defines it as a man who does nothing but athletics during a longer or shorter period of time. (1976, 81)

But this is yet again another definition. It has nothing to do with money. Rather it relates to the anti-athletic bias of the amateur movement. An amateur should never take athletics seriously; a professional is one who does take athletics seriously ("does nothing but athletics during a longer or shorter period of time"). So vague a definition might include almost any athlete. It includes Theogenes without a doubt. He took athletics seriously. A precise contemporary of Pindar, Theogenes won the Olympic boxing crown in 480 B.C., and the pancration in 476. He competed in sundry Greek athletic contests

---

94. Milo of Croton had a career comparable to Theogenes', competing for more than two decades and from a homeland across the sea. Milo also "probably...won many times in local games" (Pleket 1974, n. 59). Like Theogenes, Milo now enjoys a posthumous noble birth, a generous gift from modern scholars (Part Two, VI, below). There seems only one reason why Theogenes must be quizzed about his professional status, while Milo can pass unasked. Milo lived a half century before Theogenes, and his victories are all sixth-century. In Pleket's chronological case, the early fifth-century Theogenes serves far better as a kind of 'missing link' to the beginnings of authentic professionalism at the very end of the fifth century.

for a "longer" period of time, twenty-two years, and won on more than 1,300 occasions. Most of those many victories came in games which paid cash or valuable 'in kind' prizes.[95] During that long career, his "average" was, as Pleket says, "a victory a week." Here is a man, if any man, who "does nothing but athletics during a longer or shorter period"; at last, we think, we have found a professional athlete in Pleket's early Greece. But no. Pleket suddenly switches the definition one last time and settles on another, reaching his ultimate goal-- to deny professionalism even in Theogenes' case:

95. Some sources for Theogenes (Theagenes) are translated in Miller, 59-61. But neither Miller nor any other readily accessible book (such as Robinson, Gardiner, Harris, or Finley and Pleket) will translate the most important ancient document, Theogenes' victory inscription from Delphi (Ebert # 37). I therefore translate it here (the first two lines are heavily restored, but thereafter the text is not in doubt):

> No one else like you, son of Timoxenos, has Thasos borne; you have among all the Greeks by far the greatest praise for strength. For never before was the same man crowned at Olympia winning in both boxing and pankration. And at Delphi, of your three crowns one was uncontested; -- a thing no mortal man had done before. In nine Isthmiads, ten victories; for twice the herald proclaimed you the first man on earth to win in a single day both boxing and pancration. Nine times at Nemea; and, Theogenes, your total victories are: one thousand and three hundred. And never, I say, in twenty-two years were you ever beaten in boxing.

This inscription shows that Theogenes set new records at Olympia ("never before was the same man"), at Delphi ("no mortal man...before"); and at Isthmia ("first man on earth"); it thus also reveals how far from the mark is Gardiner's comment, "The Greek did not care for records, and he kept no records" (Gardiner 1910, 2). Gardiner did not want the Greeks to keep records, for to keep records is to take athletics seriously. Therefore they "kept no records."

> They would have accepted the title of professional if one
> defines it as a man who does nothing but athletics during a
> longer or shorter period of time; they would have rejected this
> label, if we had given the following definition: a professional
> is a man who derives *his income* from his sport. They would
> have objected because they did not earn or did not have to
> earn their daily bread; they *were* wealthy; they did not have a
> *profession*. (Pleket's emphases, 1976, 81)

Theogenes, the professional, was not a professional.

By this semantic legerdemain Pleket clears the wealthy aristocratic athlete--even Theogenes--of the dreaded charge 'professionalism.' He may dedicate his whole life to athletics, win as much money as he wishes, and still retain his non-professional standing. Not needing a profession, he cannot be a professional. His amateur credentials are stated in Pleket's next sentence: "land ownership" and "the absence of any occupation."[96] That last phrase recalls the nineteenth-century amateur clubs which spurned as "professional" anyone who had an occupation such as "mechanic, artisan, or labourer." Pleket has saved the myth simply by rejecting the modern meaning of the word "professional athlete." His approach comes more from the 1870's than the 1970's, and an ironic twist of history has brought our study full circle back to London in 1866. Like the founders of the first Amateur Athletic Club Pleket eventually defines "professional" *in terms of social origin and economic class.* Money *won* is irrelevant--but *money* is not. Pleket's early Greek athlete is, after all our pains, just another nineteenth-century British gentleman in ancient dress.

---

96. Pleket himself never calls Theogenes or any other ancient Greek an "amateur"; for he seems always to have the 1880 definition in mind. But his caution is here unnecessary; perhaps unknowingly he has hit upon the original "amateur" definition and denied Theogenes' professionalism on the original grounds.

There is a strong chance that Theogenes was no wealthy aristocrat at all (Part Two, VI, below). If he actually was an aristocrat, Pleket's 'professional non-professional' Theogenes is indisputably another case of Gardiner's "professional amateur," the wealthy noble who takes athletics seriously and wins many prizes. The "true" or "full" professional--the professional professional[97]--must, by Pleket's ultimate definition, come from the working class. He is the man who "derives *his income* from his sport." He is the man who can use the money which he wins, for he is not born to wealth. These professional athletes, Pleket argues in utter conformity to the amateur thesis, did not enter major Greek games until *after Pindar*. Even in the late fifth century they were rare. Professional athletes (i.e., "non-nobles" or "lower class") first appeared in significant numbers, Pleket asserts, "shortly before Plato's time" (that is, about 400 B.C.; Pleket 1974, 68).

*   *   *   *   *

With this precise timetable, Pleket leaves aside semantic subtleties and imaginary interviews with ancient men. The timetable concerns objective details crucial to how we view and talk about early Greek athletics; it raises substantive questions, such as: What is the evidence that all early Greek competitors were high born? Pleket's timetable, unfortunately, proves to be marred by selectivity and an uncritical acceptance of

---

97. "True professional" is Gardiner's term (n. 75, above), "full" is Pleket's; the athlete is the same. Pleket might not object to such a reduplicated term ("professional professional"), since he himself uses more than one definition. But their use of multiple meanings can cause outright frustration to Gardiner's and Pleket's readers. In hopes of reducing the confusion I list the several definitions of "professional" commonly used in our field, and present in tabular form the various possible combinations (along with translations) in Appendix Three.

others' errors. He argues a thesis that non-nobles were wholly excluded from archaic and early classical Greek sport. He does not often, therefore, write off a piece of recalcitrant evidence merely as an insignificant "exception."[98]

Sometimes Pleket simply argues the evidence away, as in the case of the first Olympic victor, Koroibos, reportedly "a cook." Seeing that Koroibos' profession flies in the face of the nothing-but-nobles thesis, Pleket leaves no doubt where his allegiance lies. "There is a way out (*Es gibt einen Ausweg*)," he cries-- with patent special pleading--and converts the word "cook" into a priestly instead of an occupational title. Since we assume that priests were always drawn from the upper classes, the obscure "cook" Koroibos becomes a landed aristocrat, after all.[99]

In general Pleket just looks the other way when probable non-nobles appear in the early evidence. That is the case with the famous farmer boy, Glaukos of Carystus, Amesinas the "cowherd," and Polymnestor the "goatherd." Goatherding thoroughly resists conversion into a priestly occupation or aristocratic activity of any kind, and I do not notice Polymnestor's name in

---

98. He states that Melesias (Part Two, n. 45, below) might be an exception, "ein frühes Beispiel eines lower-class Athleten" (1974, n. 68); but he generally avoids that course (1974, 58).

99. Pleket (1974, 60) follows Bilinski and Hönle in adducing a Hellenistic-Roman Cypriote cult, which probably had priests called "mageiroi" ("cooks, butchers"). But to put an eighth-century Elean runner into that cult (or to conjecture an eighth-century Elean equivalent to put him in)--merely to invest him with noble birth--seems a desperate expedient. Yet Pleket readily decides that Koroibos was "not an ordinary 'butcher'-'cook' but a 'priest-butcher'...therefore not from an undistinguished (*unansehnlich*) family." (It is an ironic coincidence that the 1870 Olympic victor in the foot race, E. Skordaras, was a butcher [Sec. III, above, with n. 35; cf. also n. 10, above].)

either of Pleket's papers.[100]

Pleket's presentation of the evidence, then, is far less faulty than Shorey's or Gardiner's outright misreporting; but it leaves his position nearly as vulnerable as theirs. I close with a final example of Pleket's kind of special pleading. For it well demonstrates what caution a reader must employ when reading any modern scholar on Greek athletics, even a scholar of the first rank and the highest integrity, such as Pleket. At issue is a passage which Isocrates wrote for Alcibiades' son to deliver in an Athenian court. The son explains why his aristocratic father disdained to enter one of the physical athletic events at Olympia (*gymnastika,* such as running, pentathlon, or wrestling). Alcibiades entered the Olympic *chariot race* instead, for:

> He knew that some of the athletes were of low birth, came from small towns, and were of low education (Isocrates 16.33-34)

I let Pleket interpret these words before I comment.

> [A]ccording to the well-to-do Athenian politician Alcibiades, ca 400 B.C. *some* (ἐνίους) of the athletes who performed at Olympia were of low birth and mean education. Obviously *most* participants still belonged to the upper-class; it looks as if the recruitment of lower-class Olympic athletes was a relatively recent phenomenon on the basis of which Alcibiades began to disdain the gymnastic contests....(Pleket 1976, 73; Pleket's emphases)

100. For these athletes see Part Two, VI, below (end). Gardiner indeed mentions Polymnestor, but with an amusing change in the evidence. He elevates him from a goatherd to a "shepherd boy" (Gardiner 1910, 58). For Gardiner it was bad enough that an early Olympic victor had an occupation so menial as a herdsman. But a goatherd, the lowest of the low (the bottom even of the Greek herdsmen's pecking order [Gow *ad* Theocritus 1.86]), he could not brook. A shepherd boy is at least quaint ("Spiridion Loues was a Greek shepherd ....as he watched over his sheep...," Grombach 166). But a goatherd is, well, unacceptable.

To use this passage as evidence for the "recent" appearance of lower class athletes is to maltreat the Greek, and to pervert Alicibiades' point. Pleket omits some important words from his paraphrase. I repeat Isocrates' sentence, emphasizing the words which Pleket left out:

> He knew that some of the athletes were of low birth, *came from small towns,* and were of low education.

Pleket's omission serves more than economy. For if the words "came from small towns" are allowed to remain, they destroy the chronological value which Pleket gives the entire passage.[101] They destroy any interpretation that Alcibiades refers to "a recent phenomenon." For the athletes' provincial origin offends Alcibiades as much as their lowly birth. And Olympic victors had come from small towns from the start, several centuries before Alcibiades' time. They were nothing new. Pleket's own addition of temporal words ("still" and "began to") begs the very conclusion which he draws. There is certainly nothing in Isocrates' Greek to correspond with or suggest them (Isocrates could have written "athletes *nowadays*," οἱ νῦν ἀθληταί, but he did not). Pleket's use of the Isocrates' passage, then, is just one more instance, a subtle instance, of the same old chronological sleight of hand.

Alcibiades draws here no class distinction between 'the good old days' of Pindar and his own time, as Pleket claims. Rather he draws a class distinction between the athletic events proper (*gymnastika*) and the

---

101. In his earlier paraphrase of the same passage (1974, 67) Pleket did not omit this phrase ("und aus unbekannten kleinen Städten kamen"). Significantly, the tendentious temporal words do not creep into the 1974 assessment of the same passage, nor does Pleket there attempt to turn it into chronological capital and cite it as proof of non-nobles' "recent" appearance.

equestrian events (*hippika*). Alcibiades chose an equestrian event, his son continues, "possible only for those most blest by fortune and not to be pursued by one of lowly estate" (Pleket's translation). The great expense of breeding horses, keeping stables, and transporting the animals with their entourage had always restricted equestrian events to the wealthy, from Homer's day through Pindar's time into Alcibiades' own. These events remained the domain of the wealthy long afterward and remain so today.

In my own study here I follow Alcibiades' cue, and seek to separate wealthy stable-owners, who need not even attend the games to win, from the athletes who competed personally and physically in the *gymnastika;* that is, from the runners, pentathletes, wrestlers, boxers, and pancratiasts. To do otherwise invites confusion and error.[102] And my study hereafter focuses on *gymnastika* rather than *hippika.* The study of the latter is important, too, and necessary for any comprehensive ac-

---

102. See n. 73, above. At a meeting of the California Classical Association, Southern Section (October 1982), Donald Kyle well demonstrated how some Athenians used competition in the athletic festivals for various political ends. Virtually all of his subjects were noble aristocrats; virtually all entered the equestrian events, not the *gymnastika.* For the common value of the victory (not the similarity of competition) in both athletic and equestrian events, see my essay "Pindar" in T. J. Luce, ed., *Ancient Writers: Greece and Rome* (New York, 1982), I, 157-177 (n. 13). For the truly great expense of keeping racing stables, restricting the activity to the upper classes, see Part Two, below, n. 6. It is worth noting that on at least two occasions (480 and 472 B.C.), the people of "horse-raising Argos" (*Iliad* 3.75) apparently pooled their resources (or taxed themselves) to break the chariot-racing monopoly of the wealthy kings and nobles at Olympia with a "people's entry" (Pap. Oxy. 222, translated in Miller 48f). In the athletic events proper, we know of no public entry, only those of individuals.

count of Greek athletic festivals. But mine is not a comprehensive account. My subjects here are those that
bear upon the amateur-professional controversy. That
controversy has always concerned what we call
"athletics," not the ownership of horses. We must be
careful not to repeat Mahaffy's error, and mistake gymnastic events for horse races.

PART TWO: *THE REALITY*

Πλούτῳ γάρ ἐστι τοῦτο συμφορώτατον
ποιεῖν ἀγῶνας μουσικοὺς καὶ γυμνικούς.

"To have contests in music and athletics
is the thing most suitable to Wealth."

Aristophanes *Wealth* 1162f

I

The misconceptions which we have held about Greek athletics come from decades of misleading classical scholarship and false historical analogies. It is no wonder that H. W. Pleket, an outstanding scholar, failed in his recent attempt to right all the wrongs of so many years travel in the wrong direction. He indeed denied that ancient Greece knew our current amateur ethic which refuses all money and pursues sport only "for sport's sake." He exposes the "bias" behind Harris' most blatant anachronisms and his "interesting" philological flaws: "[W]itness Harris' moving exclamation: 'Across the centuries Titus Domitius reaches out a hand to Mr. Avery Brundage'. *That is no longer acceptable"* (1976, 71; e.a.). But when Harris reverts back beyond the 1880 rule to the original 1866 ethic, when he speaks of "wealth" and "birth" instead of Brundage-style amateurism, Pleket travels with him and asks no questions. All that is acceptable and more.

Harris' Phayllos (Part One, I, above) is just as badly anachronistic as his Titus Domitius; the philology there is even worse. And the fictitious deeds which Harris assigns to Phayllos' archaic career, the fictitious motives which he places in Phayllos' archaic mind--these mislead far more than Titus' later outstretched hand. Yet this utterly make-believe athlete can march right by, unnoticed by Pleket's critical pen. For Harris' Phayllos is patterned after the idealized nineteenth century English aristocrat who seems to be Pleket's model Greek, as well (Part One, VII, above).

Imbued with the notions of Greek exclusivist sport from all sides, Pleket questioned the myth of Greek amateurism only at its outer surface. He never peered back into its almost hidden origins in the nineteenth-

century amateur movement. He apparently never im-
agined that the entire amateur thesis--including the
aristocratic monopoly--could be quite groundless, a
mere house of cards. Pleket's archaic Greek gentleman
athlete will practice and accept prizes, but otherwise he
shares most things with his Victorian counterpart;
namely, upper-class birth, inherited wealth, and a contempt for money honestly earned. This tendency to fit
ancient sport into nineteenth-century molds sometimes
leads Pleket to irrelevant, distracting questions. He
wonders why "there was never a movement in antiquity
to ban monetary rewards and prizes completely from
sport." The answer is embarrassingly simple: the concept of amateurism did not yet exist. But Pleket can only
give a wrong answer.[1] For he treats amateurism as an
"almost" anachronistic concept when applied to ancient Greece. Until we thrust fully aside the *wholly*
anachronistic concept of amateurism, we will continue
to formulate ambiguous definitions, to tinker with the
evidence or use it selectively, and to pursue irrelevant
issues which distract us from the truly important questions about the nature of Greek athletics.[2]

One of those important questions Pleket himself is
compelled to ask about the later "professionals":

1. Pleket 1976, 87 ff.; he can look only to nineteenth century
England for an answer and indeed extracts one there (see n. 69,
below). But it is the anachronistic use of nineteenth century
England that raised the irrelevant question to begin with. Equally
anachronistic, I suspect, is Pleket's recourse to Thorstein Veblen's
theory of "the leisure class" (Pleket 1976, 78). Even Pleket's frequent references to modern scholars' theories about the ancient
Greek hoplite class seem of slight use in interpreting the actual
surviving evidence for Greek athletics.
2. Section IX, below, seeks merely to sketch some of their
distinctive features, which deserve and will repay more study
when once cleared of all Victorian overgrowth.

A cardinal problem is naturally how athletes from the lower strata of the population afforded the expense of training and how they could earn a basic living to begin with (*überhaupt*).[3]

The question how the poor or even those of moderate means could afford the time and expense to compete, in any period, is a legitimate one deserving an answer. Pleket generally despairs, weakly offering the modern concept of subsidy (a controversial subject in amateurism and in the modern Olympic Games):

Subsidization would have been indispensable, but the earliest evidence for that is much later: an inscription from Ephesus (ca. 300 B.C.) .... (1976, 72)

But once we abandon the concept and the terminology of amateurism, "subsidization" may not be indispensable. There are other means.

Another legitimate question which Pleket raises was first suggested by Albrecht Dihle. Prompted by the large number of successful athletes, even *gymnastikoi,* who later participated in their cities' governmental affairs, political or military, Dihle wondered,

Can we determine whether an athlete, in a given case, rises to a position of rank *because* of his success as an athlete or whether he participates in athletics *because* he is the son of a ranking family?[4]

3. I offer a solution to this problem in the first part of Sec. VII, below, and the solution is implicit in the Panathenaic prize inscription translated in Sec. III, below. The quotation comes from Pleket 1974, 67; as in Part One, I have often translated material written in foreign languages in hopes of making it accessible to the non-specialist. Where the precise foreign word may be significant, I add the original.
4. Pleket 1974, 75, with my emphases. Pleket has slightly modified Dihle's question, and I modify it slightly more in my translation (to translate fully and literally both *"Berufsathlet"* and *"professionellen"* would add nothing but confusion). This question is more difficult than the other (there were probably cases of both types of athlete-politician). But here too I have offered some materials that bear on the question (Sec. VII, below).

Dihle has, in fact, asked the important question whether or not athletics ever served as a means for social mobility in ancient Greece. But Pleket's answers are again vague and, because he allows none but aristocrats into the earlier period, they all concern athletes of post-classical times.

In the remarks which follow here, I seek not so much to affirm professionalism (or deny amateurism) as to clarify the evidence on which these topics are usually argued. I am little concerned with semantics or theories about the origin of gymnasia or about Thorstein Veblen's leisure class. I want merely to focus on such straightforward questions as "how much could a Greek athlete win?" Scholars who discuss the professional-amateur question have carefully avoided any attempt at the obvious--for example, to translate the Panathenaic prize inscription into meaningful values. "How often and from what sources did an ancient athlete receive material gain?" In our rush to attribute nineteenth-century British amateurism to archaic and classical Greece we have ignored or misread much pertinent information of this kind. "How far back in Greek history *do* we find suggestions of athletic purses and non-noble participants?" "What inferences are to be drawn from the performances, records, and training methods of ancient athletes?" When we have properly assessed the evidence for these questions, we may more easily investigate the more difficult matters. And we may even be able to suggest answers to Pleket's legitimate but essentially unanswered questions mentioned above.

II

In Homer, men occasionally compete in athletic games or exercises for which there is no material reward. They are, incongruously, *athletai* without *athla*.[5] But in the funeral games of Patroclus, Achilles sets valuable prizes for each event: "cauldrons and tripods, horses, mules, valuable cattle, well-girded women, and iron" (*Iliad* 23.259-261). Fourth prize for the chariot race is two talents of gold; the tripod awarded the victor in wrestling is "valued at twelve oxen." These prizes may be exceptionally large, for the occasion is exceptional. But such prizes and the games of Patroclus are not unparalleled in Homer. In *Iliad* 9, Agamemnon offers Achilles a dozen prize-winning race-horses: "A man who possessed as much as these horses have won in prizes would be far from poor; he would be rich in precious gold." The horses have apparently run in repeated competitions, and are expected to continue their prize-winning role (*Iliad* 9.123-127 [= 265-269]).

Horse-racing remains the Sport of Kings, and has always belonged to the wealthy.[6] But Homer does not

5. *Odyssey* 8.97-103; 17.168 f.; 4.626 f.; *Iliad* 2.774 f. With the possible exception of *Od.* 8.97-103, these *aethloi* are more recreational than competitive pastimes. A good presentation of the Homeric evidence is in Patrucco, pp. 15-25.
6. Cf. Starr, p. 135. For the extraordinary expense of keeping a horse (to say nothing of racing stables) in ancient Greece see J. K. Anderson, *Ancient Greek Horsemanship* (Berkeley, 1961), chap. XI. Anderson deals mostly with cavalry horses, but mentions chargers and race-horses that sold for 1,000 drachmas and up in the classical period (p. 136). [The meaning of such figures is discussed in Section III, below]. Besides the cost of horses and their upkeep, a racing stable required full-time grooms and trainers. Yet a man so rich as Alcibiades could enter six teams of four (24 horses in all) in a single Olympic chariot race. It is difficult to imagine his expense.

limit mention of athletic prizes to equestrian events and
Iliad 23. A neglected passage in *Iliad* 22 is crucial; for it
clearly refers to actual athletic practice in Homer's own
time, not to fictitious events in the heroic age. As
Achilles pursues Hector around the Trojan wall, they
ran, Homer says, "very fast; for they were not competing for a sacrificial animal nor an ox-hide -- things
that are prizes for men in foot races. At stake in the race
was Hector's life. As when race-horses quickly run
around the turns, and a large prize is set, such as a
tripod or a woman, when a man has died; so Achilles
and Hector three times whirled round Priam's city on
swift feet" (*Iliad* 22.159-166).

Grand prizes for equestrian events in funeral games
were obviously well known in Homer's time; otherwise
he would not use them as a point of reference for a
simile. Furthermore, the passage proves that footraces
for a prize were common enough, and not restricted to
funeral games.[7] For most Greeks, at least, a victim or an
ox-hide was an object of real value and a prize worth
striving for. In the received view, competition even for
these prizes was forbidden to all except the nobles who
were already wealthy; but there is no supporting
evidence.

When cataloguing Hecate's powers, Hesiod cites
her aid to athletes, who proudly carry their prizes home
to admiring parents (*Theogony* 435-438). Hesiod speaks
with authority. He himself won a tripod in a poetry
event at the games (*aethla*) of Amphidamas, whose sons
set "many prizes" (*Works and Days* 654-657). But

---

7. Competition in Homeric times thus appears more extensive
than Pleket grants: "In early-archaic times (8*th*-6*th* century B.C.)
there was not much of an institutionalized agonistic system. The
agonistic 'market' offered the Olympic Games...and an unknown
number of contents, organized in honour of deceased noblemen
and on the occasion of their funerals" (Pleket 1976, p. 54).

Hesiod was no wealthy aristocrat exulting in his ancestors' noble blood and far-flung estates. His father, previously a poor sailor and traveling saleman, had fled his native land and migrated to Boeotia. In Hesiod's words, "He fled not wealth and substance, but abject poverty." Lesky even regards Hesiod a peasant.[8] In order to preserve the purely aristocratic character of early athletic games, we must conclude that the sons of Amphidamas allowed such people as Hesiod to compete in poetry, but barred them from the physical events, such as running and boxing. Such a policy makes little sense, and nothing could be cited on its behalf but modern scholars' faith in their own position.

There is a strong tradition that the Pythian games originally offered valuable prizes, and were later restructured to award only the symbolic laurel wreath of historical times.[9] The Olympics may have been "money" games at first, but in historical times the "Big Four" festivals, Olympic, Pythian, Isthmian, and Nemean games, gave only symbolic crowns as prizes. But there were many archaic athletic festivals besides these,

---

8. Hesiod's father: *Works and Days* 631-640. "There were aristocratic landowners there [Ascra] as elsewhere. Hesiod came in contact with them, but their world was not his. ...His world is that of small peasants who were indeed free, but had a hard struggle for a living" (Albin Lesky, *History of Greek Literature*, trans. by J. Willis [New York, n.d.], p. 92).

9. Pausanias 10.7.5, *scholia* Pindar *Pyth.*, preface (Drachmann II, 3-4). Gardiner claims that in the Olympics "the prizes were originally tripods and other objects of value" (1910, p. 48). It is likely that the early Olympics did give valuable prizes, but there is no literary evidence. Gardiner's statement is merely an (unwarranted--see Ziehen in *RE* 18, 31 f.) inference from a comment of Phlegon of Tralles (Jacoby no. 257, F1 [*FGH* 2.3, 1160-62]); from Gardiner this undocumented claim about the early Olympics has spread to subsequent literature. The many archaic tripods unearthed at Olympia may suggest athletic prizes (cf. *Iliad* 11.698-701), but are not conclusive.

and the other games awarded valuable prizes.[10] Even the lesser prizes at minor festivals command attention. The warm winter coat given each victor at Pellene was worth many days earnings to a humble man in ancient times. But most athletic festivals gave more valuable rewards. Objects of bronze, presumably tripods, were the prizes in Tegea and the Theban Iolaeia; silver goblets were offered in the games at Marathon and Sicyon. These are prizes of significant monetary worth. It is difficult to imagine that strong and talented men of Hesiod's class or better (but not noble and wealthy) passed up these prizes in total deference to the wealthy--if they were allowed to compete. No source says that they were excluded.

10. Our information comes mostly from Pindar. A convenient list of games and prizes in Pindar appears in F. Mezger, *Pindars Siegeslieder* (Berlin, 1880), pp. 1-6. See also Klee, pp. 20-70. I know no list of all regularly recurring athletic meets attested in the archaic period (including Pindar); in a brief search, I count over 40 (Appendix4). There must have been many more.

III

The Theban tripods and silver goblets from Sicyon were worth much money, but we do not know how much. We have no information about their weight, nor about their equivalents in wages or buying power. Fortunately, the Panathenaic games at Athens are another matter, at least for the classical period. An inscription from the first half of the fourth century records the amount of olive oil awarded as a prize to the victor in each category. The oil is priceable. We can easily arrive at an approximate value for the prizes in these games if we wish, in both modern and ancient equivalences. Gardiner, Pleket, and others write page after page speculating on class distinctions. Yet I know no serious attempt to assess this concrete data. Many classicists will be taken aback -- some in entrenched disbelief -- by the magnitude of these prizes.[11]

---

11. *IG* II² 2311 (Greek text, Appendix 6, pp. 186-7). Miller (pp. 44-47) translates the inscription into dollars, but his figures are far too low and hardly serious (see n. 15, below). I forewarn the reader of Miller's translation that he or she will do better to multiply each prize figure by ten (i.e., $9,600 in Miller = $96,000).

Miller's conservatism is misleading but forgivable. More accurate figures, I myself discover, are likely to call forth immediate and strong disagreement (even scoffing and anger) from other classicists, who may simply abjure high earnings for athletes. But whether we like or dislike the high figures is not relevant; only their accuracy matters here. We are students of Greek culture, not arbiters of Greek morals.

The fact is that a seventeen year-old youth in Plato's Athens could make almost as much money in a few seconds on the Panathenaic track as a skilled, fully employed carpenter could earn in two years -- if the lad was sufficiently πόδας ὠκύς. And the modern American counterpart of this seventeen year-old Greek would apparently need to work more than six years full time (at minimum wage) to earn an amount equal to the ancient athlete's prize. He cannot normally win it on the track.

Because the prize for the men's *stade* was an even
hundred amphoras of olive oil, it is most convenient to
base the study on that premier ancient event, a foot race
roughly equivalent to our 200 meter dash.[12] The
cheapest recorded price for olive oil in classical antiquity
is twelve drachmas an amphora (also on a fourth century
Athenian inscription). The price was usually higher,
sometimes three and four times that figure.[13] Thus
twelve drachmas per amphora is the *lowest* usable
figure, and we must estimate the value of the stade victor's prize at a *minimum* of 1,200 drachmas. It remains
to determine what that prize means in comparison with
wages, both ancient and modern, and what its ancient
purchasing power was. I turn first to the comparison
with wages.

Classical handbooks and economic histories of
Greece regularly report one drachma per day as the
normal wage for a working man in classical Athens. If
we were to equate that ancient daily wage with our

12. The men's athletic prizes are broken from the stone, but they
were precisely double the boys' prizes (Wilamowitz, *Sappho und
Simonides* [Berlin, 1913], p. 218 (see n. 19, below). Since the extant
portion of the stone gives the boys' prizes in full, we may con-
fidently restore the men's. First place in the boys' stade paid 50
amphoras, in the boys' pentathlon, 30; their adult equivalents,
therefore, paid 100 and 60 amphoras, respectively.
13. A Panathenaic prize amphora contained one *metretes* (Lang
apud Pritchett, "Attic Stelai," II, 195 [the normal Attic amphora
was a third smaller]). A *metretes* = 39.39 litres or about 10.4
gallons (Hultsch *apud* Pritchett, II, 182).
    The ancient price for a *metretes* of olive oil is often recorded; it
ranges from 55 drachmas (one instance, late fourth century B.C.)
to 11 drachmas (one instance, late second century B.C.); but 16-18
drachmas is normal (Pritchett, II, 184). The fourth century inscription with the cheapest price of 12 drachmas (*IG* II² 1356) concerns
sacrificial oil for burning (probably not premium oil). Later in that
century we find prices of 36 and 55 drachmas (in Lampsacus and
Delos).

own carpenters' actual daily wage ($101.00 per day in my own city of Santa Barbara), we would arrive at the astounding amount of $121,200.00 (U.S.1980) for the victor of a 200 meter foot race in a meet of secondary importance (1,200 × 101).

Although I believe that this calculation may be nearly correct, I do not propose to use it. Any substantial amount seems certain to arouse suspicion, and I do not seek to inflate the figures. To be on the safe and conservative side, I shall, *at every point* (as in the price of olive oil), use the data which produce the *smallest* result possible. In so controversial a matter, it seems best to give absolute minimum equivalents even at the expense of scholarly probability.

We can reduce this large figure, $121,200, based on comparative wages, in only two ways. We can reduce the modern carpenter's daily wage from $101 to something smaller; we can increase the ancient daily wage to something larger, more than one drachma. Later I shall determine a minimum modern figure, and treat the knotty question of modern equivalents for these prizes. It seems best for now to forget all modern comparisons, and to concentrate on the ancient world alone. In terms of his own economy, what did the Panathenaic stade victor's prize mean to him and to his contemporaries?

A minimum value for the prizes (compared with wages) may be found by using the maximum figure for the ancient wage. The standard wage formula (one drachma = one day's wage) refers to the end of the fifth century and the start of the fourth (about 400 B.C.). The inscription is dated "400-350" B.C. To be conservative, we may take a wage from as late as the mid-fourth century (350), when wages for a skilled worker, at least, had increased to 1.417 drachmas a day.[14] The stade victor's 1,200 drachma prize, then, was worth the equivalent of at least 847 days' wages (1,200 ÷ 1.417) for a skilled worker, or nearly three years' work (if fully employed 300 days per year). The chart on pp. 119-123 shows the number of amphoras awarded for each place in each event, the value of that prize in drachmas, the number of working days that a skilled worker would need to earn that much money, and the equivalent in years of employment (on the optimistic assumption that a workman could find work about six days a week throughout the year -- no doubt it actually took much longer to accumulate such earnings).

There is little need to inquire further in order to answer the main question. A single athletic victory, in either the men's or youths' category, paid noticeably more money than a full year's work. The average value of the men's victory-prizes is more than two years' wages (2.03). The figures are a minimum. We must

14. The standard formula (based on Acropolis building records, *IG* I² 374) is not controversial, and finds general confirmation. Two drachmas a day for the highest ranking Athenian ambassadors to Persia could hardly be presented as an unwarranted and unconscionably high salary (Aristophanes *Acharnians* 65-90) were it not about double that of an ordinary worker. But both the standard formula and Aristophanes refer to the late fifth century, and more precise information on fourth century wages is available. I summarize here the discussion in Glotz, *Ancient Greece at Work*, 282f; cf. H. Michell, *Economics of Ancient Greece*² (1957), 131f, or A. Zimmern, *Greek Commonwealth* (reprint 1961), 263f.

In the latter part of the fifth century, employed workmen in Athens, skilled (carpenter, mason) or unskilled, received one drachma per day wage. Mere assistants made only 3 obols. Wages increased in the fourth century, but only slightly. Laborers still got only one drachma, or in Eleusis in 329, one and a half drachmas. Skilled workers slowly increased to one drachma, two and a half obols (= 1.417 drachmas) by mid-century, and to two or two and a half drachmas by its end. But at the start of the fourth century, even a master mason received only two drachmas a day.

ATHLETIC EVENTS

		PRIZE IN AMPHORAS OF OIL	DRACHMA VALUE (12 drachmas per amphora)	NUMBER OF DAYS WAGES at 1.417 DRACHMAS PER DAY (skilled)	NUMBER OF YEARS FULL EMPLOYMENT (at 300 days)
STADE					
men	first	100	1,200	847	2.82
	second	20	240	169	.56
youths	first	60	720	508	1.69
	second	12	144	102	.34
boys	first	50	600	423	1.41
	second	10	120	85	.28
PENTATHLON					
men	first	60	720	508	1.69
	second	12	144	102	.34
youths	first	40	480	339	1.13
	second	8	96	68	.23
boys	first	30	360	254	.85
	second	6	72	51	.17

ATHLETIC EVENTS (continued)

		PRIZE IN AMPHORAS OF OIL	DRACHMA VALUE (12 drachmas per amphora)	NUMBER OF DAYS WAGES at 1.417 DRACHMAS PER DAY (skilled)	NUMBER OF YEARS FULL EMPLOYMENT (at 300 days)
WRESTLING					
men	first	60	720	508	1.69
	second	12	144	102	.34
youths	first	40	480	339	1.13
	second	8	96	68	.23
boys	first	30	360	254	.85
	second	6	72	51	.17
BOXING					
men	first	60	720	508	1.69
	second	12	144	102	.34
youths	first	40	480	339	1.13
	second	8	96	68	.23
boys	first	30	360	254	.85
	second	6	72	51	.17

ATHLETIC EVENTS (Continued)

		PRIZE IN AMPHORAS OF OIL	DRACHMA VALUE (12 drachmas per amphora)	NUMBER OF DAYS WAGES at 1.417 DRACHMAS PER DAY (skilled)	NUMBER OF YEARS FULL EMPLOYMENT (at 300 days)
PANCRATION					
men	first	80	960	678	2.26
	second	16	192	136	.45
youths	first	50	600	423	1.41
	second	10	120	85	.28
boys	first	40	480	339	1.13
	second	8	96	68	.26
EQUESTRIAN EVENTS					
Chariot race	first	140	1,680	1,186	3.95
	second	40	480	339	1.13
Chariot race (foals)	first	40	339	1.13	
	second	96	68	.23	

EQUESTRIAN EVENTS (Continued)

	PRIZE IN AMPHORAS OF OIL	DRACHMA VALUE (12 drachmas per amphora)	NUMBER OF DAYS WAGES at 1.417 DRACHMAS PER DAY (skilled)	NUMBER OF YEARS FULL EMPLOYMENT (at 300 days)
Missing from stone:				
more chariot races, the horse-races				
MUSICAL EVENTS [prizes in gold, silver, or cash]				
Cithara-singers*				
first		1,500	1,059	3.53
second		1,200	847	2.82
third		600	423	1.41
fourth		400	282	.94
fifth		300	212	.71
Flute-singers				
first		300	212	.71
second		100	71	.24

MUSICAL EVENTS (Continued)

	PRIZE IN AMPHORAS OF OIL	DRACHMA VALUE (12 drachmas per amphora)	NUMBER OF DAYS WAGES at 1.417 DRACHMAS PER DAY (skilled)	NUMBER OF YEARS FULL EMPLOYMENT (at 300 days)
Citharists*				
first		800	565	1.88
second		300	212	.71
third		100	71	.24
Flautists	[value of prize broken from stone]			

Broken from the stone: boys' musical prizes, etc.
Omitted from chart: prizes for military events, torch races, and boat races.

* The *cithara* was a stringed instrument of the lute class, more like the modern guitar (its etymological descendant) than the modern harp.

keep these facts in mind as we turn toward modern equivalents and approach the delicate question of a comparison in dollars.

Our first equivalent wage value for the stade prize was $121,200, founded on the formula of one drachma per day and a modern daily wage of $101. With the higher wage of the mid-fourth century (1.417 drachmas), we may reduce that amount to $85,547 (U.S. 1980; 847 days at $101). But I shall reduce it even more in order to maintain the policy of conservatism and minimums. I make the theoretical modern wage for such workmen $80 a day. Any smaller figure is unrealistic and tendentious, implying an hourly wage less than $10 an hour and annual earnings for fully employed, experienced carpenters and masons below $20,000. In our major cities, at least, it is not so.[15] In terms

15. The Santa Barbara Carpenters Local Union No. 1062 states that the official union wage (journeyman) is $101.00 per day (1979). Miller, p. iii, equates the wages of a skilled workman with $8.00 per day (1979). His figure allots a skilled modern worker in contemporary America (employed 5 days a week 52 weeks a year) an annual salary of $2,080 (so far below the official poverty level that no graduate teaching assistant receives so little [to say nothing of the unemployed]). Something is clearly wrong, for no such wage exists. The 1980 legal minimum wage of $3.10 per hour makes a minimum (8 hours) daily wage of $24.80 ($6,448 annual full time), three times Miller's figure. But no skilled worker in America receives so low a wage, nor is the minimum wage relevant to our calculations; the ancient wage more comparable to our minimum wage is that of the ancient workers' *assistants*, who received only half as much as the workers themselves (above, n. 14). On this basis alone, the comparable skilled worker's wage becomes almost $50, and we must multiply all of Miller's figures by approximately six.

Yet even $50 a day (= $13,000 full time) is not an acceptable wage for a trained workman nowadays, especially in the case of carpenters or masons who, like their ancient counterparts, work by the day without an annual stipend. The $101 per day which the Santa Barbara carpenter actually receives may be higher than average, but $80 a day is a realistic figure (= $20,800 annual only if employed every work day). I doubt that anyone in this country (on either coast, at least) can now obtain the services of a competent carpenter, mason, or plumber for less than $10 an hour.

ATHLETIC EVENTS

Stade

men	first	$	67,800
	second	$	13,560
youths	first	$	40,680
	second	$	8,136
boys	first	$	33,900
	second	$	6,780

Pentathlon

men	first	$	40,680
	second	$	8,136
youths	first	$	27,120
	second	$	5,420
boys	first	$	20,340
	second	$	4,068

Wrestling

men	first	$	40,680
	second	$	8,136
youths	first	$	27,120
	second	$	5,420
boys	first	$	20,340
	second	$	4,068

Boxing

men	first	$	40,680
	second	$	8,136
youths	first	$	27,120
	second	$	5,420
boys	first	$	20,340
	second	$	4,068

Pancration

men	first	$	54,240
	second	$	10,840
youths	first	$	33,900
	second	$	6,780
boys	first	$	27,120
	second	$	5,420

EQUESTRIAN EVENTS

keles (horse race)

[missing from stone]

Chariot race

first	$	94,920
second	$	27,120

Chariot race (foals)

first	$	27,120
second	$	5,420

MUSICAL EVENTS

(N.B.: prizes for athletic and equestrian events were given in olive oil, but the prizes for musical events were given directly, either in gold or silver crowns of assessed drachma value, or in cash (drachmas).]

Cithara-singers

first	$	84,750
second	$	67,800
third	$	33,900
fourth	$	22,600
fifth	$	16,950

Flute-singers (men)

first	$	16,950
second	$	5,650

Citharists

first	$	45,200
second	$	16,950
third	$	5,650

Flautists

[prize amount missing from stone].

[Apparently also missing from the stone are boys' prizes in the above musical categories, contests for rhapsodes, and others.]

of wages, then, the fourth-century drachma of the inscription is equivalent to $56.50 U.S. 1980 (1.417 drachmas = $80, both as daily wage). The chart on p. 125, based on those calculations, is intended to suggest the approximate minimum modern equivalents in wages for the prizes given at the Panathenaic games in Athens during Plato's time.

I make some observations on the prize-list. 1) Then, as now, a fourth-rate singing musician made more money than a second-rate athlete. 2) The amounts in the above list are actually worth far more in 1980 U.S. wages than they appear, because they were tax-free. Apparently the victorious athletes were permitted to export their oil without paying the usual duty.[16] 3) The boys who won as much as $33,900.00 for a track performance as brief as twenty-five seconds would certainly have been classed as professionals by our Amateur Athletic Union or the International Olympic Committee and barred from all modern competition. But they are *not* (whatever their social class) professionals by Pleket's new definition. They did not make their living from athletics. They did not make a living (just a large amount of money). Herein lies a possible answer to Pleket's question about the ability of non-nobles to enter the athletic profession. To this point I shall return later (below, sec. VII).

Any economic comparison of ancient and modern, such as the wage-formula expressed above, is obviously perilous and of limited use; for our standard of living is greatly improved over that of ancient Athenians. And working conditions in antiquity (such as the length of the working day) differed from ours. *But all these differences merely increase the value of the ancient athletes'*

16. D. Amyx, "Attic Stelai," III, 182 (citing Karl Peters, *Studien zu den panathenäischen Preisamphoren* [Diss. Köln, 1942], pp. 11 f.); cf. *scholia* Pindar *Nemean* 10.64b.

prizes. If we again divorce the ancient prizes from all modern comparisons and view them exclusively in their own historical context, they become perhaps even more impressive than in my calculations above.

With his 1,200 drachmas, the victorious sprinter had a small fortune in purchasing power. For example, he could buy six or seven *medium*-priced slaves (people!); or a flock of about 100 sheep. Or he could purchase outright two or three houses in Athens or elsewhere in Attica; for the full 1,200 drachmas, he could apparently buy a rather fancy house in the city.[17] This purchasing power suggests that my modern comparative figure, $67,800 U.S. 1980 is not excessive.[18]

17. For the average price of slaves (about 180 drachmas) see Pritchett, "Attic Stelai," II, 276-278; for Attic real estate, pp. 269-274.
18. $67,800 U.S. 1980 may be enough to purchase a moderate house in many parts of this country, but it will not buy the highly paid Santa Barbara carpenter even a cottage. For a modest "tract" house, he will pay twice that figure. To compare favorably with his ancient counterpart, he will do best to buy sheep (below, n. 21).

IV

The apologists of amateurism may argue that athletic prizes of this magnitude were an innovation of the classical period, that such large purses were not available much before the time of Plato. But there is good evidence to suggest that the Panathenaic program and prizes were the same in the archaic period as in classical times.[19] It is true that the officials of the Olympic games gave the victorious athletes a crown of olives, nothing more. That is because the athletes' own home cities would reward them with lavish prizes.

Solon, according to ancient sources, thought that athletes were of little importance to the well-being of the state, and therefore reduced (*synesteile*) to 500 drachmas the standing reward (*time*) which the Athenian treasury would pay any Athenian who won in the Olympics; he set the reward for an Isthmian victory at 100 drachmas, and for the other games accordingly. "For he thought it tasteless to magnify their rewards."[20]

19. Whether Simonidean or not, Simonides 43 Page (155 Bergk) shows that the early fifth-century men's Panathenaic pentathlon prize was 60 amphoras of oil, twice the boys' fourth century prize and evidence for continuity in the prize amounts from late archaic to late classical times (Wilamowitz, above, n. 12). For the same continuity of the Panathenaic *program* of events and prizes (including those for boys), see Gardiner 1910, p. 233.

20. Plutarch *Solon* 23, Diogenes Laertius 1.55 (= Nos. 484 a-b in Martina's *Solone*). Pleket (1974, n. 53) doubts Diogenes' statement that the Olympic prize was a reduction, but it suits Solon's other policies. All studies of ancient athletics seem to accept the substance of both reports as valid (see note, 24, below). Yet these passages introduce difficult questions, namely, the dates of Solon's archonship (the Isthmian games were not founded until about 582) and the introduction of money in Attica (many experts

What Olympic victors received before Solon's time we cannot guess, but we can attempt to estimate the worth of the 500 drachma prize. We cannot apply the fourth century formula 'one drachma = \$56.50 U.S. 1980' to Solon's time, for Athens had suffered runaway inflation in the intervening two centuries. A drachma in Plato's time was worth far less than in Solon's. Fortunately, Plutarch (*Solon* 23) also gives us some points of reference for Solonian prices, saying that Solon equated the value of a drachma to that of a sheep or a bushel of grain.

The cheapest price recorded for a normal size sheep in classical times is twelve drachmas (the same as an amphora of oil).[21] It therefore took the 1.417 drachma a day skilled worker of Plato's time a minimum of 8.47 days to earn the price of a sheep. 500 sheep represent to such a worker 4235 days work or more than *fourteen years wages* (at 300 working days a year). There is no reason to believe that classical sheep were any dearer than archaic sheep, or that a classical man had to work longer to earn one than his archaic counterpart (perhaps the opposite). Thus we may assume that one Platonic sheep equals one Solonian sheep.[22] In terms of 1980

20. (**continued**) believe that the drachma was not coined until after Solon's time). This is obviously no place to discuss such notorious controversies. If Solon did not himself set the Isthmian award and the cash prizes, they were probably established by one of his successors and later attributed to the more famous Solon (a common happening).

21. In "Attic Stelai" II, 259-260 Pritchett records these prices for sheep in the classical period: 16, 10 (a "small" sheep for sacrifice), 19, 12, 15, 17, 15, 15, 15, 12, 12, 12, 11, 12, 16, 17, 12, 12, and 17. To take the lowest figure here (10) would be improper, for it is a clear anomaly. I therefore take the lowest common figure (12) as the standard -- still noticeably *below* the average price. Anderson (above, n. 6, pp. 122-3) estimates the value of a sheep in Xenophon's time at a minimum of 15 drachmas.

22. 1,100 % inflation in 200 years is high, but hardly incredible if we think of our culture, where it has been greater in less time.

U.S. wages, then, one Olympic victory in Solon's time paid the equivalent of $338,800 (4235 days work at $80 a day). Even calculated at the 1980 U.S. minimum wage, the prize equals more than $100,000 (4235 × $24.80), but to use the minimum wage is unscholarly.[23]

The figure $338,800 is again likely to offend, and provoke objections. But my calculations are not so complex or conjectural as some may wish. A sheep is a sheep. Fourteen years wages, at any time in any society, is a large amount of money. Whether the proper wage-comparison figure should be $200,000 or $700,000 (it is obviously somewhere between) makes little difference to my point, which is this: an Olympic victor obtained a lot of money, and automatically became a rich man.

If we divest the Solonian prize from all modern comparisons, and view it strictly within its own cultural context, the result is essentially the same. The Olympic victor's 500 Solonian drachmas equalled 500 bushels of grain, the very amount, as an annual yield from a land-owner's estate, that placed him in the wealthiest of the five economic classes in Solon's timocratic system, the *pentacosiomedimnoi*. These "500-bushel men" were the super-wealthy elite of Solon's time, whose "rich-get-richer and poor-get-poorer" policies had brought about the social and economic crisis that Solon sought to resolve. Economically, at least (I do *not* say "socially"), any athlete's Olympic victory briefly thrust him into the same class as the few extremely wealthy aristocratic landowners whom athletic scholarship so often conjures up. If we compare our own super-rich, aristocratic or not, $338,800 as a demarcation line for the elite few is a reasonable figure. Many in our society (including some athletes) have annual incomes that large.

---

23. We would need to increase the number of working days to at least 8,470 -- more than 28 years full time (see n. 15, above).

Our information about Solon's large Olympic prizes comes from late, often unreliable sources, namely, Plutarch and Diogenes Laertius. Although other scholars seem to accept it readily enough, I would not trust it were there no corroborating evidence dating from the sixth century itself.[24] There is. The Athenian policy of lavishing large rewards on its victors was not unique. Our oldest athletic inscription was unearthed near Sybaris in 1965. It dates from the sixth century (probably the first half, and thus from Solon's very time). It records an athlete's dedication of a tithe of his Olympic prize to Athena. Epigraphers have concluded that he received a large sum from the Sybarite government as reward for his victory, and they rightly compare the Athenian prize set by Solon.[25]

Most telling of all is another sixth century document from the Greek West, the complaint of the poet Xenophanes. In a passage that harshly criticizes the role of athletes in the Greek city, Xenophanes complains that victorious athletes get free board at public expense and seats of honor at public festivals. The same policy in Athens, attested in a fifth century inscription, later provoked Socrates' indignation.[26] But it is not

24. See n. 20, above. Solon's 500 drachma prize is accepted throughout the athletic literature: Pleket 1974, pp. 62, 67; Gardiner 1930, p. 37, Harris 1964, p. 37; et al.
25. For text and commentary see J. Ebert, *Griechische Epigramme auf Sieger* (Abh. Sächs. Akad. Wiss. Leipzig, Phil. Hist.-Kl., 63, no. 2, 1972), pp. 251-255 and fig. 32. Miller, p. 93, attempts an English translation, but omits some difficult phrases. Parts of the inscription remain obscure, but all who interpret it agree that it implies a very large Olympic prize (besides Ebert see Pleket 1976, p. 80).
26. Xenophanes frag. 2 (West; Diehl). The Athenian inscription (*IG* I² 77.11-17; translated in Miller, p. 94) promises a lifetime of free meals at the prytaneum to all victors in athletic or equestrian events at Olympia, Delphi, Isthmia, or Nemea. Cf. Plato *Apology* 36e; Socrates' comment that the victorious athlete "does not need" the free board suggests that any victor in the major games was, at least after his victory, financially secure.

Xenophanes' main complaint. The athlete also gets, he says, "A (lump sum) payment that will be a treasure to him" (doron ho hoi keimelion eie). In Homer, the word keimelion, "treasure," frequently refers to valuable objects of gold and other precious metals, which the wealthy exchange as gifts of xenia.[27] Xenophanes' word doron, then, denotes a payment of substantial value, probably similar to the 500 drachmas awarded victorious athletes in Solon's Athens.

We do not know whether Xenophanes is condemning the specific policy of a specific city or the general practice in archaic Greece. He claims to have traveled throughout Greece, from East to West, for a period of sixty-seven years. He spent most of his long life in Greek colonies of Magna Graecia (Italy) and Sicily. That western Greek world, in the last half of the sixth century, is probably the primary target of his complaints. There is the inscription from Sybaris. And Athenaeus (522) reports that sixth-century Croton and Sybaris offered huge cash purses in an attempt to lure athletes away from the Olympic games to Italy for a kind of "counter-Olympics."

Athenaeus is a late author, but often reliable, and here he cites fourth-century evidence. One may still wonder about the precise accuracy of his report.[28] Indeed, if viewed as individual items, several particulars which I

27. Priam ransoms Hector's body with costly garments and linens, gold ingots, tripods, and bowls (Iliad 24.228-234) called keimelia (24.381). Adrestos promises Menelaos that his father will ransom him: "Many treasures (keimelia) lie in the house of my wealthy father, bronze, gold, and iron" (Iliad 6.47-50); cf. Odyssey 1.312 (which Xenophanes appears to echo), etc.

28. For the Sybarites Athenaeus (522a) cites Heraclides Ponticus, for Croton, Timaeus (522c); both historians are fourth century. The important fragment of Xenophanes (above, n. 26) is preserved only in Athenaeus.

have presented here may properly be questioned. But my argument does not stand or fall on any one piece of evidence. If one should prove false, the others remain in force, and wherever we find relevant sixth-century documents, such as Xenophanes' poem or the inscription from Sybaris, they corroborate rather than confute what we learn from later literature. Taken in the aggregate, the evidence for large athletic winnings in archaic times, and for archaic athletic games on a grand scale, is compelling. There is even strong circumstantial evidence that, in the very period of Xenophanes' residence there, these western Greek colonies recruited athletes and paid them handsomely.

V

Athletics apparently played an unusually strong role in many Greek colonies of archaic Sicily and Magna Graecia. The list of stade-victors (pp. 135-138) tells its own story.[29]

I focus here on a single *polis*, Croton. This city, located on the sole of the Italian boot, exhibits in an extreme degree policies that were probably common throughout the western Greek colonies. Croton was the home of the famous mathematician and mystic, Pythagoras. It was also the home of antiquity's most illustrious athletes. The wrestler Milo, who reigned as the men's Olympic wrestling champion from 532-512 B.C., was from Croton. Like Pythagoras, his contemporary, Milo became the subject of much apocryphal fancy. The Crotoniate pentathlete Phyallos entered posthumously into Aristophanes' plays and later Greek proverb.[30] But

29. From the early sixth to the late fifth centuries, western Greek colonies (Sicily, Italy, and Corcyra) eclipsed all the rest of Greece at Olympia. Of the 46 Olympic stade victories dating from 588 to 408, the colonies won 30 (65%), and the older, non-colonial cities of Greece only 16 (35% [of these: Sparta two, Corinth one, Athens none]). See note 31, below. See also the lists in Klee, 109-120, esp. 116.
30. For the later legends of Milo, see, e.g., Harris 1964, pp. 110 ff. (but cf. n. 50, below). Milo won the boys' Olympic wrestling in 540 and the first of five successive men's championships in 532. He also won seven Pythian, ten Isthmian, and nine Nemean victories. He was finally dethroned at Olympia by another Crotoniate in 512.

Milo is the first known periodonikes (i.e., winner of all four of the most prestigious festivals, Olympian, Pythian, Isthmian, and Nemean Games), and -- surprisingly -- the only periodonikes known from Croton. See Rudolph Knab's excellent *Die Periodoniken* (Giessen 1934, reprint Chicago 1980), 16ff. For Phayllos see Herodotus 8.47 and Pausanias 10.9.2. The Phayllos who appears in Harris 1964, 113ff comes not from antiquity but from an ideal conceived in modern times (above, Part One, I). See further note 33, below. In Sec. VI, below, I examine the specific question of these athletes' social class at birth.

Victors in the Olympic stade (192-meter dash), 588-408 B.C., by homeland

| Date | From the colonies | | From "Old" Greece | | Remarks |
	Name	City	Name	City	
588	Glaukias	Croton, Italy			
584	Lykinos	Croton, Italy			
580			Epitelidas	Sparta	
576	Eratosthenes	Croton, Italy			
572			Agis	Elis	
568			Hagnon	Peparethos	One of only two athletes here (see also 476 B.C.) from an Aegean island (Northern Sporades)
564	Hippostratos	Croton, Italy			
560	Hippostratos	Croton, Italy			
556			Phaidros	Pharsalos	
552			Ladromos	Sparta	
548	Diognetos	Croton, Italy			
544	Archilochos	Corcyra (Korfu)			
540			Apellaios	Elis	

Victors in the Olympic stade (192-meter dash), 588-408 B.C., by homeland (continued)

Date	From the colonies		From "Old" Greece		Remarks
	Name	City	Name	City	
536	Agatharchos	Corcyra (Korfu)			
532	Parmenides	Camarina, Sicily	Eryxias	Chalkis	(Wrestling victor: Milo of Croton)
528					(Wrestling victor: Milo of Croton)
524	Anochos*	Tarentum, Italy	Menandros*	Thessaly	(Wrestling victor: Milo of Croton)
520					(Wrestling victor: Milo of Croton)
516	Ischyros	Himera, Sicily			(Wrestling victor: Milo of Croton)
512			Phanas	Pellene	(Wrestling victor: Timasitheos of Croton)
508	Ischomachos	Croton, Italy			
504	Ischomachos	Croton, Italy			
500			Nikaistas*	Opus	
496	Tisikrates	Croton, Italy			
492	Tisikrates	Croton, Italy			
488	Astylos	Croton, Italy			
484	Astylos	Croton, Italy			The last of Croton's known victories (in any event).

Victors in the Olympic stade (192-meter dash), 588-408 B.C., by homeland (continued)

Date	From the colonies Name	City	From "Old" Greece Name	City	Remarks
480	Astylos	Syracuse, Sicily			
476			Skamandros*	Mytilene, Lesbos	The only victor from the East here (none from Ionia proper)
472			Dandis	Argos	
468	Parmenides	Poseidonia, Italy			
464			Xenophon	Corinth	
460			Torymbas*	Thessaly	
456	Polymnastos	Cyrene, Africa			
452			Lykos	Larissa	
448	Krison	Himera, Sicily			
444	Krison	Himera, Sicily			
440	**Krison**	Himera, Sicily			
436			Theopompus	Thessaly	
432	Sophron	Ambracia, Greece			(Ambracia in NW Greece, now Arta, a Corinthian colony).
428	Symmachos	Messana, Sicily			

Victors in the Olympic stade (192-meter dash), 588-408 B.C., by homeland (continued)

	From the colonies		From "Old" Greece		Remarks
Date	Name	City	Name	City	
424	Symmachos	Messana, Sicily			
420	Hyperbios	Syracuse, Sicily			
416	Exainetos	Akragas, Sicily			
412	Exainetos	Akragas, Sicily			
408	Eubotas*	Cyrene, Africa			

* Exact spelling of victor's name uncertain; sources vary.

the successes of Croton's less fabulous athletes provide the evidence most pertinent to our study.

Our Olympic records are generally complete only for the stade, the foot race of 192 meters.[31] For more than a century, from 588 to 484, Crotoniate sprinters dominated the stade, winning almost as often as runners from all other cities combined, specifically, twelve of the twenty-seven times it was contested, or 44% of the time. In the same period, Sparta won the stade only twice (7%), and Athens, including all of Peisistratid Athens, not even once. In one Olympic stade, the first seven places reportedly went to Crotoniate runners, a great show of "stable" strength (comparable to Alcibiades' famous finish of first, second, and fourth with his entry of seven chariots).[32] Croton's stade domination began with victories in 588, 584, 576, 564, 560, and 548. During Milo's brilliant Olympic career, Croton's sprinters could not win the stade. But they resumed right after it, winning in 508, 504, 496, 492, 488, and 484. Yet after 480, Croton never again won an Olympic victory in any event. Crotoniates had won

31. The complete list (to 217 A.D.) of stade victors comes from Julius Africanus and is found in Eusebius *Chronica;* a full text and commentary in I. Rutger's edition (Leiden 1862, reprint Chicago 1980; Sextus Julius Africanus). Other Olympic victories are known from various sources, literary and epigraphical. L. Moretti (*Olympionikai* [Rome, 1957]) attempts to provide a chronological list and to summarize what is known of each athlete. He catalogues 988 known Olympic victories (plus 41 dubia) and 780 individual athletes. My figures on Olympic victories are compiled from (and heavily dependent on) Moretti's work, which itself depends on Rutgers. Moretti adds to his list in "Supplemento al catalogo degli olympionikai," *Klio* 52 (1970), 295-303.

32. From the Crotoniates' finish in the first seven places arose a proverb, "The last of the Crotoniates was first of all other Greeks" (Strabo 6.1.12 [262]). Moretti (No. 345) lists sources for Alcibiades' victory.

more than a fifth (23 of 109) of all known Olympic victories in that period from 588-484. Yet of the approximately 700 Olympic victories known from the next 800
and more years, not one belongs to a Crotoniate. Nor is
there a certain Crotoniate victory recorded in any other
of the great games after that date.[33]

How could so dominating an athletic power plum-
met to absolutely nothing in one Olympiad? How could
a single colonial city in Italy enter the seven fastest men
in the whole archaic Greek world in a given Olympic
race? The most probable answer to these and other
questions is obvious. Croton recruited its athletes from
other cities, rewarding them or somehow supporting
them from the state treasury. The sudden end to
Croton's athletic empire could be explained by a sudden disappearance of the financial support that went to
the athletes. Other evidence supports this hypothesis.

After Croton's devastating victory over Sybaris in
510, Pythagoras himself retired and the Pythagoreans
who governed Croton expanded her power and
prestige. From 510 to 480, Italian coinage suggests that
Croton enjoyed economic-political control of its sur-
rounding territories (and Croton won seven of the eight
Olympic stade races run in that period). But about 480,
some of the neighboring towns began to mint their own,
independent coinage. Croton's economic domination

33. Neither Krause, *Die Pythien, Nemeen, und Isthmien* (1841,
reprint 1975) nor Klee lists a Crotoniate victor after 480 in those
three games, and there is none in Moretti, *Olympionikai.*

Harris 1964, p. 114, dates Phayllos' final Pythian victory in
478, but without cause (other than a need to buttress his own
romantic but imaginary account of an athlete who, at the peak of
his career, passed up the 480 games to fight Persians [Part One, I,
above]). Others (e.g., Krause [above], p. 97; *Olympia* [Vienna,
1838, reprint 1972], p. 350) follow the obvious suggestion of
Herodotus' Greek, that all three of this Crotoniate's Pythian victories fell sometime before 480.

was collapsing.[34] Since that date coincides with the complete collapse of Croton's athletic empire, as well, it is logical to associate the two, and to infer that some change, political or economic, internal or external, cut off the funds from this truly extraordinary athletic program.

By a stroke of fortune, we can actually observe the fall of Croton's athletic empire in the career of an individual athlete, the sprinter Astylos. Astylos won both the Olympic stade and the *diaulos* (race of two stades) in 488 B.C., and won the same two victories in 484, competing for Croton both times. He won the same two races in 480, capping them off with an additional victory in the armed race. But he did not run for Croton that year. This "super-star" athlete had switched cities. He now competed for Syracuse, "to please the Deinomenid Hieron" (brother and heir of the Syracusan monarch), who no doubt simply bought Astylos' services with a large *doron*.[35] Had Croton been able to pay

---

34. T. Dunbabin, *The Western Greeks* (Oxford, 1948), pp. 367 f.

35. Pausanias 6.13.1. Moretti (pp. 82-87) lists Astylos as a Crotoniate only in 488, and dates his transfer to Syracuse in 484 (so also Pleket, 1974, n. 60); but Gardiner 1930, 100 places the transfer in 480. My argument is not much affected by a 484 transfer date (but Croton's athletic downfall is moved back four years). Pausanias' text can be read to produce either date (the question is whether his phrase "in the last two" refers to the last two of Astylos' three Olympiads, or the last two of his six *stade* and *diaulos* victories). I favor Gardiner's dating; for in 484 Syracuse had just come under Deinomenid power (Moretti, No. 185 [not 186]; Dunbabin [above, n. 34], p. 410). Most scholars (Dunbabin, p. 373, n. 2; Moretti, p. 85; L. Drees, *Olympia* [New York, 1968: English version], p. 53) emend Pausanias' report so that the tyrant Gelon (rather than his younger brother, Hieron) is the one who attracted Astylos to Syracuse; for Hieron did not become tyrant until Gelon died in 478. But Pausanias does not say that *Hieron was tyrant* when Astylos was transferred; perhaps he was still but the brother of the regent, working on Gelon's behalf and being groomed for the throne. In that case, 480 is all the more the likely date. Julius Africanus, whom Moretti cites for Astylos' victory and Syracusan transfer in 484, lists him as a Crotoniate throughout, without mentioning Syracuse.

Astylos his reward or stipend, there is no reason, so far
as we know, for Astylos to have left it. We hear much of
Crotoniate politics, but no mention of any political
motivation for Astylos' transfer to Syracuse and its
Deinomenid monarchy.[36]

Pleket (1974, p. 63 and n. 60) includes Astylos
among the "noble lords," but we know not a thing of
Astylos' birth or social background, a point to which I
shall return. We do know more about him. His victory
in the armed race, added to his victories in both stade
and diaulos for three successive Olympiads, set a new
Olympic record, which stood for more than 300 years.
He was no miser, and could afford the best. For his
victory-ode, he commissioned Simonides; for his statue
(to be placed in the ancient Olympic equivalent of our
'Hall of Fame') he hired the noted sculptor Pythagoras
of Samos. Nor was he inexperienced in self-sacrifice for
the sake of his physical condition and athletic career.
Plato says that Astylos and some other successful
athletes abstained from sexual intercourse throughout
their period of training.[37]

36. Pausanias says nothing of politics when he relates that the
citizens of Croton turned Astylos' house into a prison and tore
down his statue upon his transfer to Syracuse. Pleket (1974, n. 60)
rejects Hönle's political motive for Astylos' move, on the grounds
that oligarchical Croton experienced no change of regime at this
time (he seems not to know the evidence from coinage). But Astylos
may not have been a "nobleman," and our knowledge of
Crotoniate politics very confused (Dunbabin [above, n. 34], pp.
361-375; K. von Fritz, *Pythagorean Politics in Southern Italy* [1940]). It
seems best not to inject them (with no ancient source) into
Pausanias' Astylos-story, much of which may be fanciful anyway (it
fits well a common pattern in the legends of athletes: J. Fontenrose,
"The Athlete as Hero," *Calif. Stud. in Class. Antiq.* 1 [1968], 73-104,
Themes D-E; F. Bohringer, "Cultes d'athlètes en Grèce classique,"
Revue des Études Anciennes 81 (1979), 5-18.
37. *Laws* 840a. Some few modern athletes have practiced the same
abstinence. Simonides' epinician for Astylos: Simonides 1 *PMG* (10
Bergk); statue by Pythagoras of Samos: Pausanias 6.13.1.

A classicist might find the most impressive item here an epinician by Simonides. But a modern Olympic athlete would surely marvel most at the length of Astylos' career. The length of ancient athletes' careers, in general, merits attention. Modern books talk only of the Greek "youth"--as if Olympics were not for grown men. Milo reigned as Olympic wrestling champion for twenty years. Our own boxers sometimes have careers longer than a decade, as do baseball and football players. But they are professionals. Our modern runners have only a few peak years, often not a full Olympiad. By contrast, running victories won by the same ancient athlete in two successive Olympiads are so common that they attract no special notice. A number of sprinters won the stade in three successive Olympiads, and one runner broke the record by adding a fourth.[38] Three Olympiads implies a peak career of about a decade, four Olympiads implies more than a dozen years. There has been no runner comparable in modern times except the distance runner, Paavo Nurmi--whose long Olympic career was finally terminated by the International Olympic Committee,

38. Among modern athletes, sprinters probably have the briefest period when their careers are at their "peak." Yet the following ancient sprinters were in Olympic championship condition for three Olympiads or more: Chionis (664-656), Olyntheus (628; 620), Astylos (488-480), Krison (448-440), Dikon (392; 384; his first Olympic victory was in the boys' competition, but his five Pythian victories suggest a long adult career). Leonidas of Rhodes won (men's) stade, diaulos, and armed race in four successive Olympiads (164-152). Many sprinters who won in only one or two Olympiads had long, profitable careers in the other games (e.g., Dandis [below in text]); this was no doubt the case with the many sixth-century sprinters who won in two but not three Olympiads. Distance runners probably had longer careers, but do not appear on Africanus' list. See also S. Miller, "The Date of the First Pythiad," *Cal. Stud. in Class. Antiq.* 11 (1978), 127-158, n. 26. Knab (16f) seems the first to notice the matter of career length.

which declared him a professional and barred him from his fourth Olympiad.

In the first half of the fifth century, Dandis of Argos had a long running career, including fifteen Nemean victories (no doubt several in several Nemeans). Ergoteles of Crete won the Olympic distance race in 472, but not in 468. He came back to win in 464, and his career covered more than a decade. But his two Olympic victories were not for the same city. Forced from Crete by discord, he had migrated to Himera, Sicily, which *polis* gave him land and other valuable considerations, apparently in return for his athletic services. Diagoras, an outstanding Rhodian boxer, seems to have spent most of his time on the mainland in athletic competition. The evidence is the number and scope of his victories. A major festival or two, Olympic, Pythian, Isthmian, or Nemean was held every year, and there were scores of lesser games, the ones which paid rewards directly. Some athletes apparently just traveled the circuit, much as a modern golf professional. The Thasian boxer and pancratiast, Theogenes, says that he won 1,300 victories in a twenty-two year career in the early fifth century. His claim meets with some modern disbelief only because we cannot imagine a wealthy aristocrat spending every week, six months a year, for decades, miles from his island home and ancestral estates -- merely for the glory of hitting and being hit in an athletic road show that toured more small towns than large ones. But Theogenes may not have been a well-born aristocrat.[39]

---

39. Dandis: Moretti No. 210, Ebert (above, n. 25) No. 15, Knab 6; Ergoteles: Moretti Nos. 224, 251, Ebert No. 20, Pindar *Ol.* 12, Knab 7; Diagoras: Moretti No. 252, Knab 9, Pindar *Ol.* 7 (see my *Three Odes of Pindar* [Leiden, 1968], pp. 91 f.). For Theogenes (Knab 4) see Sec. VI below, and Part One, VII, above. All of these athletes were contemporary with Astylos, and competed in the 470's. Finley and Pleket, p. 68, join others who simply deny Theogenes' record ("mathematically impossible") without substantial cause.

The only way that these athletes -- the case is clearest with the runners -- could have stayed in championship form for such long periods of time is by full-time devotion to training in order to maintain both physical condition and technique. This matter is hardly in dispute.[40] But the early athletes' methods of training indeed provide more circumstantial evidence that they took their careers as serious, all-engrossing business, quite unlike the amateur sportsmen of nineteenth-century England. Besides the few who practiced sexual continence, such as Astylos and Ikkos of Tarentum, most ambitious sixth- and fifth-century athletes followed strict diets and strenuous workouts, prescribed by their coaches. Various early training diets, including meat diets, are mentioned. Naturally, the question of Pythagorean diet brings a controversy to the unusual record of Croton.[41]

There was a close connection between ancient coaching and ancient medicine. During its athletic hey-day, Croton was also famous for its doctors. Harris, followed by Miller, thinks that the prominent Crotoniate doctor Democedes practiced primarily athletic medicine. From Herodotus we know Democedes' penchant for high living, high salaries, and one-year contracts let to the highest bidder. His career indeed reminds one more of the National Football League than any academy of medicine. He married an athlete's daughter, namely, Milo's. The punishing "exhaustion" drills of some modern coaches were anticipated by a doctor-coach, Herodicus of Selymbria, who supplemented his athletes' grueling workouts with

40. Cf. Pleket 1976, p. 81; 1974, p. 64.
41. See Pleket 1974, pp. 63 f.

careful dietary control.[42] The employment of these professional coaches apparently goes back beyond the mid-
sixth century, and in itself implies a milieu and importance for athletics more comparable to our own world
than to nineteenth-century England. The Victorian
Gentleman Amateur, as Mahaffy tells us, refused to use
coaches and viewed the whole coaching enterprise with
contempt (Part One, IV, above).

42. Pleket (1974, p. 64) calls the relationship between ancient
medicine and ancient coaching a "symbiosis."

Harris (1964, pp. 112 f.; cf. Miller, p. 91) infers that
Democedes specialized in athletic medicine because he married
Milo's daughter and was adept at setting dislocated joints. The
athletic propensities of Aegina and Samos tend to corroborate
Harris' conjecture. Democedes left his native Croton for Aegina,
and ("although untrained and without instruments") so outstrip-
ped other physicians that the Aeginetan government hired him for
a salary of 6,000 drachmas per year (an astonishingly high annual
salary in the late sixth century). The next year the Athenians hired
him away from the Aeginetans by paying him 10,000 drachmas.
But the following year he sold his services to Polycrates of Samos,
who set his annual salary at 12,000 drachmas. When Samos fell to
the Persians, Democedes became a prisoner of the Great King. By
properly setting Darius' ankle, he earned himself a great fortune
and a mansion in Susa, but not his freedom to leave Persia. By a
ruse, he eventually escaped back to Croton and married Milo's
daughter (Herodotus 3.129-133).

Herodicus, according to Plato (Republic 3.406a), altered the
course of Greek medicine by combining athletic training with the
healing arts (see also Patrucco, pp. 52 f.). This Herodicus generally
passes for Hippocrates' medical mentor (K. Kudlien, Kleine Pauly,
s.v. Herodikos), but the identification with Hippocrates' teacher is
not certain. For the details of Herodicus' methods and their relationship to the Hippocratic Corpus see J. Jüthner, Philostratus
(Leipzig, 1909), pp. 9-16. For his supposed destruction of Greek
athletics by developing methods of training see Part One, IV,
above.

VI

In this matter of coaches, Pleket's archaic Greek aristocrat again proves truer to Mahaffy's Victorian ideals than to the Greek evidence. For no apparent reason other than the implicit Victorian analogy, Pleket makes several unfounded claims. First, it "seems," he says, that the aristocrats viewed specialized coaches as "the innovation of an anti- or at least non-aristocratic movement" (1974, 64). But I know of no ancient source that associates athletic coaches with a social class or any social movement (Pleket cites none). Second, Pleket claims, the earliest palpable evidence for athletic coaches concerns those used by "Pindar's clients," that is, *after* 500 B.C. (*ibid.*). But that conclusion goes against the ancient reports about several early Olympic victors; namely, Arrichion (coached by Eryxias about 564 B.C.) and the much neglected Glaukos of Karystos (coached by Tisias about 520 B.C.). It better suits Pleket's notion of an exclusively aristocratic sixth century (*if* coaching was anti-aristocratic); but no other scholar dates the advent of coaching so late. Even Finley and Pleket say that Greek athletes had begun to use coaches "by 600" (p. 70).[43]

---

43. For the amateur movement's objection to the use of a coach and to specialized training see Part One, IV-V, above. For Arrichion ("il primo atleta antico di cui sappiamo che si sottoponesse alle cure di un allenatore") and Eryxias see Moretti, No. 102 (564 B.C.); for Glaukos and Tisias see Moretti No. 134 (520 B.C.). The ancient source here is Philostratus *Gymn.* 150.5ff and *Imag.* 2.6, and *Gymn.* 148.33. Philostratus' accounts of these athletes' careers may be affected by his imagination, but I hesitate to write off his naming of their trainers as pure fancy. Nor is it likely that Croton's sixth century athletic empire consisted of individual athletes acting wholly without direction from a faculty of coaches.

Third, Eryxias, Tisias, and their fellow-coaches attested in Pindar, such as Melesias and Menander, seem to have been professional trainers. The archaic aristocrats, Pleket thinks, must have contemned their own coaches; for "professionals" can come only from the lower classes. In arguing that the athletes did not view themselves as professionals, he contrasts the coaches with their non-professional (i.e., aristocratic) athlete-pupils: "A trainer had a profession, just like a sculptor, an architect, a doctor or an actor. They are contracted, hired by an individual or a community for a specific job at a specific salary (μισθός: wage). Wage labor had a low social status in Greco-Roman antiquity." He cites no Greek athletic source but quotes Cicero ("Illiberal and mean are the employments of all who work for wages"), and concludes that both those who work for clients and those who work for wages "are held by the upper class [i.e., the athletes -- D.Y.] to be of inferior status."[44] Yet there is a serious anomaly here: several early coaches were themselves former victors in the major games. Pleket himself notes that Melesias (a Nemean victor who later coached his pupils to thirty major victories) might be an exception to his rules: "an early example of a lower-class athlete...who won in one of the great international games."[45] But he

44. Pleket 1976, pp. 84 f. Gardiner (1910, p. 504) and Harris take the opposite position and regard coaching as a prestigious career ("Coaches...were men of some position in the community," Harris 1964, p. 177).
45. Pleket (1974, n. 68) thus rejects H. Wade-Gery's argument (*JHS* 52 [1932], pp. 200-211) that this Melesias was the same man as Melesias, father of the Athenian politician (not historian) Thucydides, and therefore descended from a wealthy noble family related to Cimon. C. M. Bowra (*Pindar* [Oxford, 1964], p. 150) follows Wade-Gery and claims that Melesias the coach was a noble "of Cimon's world" But the name Melesias is common, and wrestling metaphors are frequent in ancient literature. We know

neglects the athletic career of Melesias' contemporary, Ikkos of Tarentum, who was an Olympic pentathlon champion before turning to coaching.[46] If late archaic competition was really limited to wealthy aristocrats, we must conclude that some of these "upper class" athletes, even Olympic victors, voluntarily demoted themselves to the "inferior status" of a coach. Yet it is hardly conceivable that the haughty aristocrats who fill Pleket's and Gardiner's pages would stoop--without compelling need--to "employments" associated with the "illiberal and mean." There seem to be too many exceptions to Pleket's rules.

Pindar's odes, which often praise the victor's coach by name, raise another problem. Pleket believes that Pindar and his aristocratic patrons viewed the use of coaches as part of an "anti- or non-aristocratic movement."[47] Would the aristocrats, for whom scholars

---

45. (**continued**) nothing certain about Melesias except that Pindar praises his coaching several times and attributes thirty victories in major games to his pupils (*Ol.* 8.54-66). Wilamowitz (*Pindaros* [Berlin, 1922], p. 398) states that Melesias was not even an Athenian (*contra schol.* Pind. *Nem.* 4.155) but an Aeginetan, and he roundly concludes, "vornehm war er...nicht"; Krause, too, denies that Melesias was even Athenian (*Olympia* [above, n. 33], p. 156).

46. Moretti No. 307. Moretti disputes Robert's 476 date for Ikkos' Olympic victory, and places it about 444, despite Aristophanes of Byzantium, who dates Ikkos about 472. I suspect that both Robert's and Moretti's dates are too late. Aristophanes probably refers not to Ikkos' Olympic victory but to his *floruit* in his subsequent career as a coach. We know that the pentathlon champions in both 476 and 472 were Tarentines, but neither was Ikkos (Moretti Nos. 212 and 238). The obvious conclusion is that both were pupils of the noted Tarentine coach, and that Ikkos' own victory antedated theirs, probably falling between 500 and 476. Plato says that Ikkos, too, abstained from sexual intercourse while training (n. 37, above).

47. Pindar's praise of innate talent has no bearing here. He praised innate talent *augmented* by technical training: see my remarks on *Ol.* 7.53 (*Three Odes*, p. 86). In a separate article I shall argue that *doctrina sed vim promovet insitam* (Horace *C.* 4.4.33) directly translates *Ol.* 7.53.

insist Pindar wrote, brook his praise of illiberal or mean individuals in the poems for which they paid? Either they were not so aristocratic as we think, or the profession was not so mean -- or all these categories and labels are too simplistic to be of much value. I favor the last choice.

We have so little information, far too little to match our desire to place ancient men into either neat category, the nobles or the lower class. We therefore leap at conclusions. This tendency is even more pronounced when the subjects are the athletes themselves. Pleket does not hesitate to place Astylos, the last of the great Crotoniate athletes (above, sec. V), among the noble aristocrats. But there is no evidence at all for his birth or social class. He passes for a noble only because modern scholars wish it so. They have not explained why a wealthy aristocrat should choose to transfer his athletic career to a Syracusan monarchy.[48]

Similarly, no one has explained Theogenes' career. Theogenes was the Olympic, Pythian, and Isthmian record holder who won more than a thousand athletic victories in his twenty-two year career, Pleket's professional non-professional whom we examined once before (Part One, VII, above). Why would a wealthy, noble aristocrat prefer (to the luxurious life of a wealthy aristocrat) to spend the best decades of his life as an itinerant prize-fighter? An army of recent books and articles *says* he was a "wealthy noble." Pleket, for example, repeatedly calls Theogenes just that, and adds that Theogenes was *"born* rich" (*von Haus aus reich war*) with "no need to earn any money for his primary livelihood." He also endorses Pouilloux' rapturous account: Theogenes "was descended from a prominent family (*une grande famille*) whose traces may be found in

48. Pleket 1974, n. 60; cf. *ibid.* p. 63.

the course of several (*plusieurs*) generations in the lists of
[*Thasian*] magistrates" (Pleket 1964, 65f). But all that is,
as one sober scholar calls it, "nothing but fancy." There
exists no evidence that *any* of Theogenes' ancestors ever
held *any* political magistracy. The several generations
turn out to be two; namely, Theogenes' own brother,
Neilis, and his own son, Disolympios
("Twice-Olympic," obviously named after his father's
two Olympic crowns). *After* Theogenes became a
famous athlete Neilis and Disolympios received theoric
appointments, minor posts, hardly powerful
magistracies. And those appointments may well have
been spurred as much by Theogenes' own athletic pro-
minence as by the family's wealth and genes. Such is
the evidence for the *grande famille*.[49]

49. Ebert pp. 118-126 accurately presents the evidence for
Theogenes. Pleket and Moretti (No. 201) trust wholly in J.
Pouilloux, *Recherches sur l'histoire et les cultes de Thasos* (Paris,
1954), which devotes a long chapter to the athlete (pp. 62-105),
and makes much of the Pausanias passage and the theoric lists.
Pouilloux' Theogenes-chapter has met with devastating criticism
at the hands of serious scholars. Ebert (p. 120) demolishes
Pouilloux' chronology. A.D. Nock (*AJA* 1948, 298) demolishes
Launey's notion, revived by Pouilloux (p. 66), that Theogenes'
father was a priest of Herakles who fathered the athlete in a ritual
hieros gamos. In his review (*AJA* 61 [1957], 98-103), P.M. Fraser
demolishes Pouilloux' attempt to press epigraphical scraps into
evidence for Theogenes' noble birth and association with a
Herakles-cult in his own lifetime ("In all this, I can see nothing
but fancy: ... private mythology," Fraser, p. 100). Fraser also
places in gravest doubt the political activity that Pouilloux
reconstructs for Theogenes ("His arguments here seem to me
distinctly unconvincing," p. 99). Fraser prefaces his assessment of
Pouilloux' book thus: "his attempts at historical reconstruction
are rarely happy, mainly because of his determination to extract
far more from the evidence than it can fairly be expected to yield"
(p. 98); and he concludes it (after a long list of *errata*): "This is a
disappointing and unsatisfactory book in many ways ..." (p. 103).
Despite the length of Pouilloux' chapter on Theogenes, it is a very

And the evidence that Theogenes was born rich, a noble, wealthy, aristocrat -- is that evidence better? No. It is even worse. Here it is. Pausanias, a Greek of the Christian era, five hundred years after Theogenes' death, visited Olympia where he saw the statue "of Theogenes the son of Timosthenes."

> Yet the people of Thasos say that Theogenes was *not* the son of Timosthenes, but that Timosthenes was a priest of Herakles in Thasos, and that Herakles, as an apparition, in the likeness of Timosthenes, had sexual intercourse with Theogenes' mother.
>
> (Pausanias 6.11.2)

That is all. I can find no more. Obviously, half a millennium after Theogenes, there was a myth that the legendary Theogenes--whose name means "born from a god"--was the son of no human; in Thasos he was worshipped by the people and given sacrifices at this time. He was the 'son of Herakles.' But others probably rationalized the myth: no, he was not the son of Herakles but the son of a *priest* of Herakles. It would be a characteristically Greek rationalization of the story. At any rate, from nothing more than Pausanias' tale here, a clear adaptation of the Amphitryon myth, seems to come all the nonsense about Theogenes' vast inherited wealth, his land, his noble birth. A priest, Pleket and Pouilloux have already decided, can only be a wealthy, noble aristocrat (see Part One, VII, above, with n. 99). Therefore Theogenes was a wealthy noble. I note in

49. (continued) poor source which Moretti and Pleket (1976, p. 81; 1974, p. 65) cite for proof that Theogenes was a "noble" and "aristocrat" of high birth. With all of Pouilloux' "fancy" and "private mythology" removed, we know nothing reliable about Theogenes' birth. We are left with a highly successful Thasian athlete, and little more (hardly a man who was "born to great wealth").

conclusion that Pausanias himself does not subscribe his own name to any part of this fantastic story.

Time and again, the noble birth of a reportedly "aristocratic" athlete evaporates under elementary analysis. So also is the case of the renowned wrestler, Milo, winner in more Olympiads than any other archaic athlete and high on Pleket's list of nobles. Relying on a corrupt modern handbook tradition, Pleket joins others in claiming that "The famous boxer [sic] and Olympic victor Milo of Croton belonged to the aristocratic upper-class of Croton." But the evidence is downright ludicrous. A confused and notoriously unreliable historian from the Roman Period, Diodorus Siculus, tells the following fantastic tale: "When Croton fought its great battle with Sybaris, the athlete Milo almost singlehandedly routed the Sybarite troops, leading (ἡγούμενος) and attacking the enemy in the front line-- garbed as Herakles (lion skin, club and all) and wreathed in his six Olympic crowns." Diodorus misses the date of this 510 B.C. battle by some 64 years, placing it in 446 B.C. (long after the Persian Wars). Herodotus, a much better and nearer historian, knows nothing of this story.

If Diodorus had all his facts straight, Milo (whose first Olympic victory occurred in 540) would have been more than 105 years old when he routed the Sybarites in his Herakles outfit! Yet modern scholars accept the substance of Diodorus' fabulous tale *in toto*. What is more, they embellish it further. ἡγοῦμαι is more often a general, descriptive term ("go in front, take the lead") than a technical one (it implies no title). Yet modern scholars rashly infer from that participle "leading" that Milo had been voted formal command of Croton's army and bore the official title "General" (*Strategos*). Diodorus himself says nothing of the kind; modern scholars do. And Pleket and others have already decided that anyone elected *Strategos* must needs possess noble blood (*"Strategos--therefore* [*folglich*] aristocrat").

Therefore "Milo belonged to the aristocratic upper-class [*Oberschicht*]."⁵⁰ *Q.E.D.*
In this way we grasp at anything that will make an

50. I can find no other source for Milo the "Strategos" and "aristocrat"; it appears that he springs from nothing but this Diodorus passage (12.9.5). O. Reinmuth, in *Der Kleine Pauly* s.v. "Milon," claims that Milo "was chosen as leader" (*wurde zum Führer...gewählt*) for the great battle, but he cites only Diodorus 2.9.5, which concerns only prehistoric Babylonia. Reinmuth apparently wrongly excerpted Modrze's garbled and reduplicated reference in the "Big Pauly" (Pauly-Wissowa, *Realencyclopädie der classischen Altertumswissenschaft*), where both citations ("II 9, 5" and "XII 9, 10") are failed attempts to get the one reference right. Nor does Modrze's third reference "Diels *Vorsokr.*³ 32 nr. 14" refer to anything but a reprinting of the single and same ludicrous passage, Diodorus 12.9.5 (from which Modrze concludes that "the Crotoniates...chose [*wählten*] him [Milo] as their leader [*Anführer*]"). Pleket's word "*Strategos*" is apparently "*Führer*" merely translated into ancient Greek. His account of Milo: 1974, p. 63 (where another error adds to the confusion: Milo did not marry Democedes' daughter, as Pleket has it; Democedes married Milo's daughter [above, n. 42]).

Herodotus and other classical authors mention both Croton's great battle against Sybaris and Croton's great wrestler Milo, but no one before Diodorus associates the two. If there were a strong historical basis for Milo's generalship in the battle, it is surprising that Herodotus would ignore it when especially relevant to his narrative (3.137; 5.44-45).

Howsoever convincing Diodorus' account may be to others (he sets the number of defeated Sybarite soldiers at 300,000), it sounds to me like the same kind of inventive fancy that permeates the other tales of Milo's exploits: he would stand on a greased discus, and no man alive could shove him off; his normal daily diet was 20 pounds of meat, 20 pounds of bread, and 18 pints of wine; he is the Greek athlete with whom the bull is most associated: he once carried a full-grown bull around the stadium, and ate the whole animal himself the same day (cf. Harris 1964, pp. 111 f.). A Heraklean Milo, routing the enemy with a club, wearing a lion skin and his Olympic wreaths, seems of the same ilk.

early athlete a noble; but we ignore or argue away any suggestion of a humble origin. We have already observed how Pleket manages to turn Koroibos, the first Olympic victor, from a "cook" into a priest--therefore aristocrat. Yet he neglects the famous sixth-century boxer, Glaukos of Karystos. While a ploughboy on his father's self-tilled farm, Glaukos revealed the strength that marked him as a future athlete. The story places Glaukos in Hesiod's social class.[51] Nor does Pleket mention Polymnestor of Miletus, who won the boys' Olympic stade early in the sixth century. As a young goatherd, we are told, Polymnestor used to catch hares, running them down on foot. Goatherding is obviously a poor occupational choice for a child of Pleket's and Gardiner's nobles. Nor will "goatherd" easily convert to a priestly title. Despite his Achillean feat (Pindar *Nemean* 3.52), therefore, Polymnester's origins have not attracted attention equal to that of Theogenes' Heraklean birth. The list goes on. Amesinas "the cowherd" won the Olympic wrestling championship in 460 B.C. But he can win no notice from modern scholars, who seem to prefer to keep such an athlete in an obscurity that befits his origins.[52]

Aristotle cites some lines of an epigram (ascribed by

51. For Glaukos see Pausanias 6.10.1; many other sources listed at Moretti No. 134 and Knab 2. Despite his humble beginnings, Glaukos could later afford the best. For his epinician he obtained Simonides (frag. 4 *PMG*; 8 Bergk); his statue at Olympia (dedicated by his son) was the work of Glaukias of Aegina (Pausanias). Glaukias was not a poor man's sculptor. He also executed the statue of Gelon's victorious chariot (Pausanias 6.9.5).

52. Polym(n)estor (Moretti No. 79) and Amesinas (Moretti No. 261) are mentioned as "goatherd" and "cowherd" respectively (so also Moretti), in both Africanus' list (above, n. 31, Olympiads 46 and 80) and Philostratus *On Gymnastics* 144 (*aipolos*) and 168 (where for *Alesiai* read *Amesinai* with Guttman; cf. Jüthner's note). Philostratus at least knows the same story.

an ancient scholar to Simonides) for an Olympic victor
of low birth. The victor claims that he was once a fish-
monger or fish-porter, and carried pails of fish from a
yoke on his neck. We may doubt that Simonides wrote
it, but the epigram itself is obviously genuine, and probably fifth century.[53] We may also doubt that
Aeschines' father, apparently once an athlete, was a
former slave, as the orator's enemy, Demosthenes,
describes him; but Aeschines' attempt to elevate his
father's birth seems equally forced. The truth no doubt
lies somewhere in between.[54] Indeed, we perhaps
should question the stories of humble origins for
Glaukos the ploughboy and the herdsmen Polymnestor
and Amesinas; they smack of myth. Yet their humble

53. Simonides 41 Page (163 Bergk). Aristotle seems not to regard
the poem Simonidean (*Rhet.* 1365a, 1367b); the attribution comes
from Aristophanes "the grammarian" (no doubt Byzantinus) *apud*
Eustathius *Odyssey* 1761.25.
54. Aeschines' birth has been a matter of controversy since his
own day. In *de corona* 129-131, Demosthenes asserts that
Aeschines' father, "Tromes" ("Fearful"), was the slave of a
school-teacher and his mother a prostitute, that Aeschines had only
recently become a citizen and "from a slave, a free man, from a
beggar, a man of wealth." Surely this picture is exaggerated, for in
an earlier speech (19.281-2) Demosthenes says that Aeschines'
father Atrometos ("Fearless") was himself a schoolmaster and his
mother the leader of religious *thiasoi*. Even in this milder attack,
Demosthenes categorically denies that either Atrometos or
Aeschines had done a whit of service to the city. In stark contrast,
Aeschines claims that all his ancestors were free, that his father
shared a phratry with a prominent Athenian clan, distinguished
himself in Athenian military campaigns, and fought for the
restoration of the democracy. He also claims that Atrometos was a
man of substance and "competed in athletics" before losing his
money in the (Peloponnesian) war (2.147-8). Aeschines was obviously the son of neither a slave nor a noble. (Scholars regularly
assign an athletic career to his father, but I am not wholly certain
that Aeschines' words *athlein toi somati* refer to athletic competition [yet cf. *toi somati nikesanta*, Andocides *in Alcib.* 32].)

beginnings are much better attested than Theogenes' or Milo's "aristocratic" origin, and far better than Astylos' "noble" birth. The rather frequent suggestions of humble birth for sixth and fifth century athletes should at least give us pause when we want to declare an aristocratic monopoly; the Greeks themselves, it seems, found the "rags to riches" athletic tales fascinating, but not incredible.

These reports of a lowly origin for some early athletes are consonant with the earliest extant statement on athletes' origins, the speech of Isocrates written for Alcibiades' son. Alcibiades, his son says, entered the Olympic chariot race rather than one of the physical athletic events because "he knew that some of the athletes were of low birth, came from small towns, and were of low education." Alcibiades won his Olympic chariot victory about 416, so the reference is unmistakably to the fifth century.[55]

I have already discussed Pleket's misguided temporal interpretation of the Isocrates text (above, Part One, VII, end). There is no evidence at all for Pleket's claim that "Alcibiades would have been happier in Pindar's time." But Pleket's argument raises a new and important point.

Alcibiades saw that "*some* of the athletes who performed at Olympia were of low birth«, small towns,» and mean education" (Pleket's emphasis). Making much of the word "some," Pleket concludes, "Obviously, *most* participants still belonged to the upper-class" (1976, p. 73). Is there absolutely nothing between "low birth" and "upper-class"?

55. Isocrates 16.33-34; for details of Alcibiades' victory: Moretti No. 345.

VII

In a perceptive passage, Pleket himself introduces one of Artemidorus' interpretations of a standard dream, in which a pregnant woman imagines that she gives birth to an eagle. The dream clearly portends a successful life for the unborn child, and Artemidorus specifies the field of success in relation to the family's socio-economic class. The poor child will succeed as a soldier. The eagle-son of wealthy parents will become the ruler of many men. But the eagle-son born to parents of moderate *(metrios)* means will be a successful athlete. Pleket applies Artemidorus' principles only to the late period in which Artemidorus wrote. Pleket notes that men from poor families indeed achieved positions of rank in the Roman army. But the ability of middle class men to enter athletics still disturbs him: "The financing of an athletic career at the outset remains a relatively difficult problem."[56]

This problem recurs to Pleket again and again, and he fails to resolve it. The solution, however, is at hand, and may apply just as well to the archaic and classical periods. We need not posit a comfortable middle class, as in modern Europe, America, or Japan, to grasp how the Greek athletic system might accommodate non-nobles. The key lies in the large prizes available even to boy athletes who, because of their age, would not need to forgo other employment in order to train and compete. Children of the lowest economic scale, those forced to scrounge for a simple existence, probably had little

---

56. Pleket 1974, p. 76; cf. pp. 62, 67, 1976, p. 72 ("... decisive obstacles for the poor. Subsidization would have been indispensable, but the earliest evidence for that is much later...*ca.* 300 B.C. ...").

opportunity to enter organized games of any kind. But we have no reason to doubt--and some reason to believe--that to compete in local games was possible for children of moderate origin,[57] even for the son of a modest farmer, such as Hesiod or Glaukos of Karystos, or perhaps the son of a successful businessman or artisan.

Victory in boys' competitions, as in modern times, no doubt depended less on years of training and more on natural ability. A lad from a non-noble family who won a prize in a local event, a bronze vessel, for example, from Tegea, or a silver one from Sicyon, might use it to finance a trip to a larger festival, such as the Panathenaic games. If he won at any contest comparable to the Panathenaic games (above, Sec. III), he or his family could obviously afford some professional coaching, and his career would be launched. He might be able to enter one of the great Panhellenic games. Moreover, many festivals included a division for youths as well as for boys; a successful boy could go on as he matured. Thus the Greek athletic system itself removes the financial obstacle which Pleket sees in the path of non-nobles who aspired to an athletic career. Like their modern counterparts, most successful athletes in ancient times probably began their careers in their youth; they would have had adequate amounts of money available throughout their careers from boyhood on--so long as they continued to win prizes. A good boy professional needs no subsidy.

If we examine ancient athletes' careers, we find that many indeed began their Panhellenic careers before adulthood. The "goatherd" Polymnestor of Miletus won an Olympic victory as a boy. The athletic

---

57. Even Pleket (1974, p. 62) admits that "non-noble" athletes may have participated in "local games" in the archaic period; he doubts that they entered "the great international games." He does not show how the line could be clearly drawn.

ability of Glaukos, the farmer's son, was discovered while he was a boy. Melesias, whose pupils later won thirty victories in the major games, obtained his first Nemean victory in the youths' division. Even Milo of Croton began his illustrious Olympic career in the boys' competition. It is highly probable that a number of Theogenes' more than 1000 victories was won in the boys' or youths' divisions, and not all as an adult.[58]

I turn to the second of Pleket's crucial questions, suggested by the frequency of former athletes who later played a role in war or politics. "Can one determine whether an athlete, in a given case, rises to a position of rank because of his success as an athlete or whether he participates in athletics because he is the son of a ranking family?" We have always assumed that the second alternative is correct. Indeed the argument for the noble birth of most athletes *consists* of nothing more than their *subsequent* importance in non-athletic careers.[59] Often this importance itself rests on the shakiest of scholarly foundations, as in the case of Milo the wrestler turned "General" (above, Sec. VI). But some athletes certainly exerted power after their retirement from the games.

Phayllos of Croton (above, Sec. V) commanded his own warship at the Battle of Salamis, the only warship from the western colonies to participate in that famous and crucial sea-fight (Herodotus 8.47). We assume that anyone who could afford to outfit his own ship was by birth a wealthy aristocrat. Clearly he was "a man of considerable wealth" (Harris 1964, p. 144), and he may

58. So Ebert (above, n. 25), p. 120. Similarly, Dikon began his Olympic sprinting career in the boys' division (Knab 14, Moretti No. 379) and eight years later was the men's Olympic stade champion (Moretti No. 388). It is a familiar pattern in the ancient athletes whom we know (despite Aristotle *Politics* 1339a).

59. Pleket applies the principle rigidly and states its logic succinctly: "der *Strategos* (und folglich Aristokrat) Phrynon" (1974, p. 63).

have been a noble. But we have no evidence either way. There remains the obvious possibility that he could have financed his warship with his athletic earnings instead of his inheritance or the profits from his crops.

Other athletes' political careers are strangely unaristocratic. Because the former Olympic victor Philippos of Croton played a role in sixth-century Italian politics, we would make him an aristocrat. Yet his attempt to marry the daughter of Telys, the "popular" demagogue, then tyrant of Sybaris, hardly suggests settled oligarchic leanings. Pouilloux, as he insists on Theogenes' noble birth (above, Sec. VI), argues with equally scant evidence that the prize-fighter retired in order to lead a pro-Athenian (that is, democratic) faction against his peers among the Thasian oligarchy. I find most careers of retired athletes more suggestive of the soldier of fortune than of the conservative, old guard aristocrat. I could not guess which is the case with Timasitheos, an Olympic victor from Delphi whom the Athenians executed for his part in the Spartan attempt to help Isagoras wrest power from Cleisthenes in Athens.[60]

Surely some athletes turned politicians were of noble stock, but there is no proof that all were. Perhaps some entered public life *because* their athletic fame and fortune could be used to launch political careers. In this respect, the most obvious candidate is the Euboean

60. Philippos: Herodotus 5.47 (see Dunbabin [above, n. 34], p. 362). Pouilloux' claim that Theogenes retired from athletics to enter politics is founded on Dio Chrysostom's embellishment (*Or.* 31.617-8R) of a common athletic legend (see Fontenrose and Bohringer, both n. 36, above). It is rightly questioned by Fraser (see n. 49, above) and Ebert (above, n. 25), p. 37, n. 2. Why an oligarch would have an Athenian bias Pouilloux does not say. Timasitheos: Moretti No. 140; Herodotus 5.72.

farmboy, Glaukos of Karystos. We need not accept the whole story about his ploughshare to believe that his father Demylos (a rather unaristocratic name) was an ordinary farmer. The story could hardly have spread had the father been an aristocrat. Glaukos won an Olympic victory about 520, and had an unquestionably distinguished boxing career. He earned a place in the Greek memory beside Milo and other old-time strongmen. Yet he met an ignominious death, far from his native land, embroiled in the lethal business of Sicilian politics:

> "The occasion was the revolt of Kamarina against Glaukos of Karystos, the boxer, who had been set up as governor by Gelon. Glaukos, the farmer's boy who straightened a ploughshare with his fist for a hammer, was a rough-and-ready governor for a new city. His death is said to have been due to Gelon's machinations."[61]

It is a strange Sicilian end for a stable, wealthy, land-owning aristocrat of Euboea.

---

61. Dunbabin (above, n. 34), p. 416 (the sources are a scholiast to Aeschines *in Ctes.* 190 and Bekker, *Anecd. Gr.* 1.232). Pausanias (6.10.1-3) gives a far more mythological account of Glaukos' death, and Moretti (No. 134) cannot decide which to believe. Surely the tradition followed by Dunbabin prevails on grounds similar to the philological principle of the *lectio difficilior* (and the historical principle of the *eventus facilior*: Pausanias reports that the Karystians traced Glaukos' ancestry to Glaukos, the sea deity, and they claimed he was buried on an island which bore both their names, Glaukos: the island remains unidentified).

VIII

In the above study, I emphasize the case for non-noble participation in early Greek athletics; for others had badly overstated the argument for aristocratic exclusiveness. Lest I mislead, I hasten to reiterate the extensive participation of the nobility. No reliable proportion of nobles to non-nobles can be established at present. I believe both participated; but the problem of athletes' origins and social standing is very complex, and beclouded by the meagerness of the evidence. I seek here only to demonstrate the weakness of the prevailing assumptions, and to suggest what lies in other directions. I do not claim to resolve all major questions.

On the other hand, with respect to money and the so-called "ancient Greek amateurism," the results are hardly indecisive. We need to inquire further as to *how* Greek athletic festivals were financed.[62] But there is abundant proof, direct and indirect, in contemporary documents and later reports, to show that athletes could and did win large amounts of money (or "in kind" prizes).[63] The evidence covers the sixth and early fifth

---

62. One might start with the nine talents granted to the Athenian *athlothetae* for the *lesser* Panathenaic Games of 415 (*IG* I² 302.56-58)--a sum so large that it compels historians to seek extraordinary explanations (R. Meiggs and D. Lewis, *Selection of Greek Historical Inscriptions,* Oxford, 1969, p. 236).

63. Besides Xenophanes 2 and Plutarch *Solon* 23, there is a general tradition conforming to that image. Words such as *megas, hyperbole,* etc., commonly accompany mention of athletic rewards. In the *Contest of Homer and Hesiod* 288, the son of Amphidamas promises to reward both the athletes and the poets "with great prizes" (*megalais doreais timon*). In Plato (*Republic*

centuries as well as classical, Hellenistic, and Roman times. Virtually no piece of the evidence which I assemble here is new or in itself especially controversial. Mainly what is new is the actual use and accumulation of evidence long available. It has a cumulative force which I myself found compelling. What may be controversial is the magnitude of the prizes as I have calculated them, and the potential for amassing wealth which these figures imply. But my figures for the Panathenaic prizes and the Solonian rewards were as small as I could in conscience make them. And we should remember that at many games the prizes were not limited to physical and equestrian events. Hesiod won his tripod, too; and in the Panathenaic games of Plato's time, a second-rate guitar-singer won more than the victor of the youths' wrestling competition.

From Homer on, as we hear of large athletic winnings, the concept of amateurism in any sense is wholly foreign, often even antithetical, to the nature and vocabulary of Greek athletics. Yet our own interest in this matter -- our legacy from the modern Olympics and nineteenth-century British elitism -- leads us to exaggerate its importance. In classical studies "amateurism"

63. (**continued**) 10.620b) the soul of Atalanta chooses the life of an athlete upon seeing his "great rewards" (*megalai timai athletou andros;* cf. *LSJ s.v. time* I.4). Athenaeus (above, n. 28) uses the phrases "extravagance of prizes" (*hyperbole athlon*) and "very rich contest for cash" (*argyrikos sphodra plousios agon*). At the end of Aristophanes' *Plutus,* Hermes cites his various functions when seeking admission to the city, but only in his role as a "god of games" can he gain entrance to a city given over to Wealth: "For the holding of contests for music and athletics is the thing most suitable to wealth" (1161 ff.). Note also the words of an "avaricious character" (*philargyros*) in an ancient comedy quoted by Plutarch: τὰ δ᾽ Ἴσθμια ἀποδοίμην ἂν ἡδέως ὅσου ὁ τῶν σελίνων στέφανός ἐστιν ὤνιος (*Symp.* 5.3.2; I owe the reference to Frank Frost). There is probably an effective pun here, the Isthmia being both the athletic games and the throat.

is an irrelevant distraction. Whether or not ancient athletes accepted money for their agonistic achievements has nothing to do with their nobility or integrity of character. With the possible exception of Avery Brundage,[64] no one in recent times has faulted an artist, musician, doctor, or professor for making money from that activity in which each excels. Only the participants in the modern Olympic sports, especially those in track and field, have been colored with corruption for engaging gainfully in an honest activity which requires talent and training. In ancient Greece, when a few critics such as Xenophanes and Socrates objected to the large financial rewards heaped upon athletes, it never occurred to them to question the athletes' own right to accept those rewards.[65]

Instead of trying to find some form of amateurism in Greece, or systematically seeking to convert all archaic athletes into nobles, or twisting the meaning of purely modern terms, we might better examine what the Greeks' large purses and athletic system imply. At

---

64. Brundage (*apud* Schoebel) said of his own collection of expensive Oriental art-objects, "Most of them are unsigned, the artists, whose work they are, were true *amateurs,* whose reward was the satisfaction of a job well done...." Of his Oriental netsuke carvings he said, "Originally...[the netsuke artist] was an *amateur* carver. Later, after the demand for netsuke grew, there arose a class of *professional* carvers. These men were usually more accomplished and expert .... their work was perhaps more polished and displayed a superior technical skill. But it was ordinarily cold, stiff, and without imagination .... Missing was the love and devotion of the *amateur* carver, which causes these older netsuke to be esteemed more highly by the collector than the commercial product *carved for money"* (Schoebel, pp. 28, 33 f; all emphases added). Brundage does not explain how he knows that the earlier netsuke carvers received no compensation for their work. His history of netsuke carving runs amazingly parallel to his history of "strictly amateur" Greek athletics.

65. Above, n. 26.

the conclusion of his book on Greek athletics, in a passage revelatory of deep confusion, Harris wistfully defines the athletic ideal of the British amateur tradition:

> "No doubt all would agree that ideally there is one simple rule for all sport; during the few seconds, minutes or hours while the game is in progress, nothing should be so important to the participants as to win it by fair means; once the game is finished, nothing should matter less than who did win. At the less eminent levels of amateur sport this ideal is often attained today; perhaps there have been times when it was approached at the highest levels, in Britain in the nineteenth century and in Greece in the sixth and fifth centuries" (1964, p. 188).

Harris' sixth and fifth century Greece, of course, never existed. It is an utterly imaginary land. *It should not matter who won?* Nothing could be more antithetical to the spirit of Greek athletics than that notion. What of the large prizes and the "sweet smooth-sailing" that "the victor" had "for the rest of his life" (Pindar *Olympian* 1.97 f.)? What of Pindar's *Victory Odes* themselves -- their very existence? What of the "agony of defeat" which the loser suffered (below)? What of the numerous Greeks --whether aristocrats or not -- who chose athletics as a serious *career?* "Who won?" was the cardinal question from Antilochos (*Iliad* 23.541-554) on down. It had only one significant modification: "Who won *and how many times?*"[66] No one in Greece knew Harris' kind of sport, where the participants say "Good show" at the conclusion, and go off, winners and losers together, forgetting who is which, to quaff a pint of bitter. Nor does the common American phrase "It's just a game" apply to Greek athletics. Pindar leaves no doubt here.

---

66. See, e.g., the inscriptions in Ebert (above, n. 25), Nos. 7, 15, 37, 39, 43, 67. No. 37, for Theogenes, is translated in Part One, n. 95, above. There is no comprehensive study of Greek athletic record-keeping, but much is available in M. Tod, "Greek Record-keeping and Record-breaking (*Classical Quarterly* 43 [1949], 105-112) and more in K. Kramer, *Studien zur griechischen Agonistik nach den Epinikien Pindars* (Köln Dissertation, 1970).

In praising the victor of the Pythian wrestling contest of 446 B.C., Pindar contrasts the winning athlete's joy with the agony of those whom he defeated:

> For them was judged no pleasureful trip home. When they came back to their mothers, no joy burst forth, none of that laughter that gratifies. No. Rather, down back roads, hiding from their enemies, they skulk, bitten by their calamity.

In another passage, he again focuses on the loser's return trip from the games, "the most hateful homecoming of all, greetings of dishonor, a road to be traveled in secret."[67] This is not Harris' ideal of sport.

Even Harris' nineteenth-century England scarcely existed. The first amateur track and field meet worthy of note took place when the Universities of Oxford and Cambridge competed on Christ Church Field in 1864. As we saw in Part One, there were already professional runners and jumpers in England and America at that time. Anglo-American amateur athletics then developed in the latter part of the nineteenth century as physical education and recreational activity, especially for college students. They were hardly sport "at the highest level"; in those brief thirty-six years of nineteenth century Anglo-American athletics, the participants were still groping to develop techniques and equipment. No American or Englishman had ever even thrown a discus in competition until the first modern Olympic games at

---

67. Pindar *Pythian* 8.83-87, *Olympian* 8.68 f. In a remarkably similar way, Floyd Patterson, beaten badly in a boxing match, once put on dark glasses and a false beard, and disappeared into the back streets of the city for several days. We may compare Jimmy Connors' behavior after he was defeated at Wimbeldon: "To avoid reporters and photographers waiting outside the Inn on the Park, Connors was driven to a rear entrance, where he dashed inside without a word" (*The Times* of London, June 28, 1983); I owe the reference to N. J. Richardson).

Athens in 1896.[68]

In contrast, competitors such as Ikkos, Astylos, and Phayllos had not two or three decades of athletic history behind them, but three centuries in which the Greek athletes had been developing successful techniques. These were no neophyte school-boys seeking diversion and discovery in a burgeoning new trend. They were mature, seasoned veterans with illustrious models from the past to emulate, learn from and live up to. There is little in these men comparable to Harris' British gentleman. Would the nineteenth century British noble have voluntarily forgone all sexual activity for his training, as Astylos did? Would the nineteenth-century

---

68. See Part One, II, above. First inter-university track and field meet, 1864: R. Quercetani, *A World History of Track and Field Athletics*, 1864-1964 (London, 1964), p. xv. Competition between colleges began at Cambridge in 1857 and at Oxford in 1860. The first important international competition took place in New York in 1895 (a New York and a London team; Yale competed at Oxford in 1894). To indicate the improvement in technique during the three decades after 1864 and the improvement in the twentieth century, I list here marks for some events, giving first the winning mark in the 1864 Oxford-Cambridge meet, then that of the 1895 New York-London meet (in parentheses), and last the current (1980) world record [in square brackets]. 100 yard dash: 10.5 (9.8) [9.0]; 440 yard run: 56 (49) [44.5]; one mile: 4:56.0 (4:18.2) [3:48.8] (There are similarly dramatic improvements in such sports as swimming: the 1896 Olympic 100 meter freestyle was won with a time of 1:22.2; in 1924, J. Weissmuller broke the one minute mark with 59 seconds; the 1980 record is 49.44). In field events, the changes in equipment contribute to the improvement in the pole vault (no nineteenth-century vaulter cleared 12'; the 1896 Olympic pole vault winner cleared 10' 9¾''); the 1980 Olympic mark and world record is 18' 11 ½''). But in the other jumps improvement results primarily from technique: high jump: 5'5'' (6'5 5/8'') [7' 8¾'']; long jump: 18' (22' 6'') [29' 2 ½'']. (In 1854 at Chester, England, a professional jumper leaped 29' 7'' using weights like the Greek jumping weights: Gardiner 1930, p. 151). The discus throw was exclusively a (modern) Greek event before the 1896 Athens Olympics, but there an American, Garrett, won his first discus competition with a "free style" throw of 96' 7 ¾''. The current 1980 record is 233' 5''.

American college man have accepted the rigid diet and punishing exercise regimen of an Ikkos? Would the English gentleman have given up his affluent life to spend twenty years as an itinerant prize-fighter, following in the myriad footsteps of Theogenes? Would this gentleman suffer all this merely for some glory and the satisfaction of a job well done? All these things are, in fact, directly contrary to the amateur philosophy. I see no significant similarity between Anglo-American spare-time amateur sports in the nineteenth century and the Greek athletic contests of the late archaic and early classical periods.[69]

69. The utter inaptness of the analogy between nineteenth century England and ancient Greece is laid bare in Pleket's final question. "One final point: why is it that, in contrast with the conceptions of de Coubertin and others, there was never a movement in antiquity to ban monetary rewards and prizes completely from [ancient Greek] sport" (Pleket 1976, p. 87). Pleket finds a specious socio-economic explanation. The Greek *nouveaux riches* never "seriously *threatened* the predominance of the landowning elite." It was otherwise in England. When the "new-rich" began to threaten "the position of the landowning nobility ..., the old nobility focussed on its code of honour, as being its *exclusive* preserve, and refused to participate in contests for money prizes." This explanation makes for a neat theory. But if we trust the contemporary observation of a Victorian Englishman (Part One, n. 15, above), most amateurs were not "old nobility"--they *were* the "new-rich."

Unfortunately, when stripped of socio-economic theory, the amateurs' motives do not appear so noble, nor the code so honorable as Pleket suggests. Gardiner states the principle more baldly: "When the rewards of success are sufficient there arises a professional class, and when professionalism is once established the *amateur can no longer compete* with the professional" (1910, p. 130, emphasis added). In practice, those who insist most strongly that "to participate is more important than to win" (the stated amateur and Olympic code) are often the very people whose desire to win is the strongest (cf. Part One, n. 17, above). In the 1897 "Diamond Sculls" at Henley, England, an American

69. (**continued**) amateur sculler of lower class origin (E. Ten Eyke) surprised the English aristocrats by winning the race. He was denied entry when he attempted to repeat his victory in 1898. The new definition of amateurism (i.e., founded on money not birth) compelled the officials to admit that Ten Eyke was technically an amateur. But they banned him anyway, on the grounds that he had trained "in a professional manner" (*The United States Watercraft Collection*, Chapelle [U.S. Government Printing Office, 1960]).

It is a bad anachronism to imagine that the Greeks could have even conceived the nineteenth-century notion of banning prizes of monetary worth when those prizes lay at the heart of Greek athletics from the outset. Moreover, Pleket himself claims that even the aristocrat in ancient Greece was willing to train "in a professional manner" (Pleket 1974, p. 65; 1976, p. 81).

IX

The glaring difference between Harris' ideal amateur sport and Greek athletics lies in the seriousness of the latter. They were not a diversion or recreation. They were not play. The Greek verb *paizein*, "to play," comes from the word *pais*, "child." Etymologically, at least, "to play" in Greek means to act like a child and in a sportive way. The Greeks sometimes apply the verb to playing music, to dancing, to playing games (such as board games or drinking games), to playing ball,[70] to jesting, and to what we call mere "horseplay." Yet I know of no text that uses the verb *paizein*, "play," for athletic contests.[71] They were not associated with childhood behavior. The boys' events at the competitive games were secondary versions of the men's events. The men's events preceded them in historical time and eclipsed them in importance. A boy athlete was acting like a man, not the other

70. In sharp contrast with modern ball games, ancient ball games were not part of competitive athletics (except perhaps among the boys of Sparta) but merely recreation and exercise. No competitions in ball games or ball playing were held at the athletic festivals, nor were ball games played for a prize. See Harris 1972, pp. 75-111.

71. Instead of the verb "play" we find *agonizomai* ("contend for a prize, struggle": cf. English "agony") and *athle(u)o* ("contend for a prize, struggle, suffer"). Several times in Homer the Myrmidons or the suitors "delight themselves" (*terponto*) by throwing the discus or javelin when at leisure (above, n. 5). Here they engage in something like "play," but there is no mention of competition. These are recreational, not athletic games. *Odyssey* 17.168 indeed reminds one of picnickers playing "catch" with a ball or a "frisbee" until called to the meal. Even here, however, the Greek verb avoids the connotation of child's play.

way around. Neither game nor play, Greek athletics were a serious business and an organized adult activity. The more we recognize their essential nature and their distinctive character the better we will understand both the Games and the Greeks. Many Olympic victors were in their thirties, some the late thirties or even older. Our modern books should stop their prattle about "the youth of Greece" at Olympia (to say nothing of "the gilded youth").

These remarks are not meant to deny that the events themselves might have a prehistoric origin in spare-time or children's play.[72] Who can run to the other end of the field first? Who can jump or fling a stone the farthest? Who can wrestle his friend to the ground? Probably all those questions occurred to children at play from time immemorial in all societies. But the ancient Greeks differ from all other peoples in that they *institutionalized these questions as serious matters for adults,* hiring poets and artists to immortalize what others fearfully

---

72. The nature of events such as the discus throw and long jump accords better with some such origin than with the beginning in ritual which the Cambridge School (notably Cornford and Ridgeway) maintained. Apart from *Iliad* 23, mock combat, the event perhaps most suited to a ritual origin, plays no significant role in Greek athletics. Homeric games set in heroic times are sometimes joined to a funeral celebration but not to religion. In historical times, the games themselves were firmly attached to religious festivals (cf. *Iliad* 22.159 f.), but that says nothing of their origin. Most experienced students of Greek athletics discount a religious or ritual origin for Greek athletics and warn against exaggerating the association of athletics with religion (Patrucco, pp. 28, 33, Harris 1972, pp. 16 f.). Gardiner flatly states, "There is no ground for attributing any religious significance to the games themselves. The fact is that Greek athletic sports, though closely associated with religion, are in their origin independent and secular" (*History and Remains of Olympia* [Oxford, 1925], p. 67). On this point Gardiner seems to have the early evidence on his side.

relegated to the separate, inconsequential world of children. And the Greeks did not merely remove these things from the realm of child-play; they boldly placed them in the basic categories of religion, politics, and business.

No other people in history until our own day ever organized such athletic contests into large-scale, international, adult competition. The ancient Persians had no athletics, and were mystified by the Greek games. A Persian sought only certain and immediate gain. To train when there was a chance to lose the prize was something he would not comprehend. The Romans adopted almost every other aspect of Greek culture as their own. But they held aloof from Greek competitive athletics. It was probably a matter of pride. No Roman could stand the risk of losing such an individual test, of looking inferior in public. To do it naked in full view of one's enemies would have made Roman blood run cold.[73]

73. Xenophon mentions contests for prizes among the Persian youth and military personnel. But these military exercises (archery and *polemika erga*) for the young trainees compare with Greek military or ephebic training, not with international athletic competition among individual adults. Indeed their purpose was not to single out individual excellence or achievement but to provide incentive so that "the companies of soldiers perform the suitable drill" in unison, "like a chorus" (*Cyropaedia* 1.2.12; 1.6.18). Greeks delighted in noting barbarians' amazement at the Greek practice of athletic contests. Xerxes is surprised that the Greeks contend for a mere "crown, not money" (Herodotus 8.26). Herodotus' presentation, whether from patriotism or humor, leaves the impression that all Greek athletics are contended for such a symbolic prize. In his *Anacharsis*, Lucian uses that legendary Scythian visitor as a vehicle for a full study of barbarian perplexity respecting Greek athletic contests. Lucian's Solon, however, plays Herodotus' Arcadians' teasing game even further, purposely misleading the barbarian into thinking that all the prizes were of merely symbolic value, even the Panathenaic prize.

Nobody, not even a Roman, hated public humiliation more than an ancient Greek. To an important degree Greece was a shame culture, and athletic defeat was, as Pindar stresses, public humiliation. But a Greek would run that risk when others would not, and for one overpowering reason. The chance to win was worth risking all.[74] He *might* achieve victory, and leave the humdrum, workaday world behind. If he was not a rich man, there was the chance to find financial security, even great wealth, and an opportunity to rise from obscurity to fame. If he was one of Pleket's aristocrats (already so rich that "they did not earn or did not have to earn their daily bread"), he might still aspire to a place in human memory through a Pindaric ode or a statue commemorating his deeds. Perhaps his non-noble competitors could aspire to the same.[75] And all hoped to gain the pinnacle of glory: "There is no greater

73. (**continued**) He lists the Athenian "oil of the olive" in the same breath and syntax as the Olympic "wreath of olive" and the Pythian "apple" -- allowing Anacharsis to assume that the Panathenaic prize may be just a small jigger of the stuff. He carefully avoids mention of any value-prize again. Herodotus and Lucian probably played a role in misleading modern barbarians, too, about Greek "amateurism." A few Romans from wealthy or imperial families competed in the Olympic chariot races in the period of Roman domination, but Romans never trained themselves to a competitive ability in Greek athletics. In the athletic contests held in Rome the athletes were Greeks, as elsewhere in the Roman world. Jumping, foot-racing, and discus throwing did not much appeal to the Romans. They preferred to sit safely and to watch prisoners of war and convicts either hack each other to bits or die lingering, twitching deaths, torn asunder by wild beasts in full view and compulsion of Rome.

74. Cf. Pindar *Olympian* 1.81-84, where Pelops 'says it all.'

75. Simonides, who wrote an epinician for Glaukos "the ploughboy" (n. 51, above), also wrote one for Astylos who, I suspect, may have depended as much on his legs as on his forefathers in order to pay the poet his fee. (p. 142, above).

glory for a man, however long his life, than what he achieves with his hands and feet (in the games)" (*Odyssey* 8.147-8).

Yet behind the Greek willingness to run the risk lay something more complex, more specifically Greek than the almost universal thirst for money, glory, and fame. It is a love of competition, and a desire to be first; a compulsion to surpass ordinary human limitations and achieve what other men cannot. It was the Greek's nature to put himself and others to the concrete test. This side of the Greek nature reveals itself not merely in athletics, but in other activities such as poetry, music, and drama, which were contested for a victor's prize. It reveals itself even in politics, for they, too, were eventually fought for a crown.[76]

Despite all these other institutions, the physical athletic contests remained the exemplar, human competition *par excellence.* They represent elementally and in microcosm the general Greek struggle to rise above man's essentially ephemeral, abject condition and do what a man cannot ordinarily do. To compete in the nude underscored this symbolic test of the individual man. The man and all he could do were laid bare before all. Only performance and achievement counted. There

---

76. See Demosthenes *On the Crown* and Aeschines *Against Ctesipho.* Jacob Burckhardt stressed the Greeks' love of competition, and that trait has often been remarked. Even Gardiner, for example, in his brief chapter "The Meaning of Athletics," sometimes argues along the lines I argue here (1930,1-3). But he obscures these points with modern propaganda ("The athletic spirit .... arises naturally in those societies where the power is in the hands of an aristocracy .... our Anglo-Saxon ancestors"). And he spoils them entirely by ending with a contradictory and false comment on the "true amateur spirit" of ancient Greece ("Overcompetition, as we shall see, led only too soon to specialization and professionalism with its attendant evils: it proved fatal to the true amateur spirit," 2f).

were no trappings of birth or rank. On the track, noble and non-noble necessarily looked alike, and the stadium became neutral ground. But in the contest itself one man was, as Pindar says, "separated out" from the others, literally "distinguished by his excellence" (ἀρετᾷ κριθείς, *Nemean* 7.7). In that quest for distinction through excellence we find the driving force behind Greek athletics, more than in any "aristocratic code of honor," more even than in the money to be made from so lucrative a business. And in the readiness of adult men to run the naked risk of public dishonor for the chance to achieve distinction, there we find what separated the Greeks out from other people.

APPENDIX 1

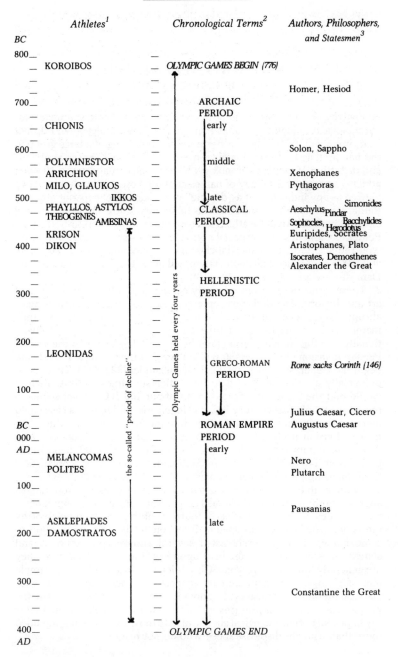

Athletes[1]	Chronological Terms[2]	Authors, Philosophers, and Statesmen[3]
BC		
800		
KOROIBOS	OLYMPIC GAMES BEGIN (776)	
		Homer, Hesiod
700	ARCHAIC PERIOD	
CHIONIS	early	
600		Solon, Sappho
POLYMNESTOR	middle	Xenophanes
ARRICHION		Pythagoras
MILO, GLAUKOS		
500 IKKOS	late	Simonides
PHAYLLOS, ASTYLOS	CLASSICAL	Aeschylus Pindar
THEOGENES AMESINAS	PERIOD	Sophocles, Bacchylides
		Herodotus
KRISON		Euripides, Socrates
400 DIKON		Aristophanes, Plato
		Isocrates, Demosthenes
		Alexander the Great
	HELLENISTIC PERIOD	
300		
200		
LEONIDAS		
	GRECO-ROMAN PERIOD	Rome sacks Corinth (146)
100		
BC	ROMAN EMPIRE	Julius Caesar, Cicero
000	PERIOD	Augustus Caesar
AD	early	
MELANCOMAS		Nero
POLITES		Plutarch
100		
		Pausanias
ASKLEPIADES	late	
200 DAMOSTRATOS		
300		Constantine the Great
400	OLYMPIC GAMES END	
AD		

(vertical text) Olympic Games held every four years

(vertical text) the so-called "period of decline"

NOTES TO APPENDIX 1

1. For reasons of space and utility I choose just a few athletes for chronological guidelines. I omit many well-known athletes who do not bear directly on my study. Furthermore, the bunching of a large group in the late archaic and early classical times (ca. 520-460) causes omissions and distortion of relative chronology. Nor are the actual dates of all these athletes certain. The paucity of names after 400, especially, should not be viewed as any indication of a "decline" or of a dearth of superior athletes. Rather it merely reflects the emphasis of my own study on the archaic and classical periods. All these athletes except the last three appear in the text. Polites of Caria deserves especial notice for his versatility as a runner. He won the stade, diaulos, and dolichos (i.e., approximately, our 200, 400, and 5,000 meter races) all at one Olympiad (69 A.D.). For Asklepiades and Damostratos see Gardiner 1930, 110ff.

2. These terms derive from scholarly convention in the study of ancient art and history. The divisions serve convenience more than they mark abrupt change, even in art and history. In athletics, in particular, they mainly indicate the march of time and little more. Classicists conventionally end the Archaic Period (and begin the Classical) with the second Persian invasion of Greece (480 B.C.). They end the Classical Period (and begin the Hellenistic) with the death of Alexander (323 B.C.). There is no universally accepted ending date for Hellenistic times. G.M.A. Richter would end the Hellenistic Period in art about 100 B.C. Pleket seems to regard the whole first century B.C. as Hellenistic, and indeed a case could be made that it extends much further, into the Roman Empire. But many make a division at 146 B.C., when Rome signaled its mastery of Greece by destroying the important Greek city of Corinth. They would then call the period from 146 to 27 B.C. the "Greco-Roman Period." Most scholars date the Roman Empire from certain acts of Caesar Augustus in 27 B.C.

3. Again, as in the case of the athletes, inclusion or omission from the list suggests nothing of an individual's importance. Again the bunching of many names in the fifth and early fourth centuries leads to noteworthy omissions (Alcibiades) and spatial distortion in the relative position of some names. I have merely listed several authors, philosophers, and statesmen, some because they bear upon my study, others because they are generally known to everyone. Chronological placement has the simple aim of giving rough, approximate signposts to readers unfamiliar with classical literature and history. It is not intended as any attempt to date the people whose names appear (several of the dates are much disputed). It is my hope that the chronological chart will help those for whom it is intended more than it might displease those who do not need it.

APPENDIX 2

The following is the text of the invitation to Coubertin's June 1894 Paris Congress, as printed (without comment) in *The Olympic,* Vol. 1, No. 6 (San Francisco, May 17, 1894). The date of Sloane's covering letter, printed with the invitation, should read "April 20, 1894" (not "1893": see Part One, n. 56, above).

* * * * *

PARIS CONGRESS

Princeton, April 20, 1893

Dear Sir:—It is, I think, about three months since I addressed this circular to the Secretary of the Olympic Club with the request that he would forward to me in its name a paper or papers on one or more of the subjects suggested. I never received any reply. It would gratify us extremely if you or any one you could trust would, even at this late day comply with the request. Yours, *Wm. M. Sloane.*

Union des So ietes Francaises de Sports Athletiques.

(Translation.)
INTERNATIONAL CONGRESS OF AMATEURS.

To be held at Paris in June, 1894, for the consideration and extension of the principles which underlie the idea of amateur sports.

Committee

France and Continental Europe. Baron Pierre de Coubertin, General Secretary of the Union des Sports Athletiques, 20 reu Oudinot, Paris.

England and the English Colonies. C. Herbert, Hon. Secretary Amateur Athletic Association, 10 John St. (Adelphi) London.

America. W. M. Sloane, Professor in Princeton University. Stanworth, Princeton, N.J. United States.

Preliminary Programme

1.—Definition of an amateur: reasons for the definition. Possibility and and utility of an international definition.

2.—Suspension, disqualification and rehabilitation. Facts which respectively sustain them and the means of proof.

3.—Can we justly maintain a distinction between different sports, in regard to what constitutes an amateur, especially in racing (gentlemen riders) and pigeon shooting? Can a professional in one sport be an amateur in another?

4.—The value of the medals or other prizes. Must it be limited? What steps are to be taken concerning those who sell prizes won by themselves.

179

5.—Gate money. Can it be divided between the associations interested or the contestants? Can it be used toward the expenses of the visiting association? Within what limits can expenses of teams on their members be borne, either by their own or by the opposing association?
6.—Can the general definition of an amateur be applied to all sports? Must it comprise special restrictions for cycling, rowing, track athletics, etc., etc.?
7.—Does betting on amateur sports lead to professionalism? Does betting on himself disqualify an amateur? Means to arrest the development of betting.
8.—The possibility of re-establishing the Olympic games. Under what conditions would it be feasible?

———

Associations which participate in the Congress do not thereby bind themselves to observe the resolutions adopted. Its object is to express opinions on the different questions submitted to it, to consider measures for international legislation, but not to inaugurate it.

The order of the sessions and the program of the festivities to accompany the occasion will be fixed at a later date.

*   *   *   *   *

Note: the above reproduces exactly what *The Olympic* prints, including the misspellings ("reu"), omitted type ("So ietes") and French accents, typographical error in the date on Sloane's letter, etc.

This document differs so sharply from that described in the histories of the Modern Olympics that it calls for an explanation. I can imagine only five possibilities. 1) The Olympic Club of San Francisco misrepresented what it received, rewriting it and printing what Coubertin did not say. 2) Unknown to Coubertin, Sloane rewrote what the Baron had given him, and sent his own version (shortened to eight points and with a contrary conclusion). 3) Sloane sent the Olympic Club a circular wholly different from that sent to all the other athletic clubs of the world. 4) Some or all American clubs were sent a document different from that sent to British and Continental clubs. 5) The document which Olympic historians (such as MacAloon and Mandell) think was the January 1894 circular was not the January 1894 circular.

Perhaps there are other possible explanations, or combinations of the above. But until another original exemplar is adduced, it seems pointless to speculate on even more remote possibilities (such as an *Olympic* editor substituting an earlier version for a later but mislaid version, *vel sim.*). Of the potential solutions mentioned above, neither One nor Two is at all likely. For *The Olympic* appears to print precisely what the USFSA approved in August 1893 (Coubertin 1908, 90f; 1931, 13) --the eight points are the same. Coubertin himself later spoke of "two versions" (*deux formules*), an original of just eight points, and a later one expanded to ten (1931, 13-15). That of ten points appeared *sometime* in

1894 (it is printed in the Dec. 1894 *Review of Reviews,* 645). But did people actually receive it in January--or a version that contradicts points nine and ten?

Nor is solution Three likely. The Olympic Club had itself held an elaborate "Revival of the Ancient Greco-Roman Games" at the San Francisco Mechanics Institute in April 1893 (they were mostly theatrical, replete with mock gladiator bouts). And Coubertin visited the Olympic Club on his California tour in the Fall of 1893. But neither of these facts seems sufficient to explain why the Olympic Club should receive such special treatment as to be sent their own version of the Agenda, at variance with that sent to all other clubs.

Nor is solution Four likely, i.e., that Sloane and Coubertin would send some or all American clubs a circular that tended to hide their plans for an Olympic revival--while sending British and Continental clubs a circular that "boldly stated the Olympic project" (International Committee, and all: MacAloon 167). For Sloane was probably Coubertin's strongest supporter in the idea of an Olympic revival. His sponsor in England, on the other hand, C. Hebert, was willing to support debate on questions of amateurism--but had no interest at all in reviving the Olympic Games (a project which he regarded as neither "viable nor useful": see Mandell 84, MacAloon 166). One wonders if Hebert would have attached his name to the strongly Olympic ten-point version (also whether the ordinarily politic Coubertin would have forced it down his throat).

Solution Five, though not certain, is the most likely; i.e., that what MacAloon and other historians print as the "January 1894" circular is not, in fact, the version which was sent in January 1894. If that is so, they have been misled by a later recasting of the document (the sources which they cite are writings which Coubertin published *after* the June 1894 congress). This solution would explain Coubertin's otherwise exceptionally odd comment that the January 1894 circular "was drawn up in such a way as to disguise its main object: 'the revival of the Olympic Games'; ...I carefully refrained from mentioning such an ambitious project" (p. 63, above). While the eight-point agenda does not wholly avoid mention of the Olympics, it treats the project lightly. The ten-point agenda does not treat it lightly at all (contrast Point Ten with "not to inaugurate it").

If Five is correct, I hazard no guess when the ten-point agenda was first drawn up, distributed, or published. The entire question will be clarified when we find additional, authentic exemplars of the January 1894 circular (or of the 'follow up' version such as Sloane sent to San Francisco in April 1894). Some probably exist. The New York Athletic Club seems to have no record of the copy sent to it (I thank Fred Jarvis for searching the archives for me); many other clubs have disappeared. But someone, no doubt, will turn up another exemplar--either an eight- or a ten-point version--somewhere (at the IOC in Lausanne or in this country, I suspect) and demonstrate its authenticity and its January 1894 date.

Coubertin (1931, 13) says the eight and ten point versions were separated by "about ten months"--hard to reconcile with August 1893 for the former (1931, 13f with 1908, 90 ["août 1893"] and January 1894 for the latter (1931, 14f with 1908, 90f ["15 Janvier 1894"]. I suspect there are at least three versions.

APPENDIX 3

Several different definitions of "amateur" and "professional athlete" have been in common use over the years, and the question of a proper definition has excited much controversy. Coubertin's announced aim in convening the 1894 Congress at the Sorbonne was to end the confusion over the meanings and application of these terms. Moreover, sportsmen and scholars alike often use now one meaning, now another, or several meanings simultaneously, without explaining precisely how they define their terms. While a few other definitions are sometimes found[1]--or even additional combinations[2]--I here focus on the three meanings to which most usages may be referred, and on the combinations possible when two or more distinct meanings are used at the same time. By the tabular arrangement I hope to make the reading of other works easier for my own readers.

Almost all occurrences of the terms will fall into one of these three categories:

1) An amateur is an athlete who makes no financial gain from sports; whoever makes financial gain is a professional. (The basic definition of the AAA [1880], AAU, and IOC [to 1979]; Pleket, Gardiner, and others, at times; the popular twentieth-century definition.) Coded below as *no money* = "amateur" and *money* = "professional."

2) An amateur is one who devotes only a (small) part of his time to athletics or, especially, participates for only a brief period of time. He knows there are "more important things than athletics"; he may, therefore, train very little and deprecate training in others. The professional is the man who takes athletics so seriously as to pursue a full-time training program or, especially, to pursue them as an adult. (Seldom an official definition [but see Part Two, n. 69, end, above]; often implicit, sometimes rather explicit in Mahaffy, Gardner, Gardiner, Pleket; cf. Brundage; it lies behind the objections to the use of coaches.) Coded below as *brief career* = "amateur" and *long career* = "professional."

3) An amateur is a Gentleman by birth, or at least from the upper socio-economic class; a professional is an athlete from the working class. (The original 1866 AAC definition; many English sportsmen, even into the mid-twentieth century; Whitney; Gardner, Gardiner, Pleket [the last avoiding the word "amateur"].) Coded below as *upper class* = "amateur" and *lower class* = "professional."

Note: in the following chart, these meanings are coded in the order 1, 2, 3:

A. amateur amateur amateur   =   no money, brief career,   upper class
B. professional amateur amateur   =   money, brief career,   upper class
C. amateur professional amateur   =   no money, long career,   upper class
D. professional professional amateur   =   money, long career,   upper class
E. amateur amateur professional   =   no money, brief career,   lower class
F. professional amateur professional   =   money, brief career,   lower class
G. amateur professional professional   =   no money, long career,   lower class
H. professional professional professional =   money, long career,   lower class

All these athletic types are feasible (with the probable exception of type G), and can be easily exemplified in specific individual modern athletes.

NOTES TO APPENDIX 3

1. Early in the history of rowing, for example, a "professional" was a professional waterman, i.e., one who made a living by rowing, apart from competitive races. Even in the earliest history of pedestrianism a "professional" could be a man who made a living as a courier, i.e., apart from races against other runners. But these rather normal definitions generally disappeared as the amateur movement took hold, and they were not a consideration in amateur athletics proper. No one, furthermore, could make a living by pole-vaulting or hurdling apart from competition or public performance.
2. For example the question "Can a professional in one sport be an amateur in another?" (item three on Coubertin's 1894 agenda)--if answered "Yes"--gives rise to many more combinations than the eight which I have listed here (e.g., if one contemplates the case of R. Nehemiah).

APPENDIX 4

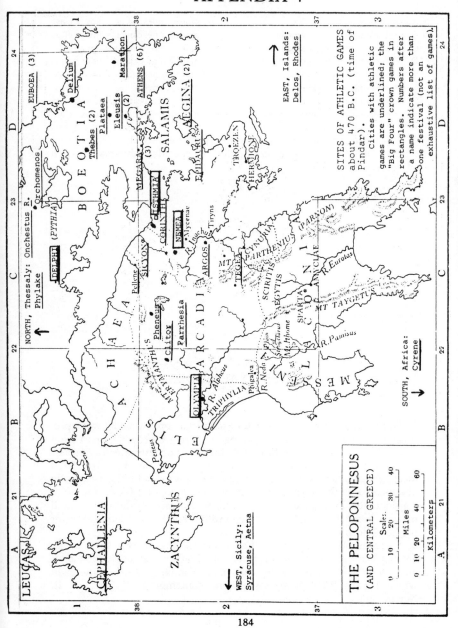

THE PELOPONNESUS
(AND CENTRAL GREECE)

SITES OF ATHLETIC GAMES about 470 B.C. (time of Pindar). Cities with athletic games are underlined; the "Big Four" crown games in rectangles. Numbers after a name indicate more than one festival (not an exhaustive list of games).

NORTH, Thessaly: Onchestus R., Phylake

EAST, Islands: Delos, Rhodes

SOUTH, Africa: Cyrene

WEST, Sicily: Syracuse, Aetna

APPENDIX 5

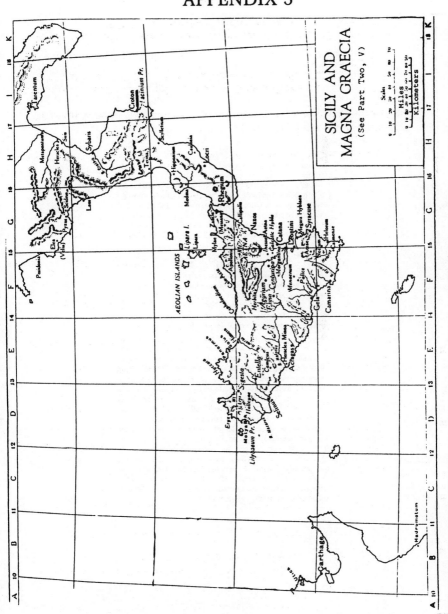

SICILY AND
MAGNA GRAECIA
(See Part Two, V)

Scale

Miles

Kilometers

APPENDIX 6

IG II² 2311

The reader may wish to refer to the Greek text of the Panathenaic prize inscription in *IG* II² 2311 (*Inscriptiones Graecae*. vol. II et III Editio Minor, Berolini 1931) which we have already mentioned in p. 115 n. 11. So we are reprinting the text as edited by J. Kirchner on p. 187 and his commentary below. For the restoration of the men's prizes (missing from the stone) see p. 116, n. 12.

Suppl. †Koe. ‖ supra v. 1 παιϲι κιθαριϲταῖϲ collato tit. Oropio Pr. 92³. ‖ 81 fortasse τη[ι δὲ δευτέραι κτλ. Koe. V. 67 I in rasura, ubi quadratarius primum posuit ΝΙΚ ad v. 71 oculis aberrans. ‖ Quae 50. 79—81 lineis subpositis distinximus, Koe. vidit, nunc perierunt. ‖ v. 18. 39. 54. 61. 70 lineam subductam omisit Koe., idem v. 33. 34 perperam posuit.

Pr. 92 in frag. *a* haec certamina musica fuisse iudicat: 1) προϲοδίου ποιηταί? 2) ῥαψωιδοί. 3) παῖδεϲ αὐλωιδοί. 4) παῖδεϲ κιθαριϲταί. 5) κιθαρωιδοί. 6) ἄνδρεϲ αὐλωιδοί. 7) ἄνδρεϲ κιθαριϲταί. 8) αὐληταί. 9) παρωιδοί. 10) ϲοφιϲταί. v. 24 ἀμφορῆϲ ἐλαίο· cf. Aristot. Ἀθπ. LX 2 οἱ ἀθλοθέται τὸ ἔλαιον τοῖϲ ἀθληταῖϲ ἀποδιδόαϲι. ϲυλλέγεται δὲ τὸ ἔλαιον ἀπὸ τῶν μορίων. Ibid. 3 οἱ δὲ ταμίαι τὸν μὲν ἄλλον χρόνον τηροῦϲιν ἐν ἀκροπόλει, τοῖϲ δὲ Παναθηναίοιϲ ἀπομετροῦϲι τοῖϲ ἀθλοθέταιϲ, οἱ δ᾽ ἀθλοθέται τοῖϲ νικῶϲι τῶν ἀγωνιϲτῶν. ἔϲτι γὰρ ἆθλα τοῖϲ μὲν τὴν μουϲικὴν νικῶϲιν ἀργύριον καὶ χρυϲᾶ (cf. Pr. 95. 96), τοῖϲ δὲ τὴν εὐανδρίαν (vide v. 75) ἀϲπίδεϲ, τοῖϲ δὲ τὸν γυμνικὸν ἀγῶνα καὶ τὴν ἱπποδρομίαν ἔλαιον. Vasa fictilia cum inscriptione τῶν Ἀθήνηθεν ἄθλων (v. Brauchitsch *Panath. Preisamphoren* 1910) non modo in Attica sed etiam extra Atticam haud pauca reperta sunt. Scilicet eis qui Panathenaeis vicerant oleum ex Attica vectigali nullo imposito exportare licebat. Schol. Pind. Nem. X 64 οὔκ ἔϲτι δὲ ἐξαγωγὴ ἐλαίου ἐξ Ἀθηνῶν εἰ μὴ τοῖϲ νικῶϲι. Boeckh *Sth.* I³ 54 not. Sauppe. 55 ἵππων ζεύγει λδηθάγωι = τελείωι· Cf. Harpocr. λδηθάγουϲ τριήρειϲ. Isocr. VI 55 ζεύγη ἵππων λδηθαγούντων. Theopomp. apud Didym. ad Demosth. 5, 26 = FGH II 589 fr. 250 λδηθάγοιϲ ζεύγεϲιν ἐν ταῖϲ πανηγύρεϲιν ἀγωνίζεται. 71 νικητήρια· Recte Dttb. haec praemia refert ad eos qui primum locum in certaminibus πυρρίχη, εὐανδρίᾳ, λαμπάδι κτλ. obtinuerant. Pr. 97. 76 φυληι νικῶϲηι· Ante φυληι omissum est λαμπάδι. Momms. Pr. 97³. 78 νεῶν ἁμίλληϲ· cf. n. 1028₃₀. Syll.³ 717¹¹.

a. 400—350.

col. I

a - - - [ΠΑΙϹΙ ΚΙΘΑΡΙϹΤΑῖϹ]·
   - - - [ΠΡΏΤΩΙ] ϹΤ[ΈΦΑΝΟϹ]
   - - - [ΔΕ]ΥΤΈΡΩΙ
   - - - [Τ]ΡΊΤΩΙ
   ⁵   ΚΙΘΑΡΩΙΔΟῖϹ·
   Χ   ΠΡΏΤΩΙ ϹΤΈΦΑΝΟϹ
   Ⴖ   ΘΑΛΛΏ ΧΡΥϹΟῦϹ
   Ⴖ   ἈΡΓΥΡΊΟ   col. II
   [Χ] Η Η ΔΕΥΤΈΡΩΙ   Ⴖ - - - -
   [Ⴖ] Η   ΤΡΊΤΩΙ   Δ - - -
¹⁰ [Η Η] Η Η ΤΕΤΆΡΤΩΙ   - - -
   Η Η Η   ΠΈΜΠΤΩΙ   ²⁵ Ⴖ - - -
            ἈΝΔΡΆϹΙ ΑΥΛΩΙΔΟῖϹ·   Δ - - -
   Η Η Η   ΠΡΏΤΩΙ· ΤΟΎΤΟ [Ϲ]ΤΈΦΑΝΟϹ
   Η   ΔΕΥΤΈΡΩΙ
¹⁵   ἈΝΔΡΆϹΙ ΚΙΘΑΡΙϹΤΑῖϹ·
   Ⴖ   ΠΡΏΤΩΙ· ΤΟΎΤΟ
            ϹΤΈΦΑΝΟϹ Η Η Η·
   [- Η Η] ΔΕΥΤΈΡΩΙ
       Η   ΤΡΊΤΩΙ
²⁰   ΑΥΛΗΤΑῖϹ·
   - Η   ΠΡΏΤΩΙ· ΤΟΎΤΟ ϹΤΈΦΑΝΟϹ
   [-   ΔΕΥΤΈ]ΡΩΙ
            - - -

col. I

b - - - -
   - - - -
   - - - -
   - - - -
            [ΠΑΙΔῚ ϹΤΆ]ΔΙΟΝ ΝΙΚῶΝΤΙ·
            [Ⴖ ἘΛΛ]ῖΟ ἈΜΦΟΡῆϹ
²⁵ Δ ΔΕΥΤΈΡΩΙ
            ΠΑΙΔῚ ΠΈΝΤΑΘΛΟΝ ΝΙΚῶΝΤΙ·
   Δ Δ Δ ἈΜΦΟΡῆϹ ἘΛΛΊΟ
   Ⴒ Ι ΔΕΥΤΈΡΩΙ
            ΠΑΙΔῚ ΠΑΛΛΑΙϹΤΕῖ ΝΙΚῶΝΤΙ·
³⁰ Δ Δ Δ ἈΜΦΟΡῆϹ ἘΛΛΊΟ
   Ⴒ Ι ΔΕΥΤΈΡΩΙ
            ΠΑῖΔΑϹ ΠΎΚΤΕΙ ΝΙΚῶΝΤΙ·
   Δ Δ Δ ἈΜΦΟΡῆϹ ἘΛΛΊΟ
   Ⴒ Ι ΔΕΥΤΈΡΩΙ
³⁵   ΠΑΙΔῚ ΠΑΓΚΡΆΤΙΟΝ ΝΙΚῶΝΤΙ·
   [Δ] Δ Δ Δ ἈΜΦΟΡῆϹ ἘΛΛΊΟ
   Ⴒ Ι Ι Ι ΔΕΥΤΈΡΩΙ
            ἈΓΕΝΕΊΩΙ ϹΤΆΔΙΟΝ ΝΙΚῶΝΤΙ·
   Ⴖ Δ ἈΜΦΟΡῆϹ ἘΛΛΊΟ
⁴⁰ Δ Ι Ι ΔΕΥΤΈΡΩΙ
            ἈΓΕΝΕΊΩΙ ΠΕΝΤΆΘΛΩΙ ΝΙΚῶΝΤΙ·
   Δ Δ Δ Δ ἈΜΦΟΡῆϹ ἘΛΛΊΟ
   Ⴒ Ι Ι Ι ΔΕΥΤΈΡΩΙ
            ἈΓΕΝΕΊΩΙ ΠΑΛΛΑΙϹΤΕῖ ΝΙΚῶΝΤΙ·
⁴⁵ [Δ Δ] Δ Δ ἈΜΦΟΡῆϹ ἘΛΛΊΟ
   [Ⴒ Ι Ι Ι Δ]ΕΥΤΈΡΩΙ
            [ἈΓΕΝΕῚ]ΩΙ ΠΎΚΤΗΙ ΝΙΚῶΝΤΙ·
   [Δ Δ Δ Δ ἈΜΦΟΡῆϹ ἘΛ]ΛΊΟ
   [Ⴒ Ι Ι Ι ΔΕΥΤΈΡΩΙ]
⁵⁰   [ἈΓΕΝΕΊΩΙ ΠΑΓΚΡΆΤΙΟΝ ΝΙ]ΚῶΝΤΙ·
            - - - -

col. II

   [- - - ἈΜΦΟΡῆϹ ἘΛΛΊ]Ο
   [- - - ΔΕ]ΥΤΈΡΩΙ
            ἽΠΠΩΝ ΠΩΛΙΚῶΙ ΖΕΎΓΕΙ·
   Δ Δ Δ Δ ἈΜΦΟΡῆϹ ἘΛΛΊΟ
            Ⴒ Ι Ι Ι ΔΕΥΤΈΡΩΙ
⁵⁵   ἽΠΠΩΝ ΖΕΎΓΕΙ ΛΔΗΦΆΓΩΙ·
   Η Δ Δ Δ Δ ἈΜΦΟΡῆϹ ἘΛΛΊΟ
   Δ Δ Δ ΔΕΥΤΈΡΩΙ
            ΠΟΛΕΜΙϹΤΗΡΊΟΙϹ·
            ἽΠΠΩΙ ΚΈΛΗΤΙ ΝΙΚῶΝΤΙ·
⁶⁰ Δ Ⴒ Ι ἈΜΦΟΡῆϹ ἘΛΛΊΟ
   Ι Ι Ι Ι ΔΕΥΤΈΡΩΙ
            ἽΠΠΩΝ ΖΕΎΓΕΙ ΝΙΚῶΝΤΙ·
   Δ Δ Δ ἈΜΦΟΡῆϹ ἘΛΛΊΟ
   Ⴒ Ι ΔΕΥΤΈΡΩΙ
⁶⁵   ΖΕΎΓΕΙ ΠΟΜΠΙΚῶΙ ΝΙΚῶΝΤΙ
   Ι Ι Ι Ι ἈΜΦΟΡῆϹ ἘΛΛΊΟ
   Ι ΔΕΥΤΈΡΩΙ
            ἈΦ' ἽΠΠΟ ἈΚΟΝΤΊΖΟΝΤΙ·
   Ⴒ ἈΜΦΟΡῆϹ ἘΛΛΊΟ
⁷⁰ Ι ΔΕΥΤΈΡΩΙ
            ΝΙΚΗΤΉΡΙ[Α]
   Η ΠΑΙϹΙΜ ΠΥΡ[ΡΙ]ΧΙϹΤΑῖ(Ϲ) ΒΟῦϹ·
   Η ἈΓΕΝΕΊΟΙϹ ΠΥ[Ρ]ΡΙΧΙϹΤΑῖϹ ΒΟῦϹ·
   Η ἈΝΔΡΆϹΙ ΠΥΡΡΙΧΙϹΤΑῖϹ ΒΟῦϹ·
⁷⁵ Η ΕΥΑΝΔΡΊΑΙ ΦΥΛῆΙ ΝΙΚΏϹΕΙ ΒΟῦϹ·
   Η ΦΥΛῆΙ ΝΙΚΏϹΗΙ ΒΟῦϹ·
   Δ Δ Δ ΛΑΜΠΑΔΗΦΌΡΩΙ ΝΙΚῶΝΤΙ ὙΔ[ΡΊΑ]·
   ΝΙΚΗΤΉΡΙΑ ΝΕῶΝ ἈΜΊΛΛΗϹ
   Η Η Η ΤῆΙ ΦΥΛῆΙ ΤῆΙ ΝΙΚΏϹΕ[Ι ΒΌΕϹ ΤΡΕῖϹ]?
⁸⁰ Η Η Κ[Α]ὶ ΕἸϹ ἙϹΤΊΑϹΙΝ
   Η Η ΤῆΙ Δ]Ε[Υ[ΤΈ]ΡΑΙ Β[ΌΕϹ ΔΎΟ]
            - - -

BIBLIOGRAPHY

Note: if only one work of an author appears in the following bibliography, it is cited by the author's name alone. If I cite more than one work of an author I include the date. The abbreviation "e.a." means "e(mphasis) a(dded)." For ancient authors see Liddell-Scott-Jones, *A Greek-English Lexicon*.

American Olympic Committee, *Report: Seventh Olympic Games, Antwerp, Belgium, 1920*, Greenwich, Conn., n.d.

Amyx, D., see Pritchett, W. Kendrick and D. A. Amyx.

Bailey, Peter, *Leisure and Class in Victorian England: Rational Recreation and the Contest for Control*, London, 1978.

Banciulesco, V., "A Forerunner of the Revival of the Olympic Games," *Bulletin du comité international olympique* 83 (1963), 55f.

(Bourdon, Georges = G.B.), "Athènes essaye de faire revivre Olympie," *Les jeux de VIIIe Olympiade*, Paris (Comité olympique français) 1924 (1926), 19-21.

Brundage, Avery, "Why the Olympic Games?" *Report of the United States Olympic Committee; Games of the XIVth Olympiad, London, England, 1948;* n.p., n.d., 21-26.

Buhmann, Horst, *Der Sieg in Olympia*, Munich, 1972.

Chrysafis = Χρυσάφης, Ἰ(ωάννης) Ε., οἱ σύγχρονοι διεθνεῖς Ὀλυμπιακοὶ ἀγῶνες, Athens, 1930.

Cohen, Steven, "More than Fun and Games: A comparative study of the role of sport in English and American society at the turn of the century" (unpublished 1980 Brandeis U. Dissertation).

Coubertin, Pierre, *Batailles de l'éducation physique: Une campagne de vingt-et-un ans, 1887-1908*, Paris, 1908.

(Coubertin, P.), "International Congress of Amateurs" (translation), *The Olympic* (San Francisco), Vol. 1, No. 6 (May 17, 1894), 55.

Coubertin, Pierre, *Mémoires Olympiques*, Lausanne, 1931.

Coubertin, Pierre, *The Olympic Idea* (ed. by Carl-Diem-Institut), Stuttgart, 1967.

Coubertin, Pierre, pp. 1-8 in: S. Lambros and N. Politis, edd., *The Olympic Games of 1896* = Part Two of *The Olympic Games: B.C. 776.--A.D. 1896*, Athens, 1896-7.

Coubertin, Pierre, "La préface des jeux olympiques," *Cosmopolis* 2 (1896), 146-159.

Coubertin, Pierre, *Souvenirs d'Amérique et de Grèce*, Paris, 1897.

Coubertin, Pierre, "Why I revived the Olympic Games," *Fortnightly Review* 90 (1908), 110-115.

Drees, Ludwig, *Olympia: Gods, Artists, and Athletes*, New York, 1968.

Dunbabin, T., *The Western Greeks*, Oxford, 1948 (reprint, Chicago, 1979).

Duruy, Victor, *History of Greece* (trans. by M. M. Ripley), Boston, 1892; with an Introduction by J. P. Mahaffy.

Ebert, Joachim, *Griechische Epigramme auf Sieger an gymnischen und hippischen Agonen*, Berlin, 1972 (= Abhandlungen der sächsischen Akademie der Wissenschaften zu Leipzig, Philologisch-historische Klasse, 63.2).

Finley, M. I., and Pleket, H. W., *The Olympic Games: The First Thousand Years*, New York, 1976.

Gardiner, E. Norman, *Athletics of the Ancient World*, Oxford, 1930 (reprint, Chicago, 1980).

Gardiner, E. Norman, *Greek Athletic Sports and Festivals*, London, 1910.

Gardiner, E. Norman, *Olympia: Its History and Remains*, Oxford, 1925.

Gardner, Percy, *New Chapters in Greek History*, London, 1892.

Grombach, John, *The Official 1980 Olympic Guide*, New York, 1980.

Guttmann, Allen, *From Ritual to Record; The Nature of Modern Sports*, New York, 1978.

Harris, H. A., *Greek Athletes and Athletics*, with an introduction by the Marquess of Exeter, Chairman of the British Olympic Association, London, 1964.

Harris, H. A., *Sport in Greece and Rome*, Ithaca, 1972.

Henry, Bill, *An Approved History of the Olympic Games*[2], 1976 (revised by P. H. Yeomans).

Hönle, Augusta, *Olympia in der Politik der griechischen Staatenwelt*, Bebenhausen, 1972.

Holliman, Jennie, *American Sports (1785-1835)*, Philadelphia, 1975.

(International Olympic Committee), *The International Olympic Committee and the Olympic Games*, Aigle, Switzerland, 1950.

Jenkyns, Richard, *The Victorians and Ancient Greece*, Oxford (Blackwell), 1980.

Jüthner, J., *Die athletischen Leibesübungen der Griechen*, 2 vols., Vienna, 1965, 1968.

Jüthner, Julius, *Philostratus über Gymnastik*, 1909 (reprint Amsterdam, 1969).

Ketseas, John, "A Restatement," *Bulletin du comité international olympique* 83 (1963), 56.

Kieran, John, *Story of the Olympic Games*[2], Philadelphia, 1973.

Klee, Theophil, *Zur Geschichte der gymnischen Agone an Griechischen Festen*, Leipzig, 1918 (reprint Chicago, 1980).

Knab, Rudolf, *Die Periodoniken*, Giessen, 1934 (reprint Chicago, 1980).

Krause, J. H., *Olympia*, Vienna, 1838 (reprint Hildesheim, 1972).

Lucas, John, "Baron Pierre de Coubertin and the Formative Years of the Modern International Olympic Movement" (unpublished 1962 University of Maryland Dissertation).

Lucas, John, *The Modern Olympic Games*, South Brunswick, New York and London, 1980.

Lucas, John, and Smith, Ronald, *Saga of American Sport*, Philadelphia, 1978.

MacAloon, John J., *This Great Symbol: Pierre de Coubertin and the Origins of the Modern Olympic Games*, Chicago and London, 1981.

Mahaffy, John P., "Old Greek Athletics," *Macmillan's Magazine* 36, (1879), 61-69.

Mahaffy, John P., *Old Greek Education*, New York and London, 1881.

Mahaffy, John P., *Old Greek Life*, London 1876 (reprint New York, n.d.).

Mahaffy, John P., "The Olympic Games at Athens in 1875," *Macmillan's Magazine* 32 (1875), 324-327.

Mahaffy, John P., *Social Life in Ancient Greece from Homer to Menander*[7], 1890 (reprint London and New York, 1894).

Mandell, Richard, *The First Modern Olympics*, Berkeley, 1976.

Manning, C. A., "Professionalism in Greek Athletics," *Classical Weekly* 11 (1917), 74-78.

Μέγα Ἑλληνικὸν Βιογραφικὸν Λεξιχόν, I, Athens, n.d. (1962).

Menke, Frank G., *The Encyclopedia of Sports*[5], South Brunswick, New York and London, 1975.

Mezö, F., *The Modern Olympic Games* (preface by A. Brundage), Budapest, 1956.

Miller, Geoffrey, *Behind the Olympic Rings*, Lynn, Mass., 1979.

Miller, Stephen, *Arete: Ancient writers, papyri, and inscriptions on the history and ideals of Greek Athletics and Games*, Chicago, 1979.

Moretti, Luigi, *Olympionikai, i vincitori negli antichi agoni olimpici*, Rome, 1957 (Atti della accademia nazionale dei Lincei).

Patrucco, Roberto, *Lo sport nella Grecia antica*, Florence, 1972.

Pleket, H. W., "Games, Prizes, Athletes and Ideology," *Arena* (now *Stadion*) 1 (1976), 49-89.

Pleket, H. W., "Zur Soziologie des antiken Sports," *Mededelingen van het Nederlands Instituut te Rome*, N.S. 36 (1974), 56-87.

Poole, Lynn and Gray, *History of the Ancient Olympic Games*, New York, 1963.

Pouilloux, J., *Recherches sur l'histoire et les cultes de Thasos*, Paris, 1954.

Pritchett, W. Kendrick, and D. A. Amyx, "The Attic Stelai," I, *Hesperia* 22 (1953), 225-299; II, *Hesperia* 25 (1956), 178-328; III, *Hesperia* 27 (1958), 163-310.

Redmond, Gerald, *The Caledonian Games in Nineteenth-Century America*, Cranbury, N.J. (Associated University Presses), 1971.

Rudolph, W., "Zu den Formen des Berufssport zur Zeit der Poliskrise," in E. C. Welskopf, ed., *Hellenische Poleis* (1974), III, 1472-1483.

Rutgers, I., ed., Sextus Julius Africanus, *Olympionicarum fasti*, Leiden, 1862 (reprint Chicago, 1980).

Santas, Alex., *Olympia; Olympiakoi agones; Olympionikai*, Athens, 1966.

Schoebel, Heinz, *The Four Dimensions of Avery Brundage*, Leipzig, 1968.

Shorey, Paul, "Can We Revive the Olympic Games," *Forum* 19 (1895), 313-323.

Sloane, Wm., see American Olympic Committee.

Stanford, W. B. and R. B. McDowell, *Mahaffy: A Biography of an Anglo-Irishman*, London, 1971.

Starr, Chester, *Economic and Social Growth of Early Greece, 800-500 B.C.*, New York, 1977.

Trollope, Anthony, *British Sports and Pastimes*, London, 1868.

Walvin, James, *Leisure and Society 1830-1950*, London and New York, 1978.

Weiler, Ingomar, *Der Agon in Mythos*, Darmstadt, 1974.

Weiler, Ingomar, *Der Sport bei den Völkern der Alten Welt*, Darmstadt, 1981.

Whitney, Caspar, *A Sporting Pilgrimage*, New York, 1895.

Yalouris, Constantinos, *The Olympic Games throughout the Ages*, New York, 1976.

Young, David C., "Pindar," in: T. J. Luce, ed., Scribner's *Ancient Writers: Greece and Rome*, New York, 1982 (vol. 1, 157-177).

Young, David C., *Three Odes of Pindar*, Leiden, 1968 (= *Supplements to Mnemosyne* 9).

INDICES

I. MODERN

"Amateur" (the word): 7f, 16
"Amateur" and "Professional,"
definition of: 19f, 24, 63, 66,
77, 80, 93-98, 126, 182f
Amateur Athletic Association:
21f, 24
Amateur Athletic Club: 19-21,
97
Amateur Athletic Union: 24f, 83
Arnold, Thomas: 58

Baseball: 22f
Bourdon, Georges: 28f, 32f, 39,
60
Brookes, Dr. W.: 59
Brundage, Avery: 16, 49, 83-88,
92, 94, 107, 165
Brundage's use of ancient
Greece: 85-87
Burckhardt, Jacob: 175

Christianity: 1, 53, 58, 79
Chronological sleight of hand:
10-14, 45, 55, 73f, 76f, 81f,
89, 101, 166
Chrysafis, Ioannis: 32, 39f,
41-43
Concepts and catch-phrases:
"Creeping professionalism/
socialism": 86
"duty to country," etc.: 13f,
78, 80
"irreproachable": v, 73
"more important things than
athletics": 13f: cf. 18, 45,
48, 56, 78f
"over-specialization": 48f, 78f
"sport for sport's sake": 48f, 86
"to participate is more important than to win": 91, 169
Congress of the Sorbonne, 1894:
60-67, 179-181

Connors, Jimmy: 167
Coubertin, Pierre de: v, 28f, 30,
49-51, 56-74, 79, 82, 91, 169,
179-181
Coubertin's use of ancient
Greece: v, 10, 59f, 67, 73
Cornell University: 23

Degeneration-theory of Greek
athletics: 2, 9-12, 53, 55f, 77f,
81f, 86, 89-92
Dihle, Albrecht: 109f
Discus throw (19th cent.): 30f,
37, 167
Duruy, Victor: 10, 51

Early amateur marks: 167f.

Exeter, Sixth Marquess of
(=David George Brownlow
Cecil): 14

Gardiner, E. N.; 2, 49, 51f,
76-82, 84f, 88-90, 92, 96, 100,
175
Gardner, Percy: 11, 51-56
Grace, W. G.: 20
Greek athlete, ancient, idealized
as Victorian: 12-14, 47f, 51-53,
76, 97, 107f, 166, 169
Greeks, ancient, misrepresented:
"Euripides," 45f, 56;
"Herodotus," 46f.;
"Pausanias," 77;
"Phayllos," 12-14, 107, 140
"Pindar," 9f, 36, 45f, 78, 91f
Grombach, John: 30, 39, 42, 74,
100

Hamilton, Edith: 10
Harris, H. A.,: 12-14, 49, 90-92,
107, 166-169, 171
Henley Regatta: 20, 170

195

International Olympic Committee
  (IOC): 27, 39, 65f, 72, 73, 82f,
  85, 87; its preference for titled
  nobility and royalty: 73; its
  use of antiquity: v, 5f, 10, 67,
  85-87 (cf. 14)
Ioannou, Philippos: 32f, 43

Jarrett (Holm), Eleanor: 85

Kardamylakis, K.: 32
Kelly, John: 20
Kieran, John: 74

Loues, Spiridon: 72, 100
Lucas, John: 58

MacAloon, John: 38-42, 58,
  61-64, 181
Mahaffy, John: 10, 29, 34-40,
  44-53, 56, 60, 78, 94, 103, 146
Mandell, Richard: 38f, 42, 58, 62
"Mechanics Clause": 20f, 26
Mercati, Count: 70f
Mezö, F.: 39, 41

Nehemiah, R.: 66, 183
New York Athletic Club: 22f,
  181
NYAC-LAC, 1895 contest: 168

Olympic Club of San Francisco:
  19, 61f, 179-181
Olympic Games, Modern.
  Greek (1859-1889): 18, 28-43,
  69-71
Olympic Games, Modern.
  International:
  1896; 8, 66, 68-72
  1900; 71f, 74f
  1904; 74f
  1906; 74f
  1908; 57, 75
  1912; 57, 75, 82f
  1936; 85
"Olympics" of Dr. Brookes in
  Shropshire: 59
"Olympism": 66f
Owens, Jesse: 57
Oxford-Cambridge, 1864 contest:
  168

Panathenaic Stadium: 31, 34,
  36, 41, 69f; see also 115-127
Patterson, Floyd: 167
Philadelpheus, A.: 41
Phokianos, Ioannis: 32-35, 37,
  40-43
Pleket, H.W.: 89-102, 107-110,
  149-155, 157, 169
Pooles, L. and G.: 10, 84-86, 92
Pouilloux, J.: 151f, 161
Pre-amateur modern sports:
  America, 16f; "Caledonian,"
  17, 22f; Highland Games, 17;
  prizes, 16; 23 (university), 30f,
  33 (Greece); university, 17, 19
  (England), 23 (American)

Robert, L: 91

Schranz, W.: 87
Schuylkill Navy regatta: 22
Scotland: 17, 77
Shorey, Paul: 8-12, 49, 51f, 56,
  68, 74
Skordaras, E.: 32, 99
Sloane, Wm.: 61f, 70f, 74,
  179-181
Soccer (Association Football):
  23f, 76f
Stannard, Henry: 16

Ten Eyke, E.: 170
Thorpe, James: v, 57, 66, 82-84
Times of London: 19, 21

Trollope, Anthony: 18
Trounkas, K.: 32
Turnen: 19, 37, 41f, 50

United States Olympic Committee
    (American Olympic Committee,
    and other names before 1961):
    27, 39, 74, 83, 86

Vikelas, Demetrius: 65-67, 72f

Weiler, I.: 91
Weissmuller, J.: 168
Whitney, Caspar: 17f, 25-27, 49,
    56f, 73f

Yale University: 23

Zappas, E.: 29f, 42, 70f
"Zappas Olympics": see Olympic
    games, Modern. Greek

INDICES

II. ANCIENT (General)

Adult nature of games: 171f
Age divisions: 74, 159
Alcohol "taboo"?: 74
Amateurism, no word or concept for: 7f, 77f, 90, 108, 164, 169f
Argos: 102

Ball games: 171
Boxing: 44, 52
Boys as professionals: 158f
"Breach in city wall" for victor?: 53-55

Career length of athletes: 95f, 143-145, 159f, 172
Coaching and medicine: 145-150
Coinage: Attica, 129; Croton, 140
Colonial Olympic victories: 134-142
Competitive nature of Greeks: 175f
Criticism of athletes or athletic rewards: 46, 131-133, 165
Croton: 81f, 134-142, 145-147, 154

Defeat as humiliation: 166f
Diets: 55, 145

Equestrian events: 77, 100-103, 111f, 157

Financing of athletic festival: 163
Frequency of competition (traveling circuit): 144

Gelon: 141

"Hall of Fame" (walkway of fame, Olympia): 142
Hieron: 141
Hippocrates medicus: 146

Homeric times, athletics in: 112f

Ideals of athletes: 92, 174-176
Inflation: 129
"irreproachable" personal life and ancestors required?: 73f
"It's just a game," non-Greek: 166f

Mock combat: 172
Musical contests and prizes (called "athletics" in Greek): 112, 122f, 125f, 164

Nero: 54f
Nudity: 176

Olympics, eligibility: 73f; end of: 1; see also 135-140 and passim

Panathenaic Games (Athens) and prize inscription: 47, 115-127
Pensions of athletes, archaic and classical periods: 131; Roman period: 1
Pentecosiomedimnoi: 130
Periodonikes: 134
Persian athletics: 173
"pic-nic" style athletics: 111, 171
Political activity of athletes: 160-162
Prices and values (Attica): grain, 130; horses, 111; olive oil, 116, 119-123; real estate, 127; sheep, 127, 129f; slaves, 127
Prizes: 1, 81f, 91f, 111-133, 163f
Purchasing/economic power of prizes: 127, 129
Pythagoras and Pythagoreans: 134, 140, 145

Pythagoras of Samos (sculptor):
142

Record-keeping: 96, 142, 166
Recruiting: 140-142
Ritual origin of athletics?: 172

Second place: 47, 119-126
Seriousness of athletics: 166f,
171-176
Sexual abstinence: 142, 145, 149
Social mobility (?): 109f, 151,
161f
Social origins of athletes: 92f,
95-102, 112-114, 144, 147-163,
174-176
Socrates: 131

Solon: 128-132
Standard of living: 126
Stade (= [ca.] 200 meter dash):
116, 119, 125, 135-143, 178
State entries (equestrian): 102
Subsidization?: 109, 159
Sybaris: 81f, 154
Syracuse: 138, 141f

Tax exemption for prizes: 126

Wages: 117-124; 146
Words: ἀθλεύω/ἀθλητής, 7, 45
γυμνάζω/γυμναστής, 45
ἰδιώτης, 7
χειμήλιον, 132
παίζειν, 171

INDICES

III. ANCIENT ATHLETES AND COACHES

Names without a symbol "E" or "C" are athletes. E = equestrian events *only*. C = Coach *only;* A & C = Athlete and Coach. *See also pp. 135-138.*

Alcibiades of Athens (E):
100-102, 111, 139, 157, 178
Amesinas of Barca, Africa: 99,
155, 156
Aratus: 77
Arrichion of Phigalia (Arcadia):
11, 147
Asklepiades: 178
Astylos of Croton and Syracuse:
92f, 141-145, 150, 157, 168,
174
?Atrometos of Athens (father of
Aeschines): 156

Chionis of Sparta: 143

Damostratos: 178
Dandis of Argos: 143f
Democedes of Croton (C?),
medicus: 145f, 154
Diagoras of Rhodes: 144
Dikon of Caulonia, Italy and
Syracuse (Sicily): 143, 160

Ergoteles of Knossos and
Himera: 144
Eryxias (C): 147f

Gelon (E): 155
Glaukos of Karystos: 99, 147,
155f, 159f, 162, 174
Gorgus: 77

Hesiod of Askra (*poeta*): 112f
Herodicus of Selymbria (C),
(*medicus*): 55, 145f

Ikkos of Tarentum (A&C): 145,
149, 169

Koroibos of Elis: 99, 155
Krison of Himera: 143

Leonidas of Rhodes: 143
Leontiskos: 11

Melancomas: 8
Melesias of Athens or Aegina
(A&C): 99, 148f, 160
Menander (C): 148
Milo of Croton: 11, 74, 92f, 95,
134, 136, 139, 145f, 153f, 157,
160, 162

Olyntheus of Sparta: 143

Pantakles of Athens: 92f
Phayllos of Croton: 12-14, 134,
140, 160, 168
Philippos of Croton: 161
Phrynon of Athens: 160
Polites of Caria: 178
Polym(n)estor of Miletus: 99f,
155, 159
Poulydamos: 11

Sostratos: 11

Theogenes of Thasos: 92f,
95-98, 144, 150-152, 155-157,
160f, 166, 169
Timasitheos of Croton: 136
Timasitheos of Delphi: 161
Tisias (C): 147f
Titus Domitius: 107

INDICES

IV. ANCIENT AUTHORS AND TEXTS

Abbreviations as in Liddell, Scott, and Jones (*Greek-English Lexicon⁹*) or fuller; sometimes an English title is used in the text.

Aeschines 2.147-8: 156; 3
(*Against Ctesipho*): 175; *schol.
ad* 3.190: 162
Andocides *in Alcib.* 32: 156
Anecdota Graeca 1.232 Bekker:
162
Aristophanes *Ach.* 65-90: 118;
Pl. 1161 ff.: 106, 164
Aristophanes of Byzantium: 156
Aristotle *Pol.* 1339a: 160; *Rh.*
1365a, 1367b: 156
Artemidorus Daldianus *Onir.*
2.20 Pack: 158
Athenaeus grammaticus *Deip.*
522: 132, 164

Cicero: 148
Contest of Homer and Hesiod
(*Certamen*) 228: 163

Demosthenes 18 (*On the Crown*):
175; 18.129-131: 156;
19.281-282: 156
Dio Cassius 63.20: 54
Dio Chrysostom *Or.* 31.617-618
R: 161
Diodorus Siculus 12.9.5: 153f
Diogenes Laertius 1.55: 128

Euripides *frag.* 282 Nauck;
frag. 755 Page; *Hipp.* 1016f:
all 46
Eustathius *ad Od.* 1761.25: 156

Heraclides Ponticus: 132
Herodotus 3.129-133: 146; 3.137:
154; 5.44-45: 154; 5.47,72:
161; 8.26: 173; 8.47: 13, 134,
140, 160, see also 153

Hesiod *Works and Days*
289-292: 10; 631-640: 113;
654-657: 112; *Theogony*
435-438: 112
Homer *Iliad* 2.774 f.: 111;
6.47-50: 126; 9.123-127 (=
265-269): 111; 11.698-701:
113; 22.159-166: 112, 172;
23.259-261: 111; 23.541-554:
166; 23.802-823: 172;
24.228-234: 132; 24.381:
132; *Odyssey* 1.312: 132;
4.626 f.: 111; 8.97-103: 111;
8.147f: 175; 17.168 f.: 111,
171
Horace *C.* 4.4.33: 149

Inscriptions
IG I² 77: 131; *IG* I² 302.56-58:
163; I² 374: 118; II² 1356: 116;
II² 2311: 115-126; Appendix 6;
Ebert (see p. 131) 7, 15, 37,
39, 43, 67: 166; Ebert pp.
251f. (Sybaris): 131-133
Isocrates 16.33-34: 100-102, 157

Julius Africanus (*apud* Eusebius
Chron.): 139, 141, 155

Lucian *Anach.:* 173f

Pausanias 5.24.9: 74; 6.9.5: 155;
6.10.1-3: 155, 162; 6.11.2:
152; 6.13.1: 141f; 10.7.5: 113;
10.9.2: 13, 134
Philostratus *Gym.* 144: 155; 148:
147; 150: 147; 152: 74, 168:
155 (Juthner's pages)

Phlegon of Tralles, *frag.* 1
  Jacoby: 113
Pindar: *Ol.*1.81.84: 174; *Ol.*1.97:
  166; *Ol.*7: 144; *Ol.*7.53: 149;
  *Ol.*8.54-66: 149; *Ol.*8.68 f:
  167; *Ol.*12: 144; *Py.*8.83-87:
  167; *Py.*11.50 f: 9f; *Ne.*3.52:
  155; *Ne.*7.7:176; *Schol. ad Py.*
  Preface: 113; *ad Ne.*4.155:
  149; *ad Ne.*10.64b: 126, 149f
Plato *Ap.*36d-e: 46, 131, 165;
  Cratylus 406c: 10; *Lg.* (*Laws*)
  840a: 142; *Re.*3.406a: 146;
  10.620b: 164
Plutarch *Aratus* 3: 77; *Solon* 23:
  128f., 163; *Quaest. Symp.*
  2.5.2: 54; 5.3.2: 164

Simonides *frag.* 1 *PMG* (10
  Bergk): 142; *frag.* 4 *PMG* (8):
  155, 174; *epigram* 41 Page:
  156; *epigram* 43 Page: 128
Strabo 6.1.12: 139
Suetonius *Nero* 25: 54

Timaeus: 132

Vergil *Aeneid* 5.425ff: 52

Xenophanes 2: 46, 131f, 163,
  165
Xenophon *Cyr.* 1.2.12, 1.6.18:
  173; *Hiero* 4.6: 8

ABOUT THE AUTHOR

David C. Young received his B.A. in Greek from the University of Nebraska in 1959 (ΦBK) and his Ph.D. in classics from the University of Iowa in 1963. He then joined the faculty at the University of California, Santa Barbara, where he was Chairman of the Department of Classics from 1968-1972. He has been Professor of Classics at UCSB since 1972. He has occasionally served as Visiting Professor of Classics at Stanford University and the University of Michigan, Ann Arbor, and has lectured at many universities in the United States and England.

Professor Young is an internationally recognized authority on Pindar (ca. 518-444 B.C.), the poet who composed the *Odes of Victory* for the athletes victorious in the Olympics and other ancient Greek games. He is the author of *Three Odes of Pindar* and of *Pindar Isthmian 7* (Leiden, Brill, 1968; 1971). His history of Pindaric scholarship (pp. 1-95 in *Pindaros und Bakchylides, Wege der Forschung*, 134, Darmstadt, 1971) is regarded the standard. He has also published numerous articles in scholarly journals, most recently (1983) in *Harvard Studies in Classical Philology; The Ancient World* (Ares, Chicago); and *Classical Antiquity* (University of California).

His athletic career was much shorter, terminating in a three-way tie for first place, high jump, 1954 Nebraska State High School Meet.

TWO SPECIAL ISSUES ON ANCIENT ATHLETICS OF

THE ANCIENT WORLD

A JOURNAL THAT PROMISED TO BRING YOU THE BEST ARTICLES ON THE ANCIENT WORLD, PROUDLY PUBLISHED A SPECIAL ISSUE IN 1983 ON "ATHLETICS IN ANTIQUITY" WITH ARTICLES LIKE "THE ANCIENT STADIUM: ATHLETES AND ARETE", BY D. ROMANO; "HERODOTUS' VIEWS ON ATHLETICS", BY T. BROWN; "ATHLETIC ARETE IN PINDAR", BY H. LEE; "SPORT AT ROME", BY H. BENARIO; "PROFESSIONALISM IN ARCHAIC AND CLASSICAL GREEK ATHLETICS", BY D. YOUNG; ETC.

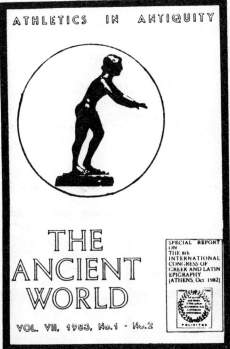

ATHLETICS IN ANTIQUITY

THE ANCIENT WORLD

VOL. VII, 1983, No.1 - No.2

SPECIAL REPORT ON THE 8th INTERNATIONAL CONGRESS OF GREEK AND LATIN EPIGRAPHY (ATHENS, Oct 1982)

THE ANCIENT WORLD IS PRESENTLY PREPARING ONE MORE SPECIAL ISSUE ON ANCIENT ATHLETICS.

Don't miss the opportunity to follow up on what scholarship adds to our knowledge of this subject.

FOR ONLY **$10.00** YOU CAN HAVE THESE TWO SPECIAL ISSUES IN YOUR HAND.

SEND YOUR REQUEST TO

ARES PUBLISHES, INC.
7020 N. Western Ave.
Chicago, Illionis 60645

COMPLETE YOUR LIBRARY

NEW

$10.00

DAVID YOUNG

THE OLYMPIC MYTH OF GREEK AMATEUR ATHLETICS

ISBN:
0-89005-523-8

No amateur ever competed at the ancient Olympics. All Greek athletes competed for prizes, with no restriction on winnings. Many ancient athletic meets paid cash or in-kind prizes. At the games in Plato's Athens, the men's 200-meter victor won a prize worth $67,000.

The Olympics awarded a mere olive crown. But in 600 B.C., Athens paid any Athenian winning at Olympia a cash prize of $300,000. Other cities did the same. If we prefer "amateurism" for our own Olympics, that is our choice. But we must stop blaming the ancient Greeks. They didn't even have a word for it.

This book has arisen from a need to put into the hands of the students ancient readings which provide evidence for and reveal various aspects of Greek athletes. These students who are, for the most part, with no prior experience of classics and the Classical world are eager and willing to confront the problems of a lack or conflicting evidence from antiquity, but they do not have the ancient languages necessary to do so. This book should be used together with a handbook such as Gardiner's *Athletics of the Ancient World* which will provide a general background of the physical evidence for the study of the Greek Athletics.

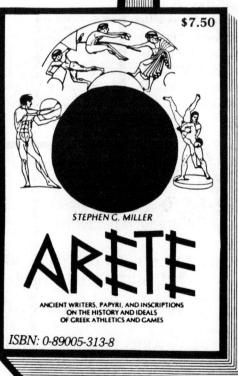

$7.50

STEPHEN G. MILLER

ARETE

ANCIENT WRITERS, PAPYRI, AND INSCRIPTIONS
ON THE HISTORY AND IDEALS
OF GREEK ATHLETICS AND GAMES

ISBN: 0-89005-313-8

Just Mail your order form to: **ARES PUBLISHERS, INC.,**

ON ANCIENT ATHLETICS

An extensive bibliography covering both Greek and Roman athletics and including works from as early as 1573 to the present (1983) cannot be absolutely complete. This is due somewhat to the interdisciplinary nature of the topic, to the occasionally obscure and scattered sources, and to deliberate selectivity. But such a comprehensive research tool long overdue for students and scholars in a growing field should foster research and teaching at all levels.

$10.00

NEW

THOMAS SCANLON

Greek and Roman Athletics
A Bibliography

ISBN:
0-89005-
522-X

$12.50

E. NORMAN GARDINER

ATHLETICS
OF THE
ANCIENT WORLD

ISBN: 0-89005-257-3

The principal reason for the continued usefulness of the *Athletics of the Ancient World* lies with its author. E. Norman Gardiner was recognized during his own lifetime as the unrivaled authority on Greek Athletics. The timelessness of Gardiner s work lies, then partly in his enormous learning. It lies even more however, in his ability to write intelligibly for both the interested layman and the specialized scholar. The status of our problems well defined, but never to the confusion of the reader. His learning sits gracefully upon his lucid prose, and one cared for it tremendously, and wanted to share it generously.

7020 N. WESTERN AVENUE, CHICAGO, ILLINOIS 60645

COMPLETE YOUR LIBRARY

NEW

$20.00

W. W. TARN

The Greeks
in Bactria and India

3rd Edition
by
FRANK LEE HOLT

ISBN:
0-89005-524-6

The preface to the 3rd edition of Tarn's pioneer work, tells the reader what has happened in historical and archaeological research since its 2nd edition (1951). Also the new bibliography brings to the researcher a complete and impressive survey of what has been published up to 1984.

This book belongs to the library of every school, college and university where ancient history is taught. It is also a good personal copy for every teacher and scholar interested in Hellenistic, Central Asian and Indian history. For the military historian and the student of cultural interchanges between Europe and Asia.

$10.00

It has been a source of great satisfaction to me, on returning to my long-planned book on Greek athletics, to find that a need for it still exists. In the present edition 3 new chapters have been written: The Legendary Origins of Games at Olympia; The Rise of Organized Athletics; The Hellenistic Age. Many new translations have been added and representative evidence from inscriptions and papyri has now been included. The rather full notes seek not only to explain certain aspects of the translations but also to provide essential information for those who would investigate more deeply the many unresolved problems of athletic history.

Sources For The History
Of Greek Athletics

RACHEL SARGENT ROBINSON

ISBN: 0-89005-297-2

Just Mail your order form to: ARES PUBLISHERS, INC.,

ON ANCIENT ATHLETICS

Sport in Classic Times was originally published in a small edition in England in 1930, and until now it has been extremely difficult to obtain. The first general book written about the field sports of the Greeks and the Romans, it masterfully combines scholarship with a witty, interesting and unfailingly charming style of writing. It opens out for contemporary readers a whole province of the classical world which had been left almost entirely unsurveyed.

NEW

$12.50

ALFRED JOSHUA BUTLER

Sports in Classics Times

ISBN:
0-89005-
525-4

$12.50

K. F. VICKERY

FOOD IN EARLY GREECE

ISBN: 0-89005-339-1

The title of this study, *Food in Early Greece*, requires, perhaps, some explanation. The expression *Early Greece* refers geographically to mainland Greece. In the almost complete absence of literary records, the study is based largely on archaeological evidence, and to a lesser extent on that of language.

The facts so gathered are presented: what food produces were known to the peoples of the various regions of the Aegean in each period of prehistory; what was the relative importance of each sort of food in the diet of those peoples; to what extent food products were articles of trade and transport; and how food was prepared.

7020 N. WESTERN AVENUE, CHICAGO, ILLINOIS 60645

COMPLETE YOUR LIBRARY

$25.00

SEXTIUS JULIUS AFRICANUS

List of Olympian Victors

Edited by

I. Rutgers

ISBN:
0-89005-351-0

The text of Sextus Julius Africanus, is an essential reference for the students of ancient Greek history and athletics.

This work is extremely rare; according to the *National Union Catalogue*, only three copies existed in the United States and Canada, previous to our printing. We do not know how long our edition will remain in print. To be sure that you secure a copy, order now.

$12.50

T. KLEE

Zur Geschichte der Gymnischen Agone an Griechischen Festen

Klee's well-known monograph on the Greek games and the festivals connected with them is heavily based upon the epigraphical evidence available before WWI. Despite this fact, however, his work is internationally recognized as one of the few major classics of the history of Greek athletics.

ISBN: 0-89005-336-7

Just Mail your order form to: ARES PUBLISHERS, INC.,